On Psychological and Visionary Art

A list of Jung's works appears at the back of the volume.

Frontispiece. Interior of the catacombs, Paris. Nadar, 1861

On Psychological and Visionary Art

*Notes from C. G. Jung's Lecture on
Gérard de Nerval's "Aurélia"*

C. G. JUNG
CRAIG E. STEPHENSON, EDITOR

Ⓟ PHILEM☉N SERIES

Published with the support of the Philemon Foundation
This book is part of the Philemon Series of the Philemon Foundation

PRINCETON UNIVERSITY PRESS
Princeton and Oxford

Copyright © 2015 by Princeton University Press
Published by Princeton University Press, 41 William Street, Princeton, New Jersey 08540
In the United Kingdom: Princeton University Press, 6 Oxford Street, Woodstock, Oxfordshire OX20 1TW
press.princeton.edu

Section 2 was translated by R.F.C. Hull. Sections 3, 4, 5, and 6 were translated from the German by Gottwalt Pankow. Section 7 (*Aurélia*) was originally published in *Selected Writings* by Gérard de Nerval, translated and with an introduction by Richard Sieburth (Penguin Classics, copyright © 1999 by Richard Sieburth) and is reproduced by permission of Penguin Books Ltd.

Jacket art © Alfred Kubin, *Aurélia* © 2015 Eberhard Spangenberg/Artists Rights Society (ARS), New York/ VG Bild-Kunst, Bo

Library of Congress Cataloging-in-Publication Data
Jung, C. G. (Carl Gustav), 1875-1961.
On psychological and visionary art: notes from C. G. Jung's lecture on Gérard de Nerval, 1945 / C. G. Jung; Craig E. Stephenson, editor.
    pages cm.—(Philemon Foundation Series)
Includes bibliographical references and index.
ISBN 978-0-691-16247-8 (hardcover: alk. paper) 1. Nerval, Gérard de, 1808–1855. Aurélia. 2. Nerval, Gérard de, 1808–1855—Psychology. 3. Nerval, Gérard de, 1808–1855—Mental health. 4. Jung, C. G. (Carl Gustav), 1875–1961. 5. Literature and mental illness. 6. Symbolism in literature. 7. Symbolism (Psychology) 8. Psychology in literature.
I. Stephenson, Craig E., 1955– editor. II. Sieburth, Richard, translator. III. Nerval, Gérard de, 1808–1855. Aurélia. IV. Title. V. Title: C. G. Jung's lecture on Gérard de Nerval, 1945.
PQ2260.G36Z74 2015

843'.7—dc23

British Library Cataloging-in-Publication Data is available
This book has been composed in Sabon Next LT Pro
Printed on acid-free paper. ∞
Printed in the United States of America
10 9 8 7 6 5 4 3 2 1

Contents

Illustrations

Halftones

The illustrations in this text are reproduced from the 1910 German
edition of *Aurélia*, illustrated by Alfred Kubin. Copyright © Eberhard Spangenberg, Munich.

Acknowledgments

Thanks to Ulrich Hoerni, Andreas Jung, Thomas Fischer, and the Foundation of the Works of C. G. Jung, Zurich, for permission to research this unpublished material and their interest in seeing it published.

Appreciation to Sonu Shamdasani, general editor, Philemon Foundation, for his historical and editorial expertise, and President Judith Harris and the board of directors of the Philemon Foundation for taking up the project.

Gratitude to Gottwalt Pankow for his precise translations and Lucie Pabel for charting line by line the progression of Jung's text from the first notes through to the final version. Without their passionate and painstaking intelligent work, this project would not have been possible.

Thanks to Dr. Richard Sieburth, New York University, for generously allowing the use of his translation of Nerval's *Aurélia*. Thanks to John Siciliano, Penguin US, and Simon Winder, Penguin UK, for granting permission to reprint Sieburth's translation, and also to Hayley Davidson, Penguin UK, for her assistance.

Appreciation to Helga Kopecky, librarian at the International School of Analytical Psychology (Zurich), for launching this research in 1996 while I was at the C. G. Jung Institute Zürich (Kusnächt). Thanks to Irving Wardle for first translating Jung's 1945 lecture for research purposes. Gratitude for assistance with many research questions: Amanda Corp, London Library; Lloyd A. Busch, Woodruff Library, Emory University; Martin Liebscher, University College London; Valerie Millet; and Dr. Yvonne Voegeli, ETH-Bibliothek Zürich. A special thank you to Philemon Foundation director Beverley Zabriskie for linking Nerval and Jung with the Enigma of Bologna.

Appreciation to Laurel Boone, once again, for her keen-eyed editorial expertise.

Gratitude to Fred Appel, Juliana Fidler, Cindy Milstein, Debbie Tegarden, and Jess Massabrook at Princeton University Press, and to indexer Dave Luljak.

Personal thanks to my partner, Alberto Manguel, *compagnon et inspirateur*, to whom this book is lovingly dedicated.

Thanks to various organizers for inviting me to present aspects of this research at these venues: Sonu Shamdasani, C. G. Jung: "Le Rouge et le Noir," Martin Bodmer Foundation and Philemon Foundation, Geneva, March 2013; Alessandra Benedicty, "Money/L'argent," 20th and 21st Century French and Francophone Studies International Colloquium, New York University, City University of New York Graduate Center, and Columbia University, March 7, 2014; Joe Cambray and Donald Fredericksen, Psyche, Spirit and Science, joint conference of the International Association for Analytical Psychology and the International Association for Jungian Studies, Yale University, July 9–12, 2015.

In memoriam, our *humanitas*: Don Fredericksen, Bettina Knapp, Claude Rouquet, Edith Sorel, Eugene Taylor, and Ross Woodman.

Permissions

Text

Aurélia, from *Selected Writings* by Gérard de Nerval, translated with notes by Richard Sieburth (London: Penguin Classics, 1999). Translation and notes, copyright Richard Sieburth, 1999.

Image Permissions

For assistance with image permissions, thanks to Dr. Thekla Weissengruber, Oberösterreichisches Landesmuseum, Linz; Ingrid Simson, on behalf of Eberhard Spangenberg, Munich, the estate of Alfred Kubin; Susanne Schneider at ETH Bibliothek, Zurich; Kajette Solomon and Isabelle Toromanof, Bridgeman Images; Anne-Catherine Biedermann, Réunion des Musées Nationaux, Paris; Lorraine Goonan, The Image Works.

On Psychological and Visionary Art

ONE

Introduction

Craig E. Stephenson

THE FRENCH ROMANTIC POET GÉRARD DE NERVAL EXPLORED THE IRRATIONAL with lucidity and exquisite craft, and Carl Gustav Jung regarded those explorations as a work of "extraordinary magnitude." Like the German poet-philosophers Novalis and Johann Wolfgang von Goethe, Nerval rejected the rationalist universalism of the Enlightenment and privileged instead the individual subjective imagination as a way of fathoming the divine to reconnect with what the Romantics called the "life principle." During the years of his greatest creativity, Nerval suffered from madness, for which he was institutionalized eight times, occasionally for extended periods. Eventually, at the request of his physician, Dr. Émile Blanche, he wrote his visionary memoir *Aurélia* in an ambivalent attempt to emerge from these episodes of insanity. In *Aurélia*, Nerval acknowledges the value of his medical treatment, and at the same time asserts that his doctor's psychiatric strategies and scientific vocabulary relegate his visionary convictions to a mental illness from which he may be released only through atonement. He published the first part of *Aurélia* in *La Revue de Paris* in January 1855. The second part and then the entire book were printed posthumously in that same year.

Almost a century later, in 1942 Jung lectured on *Aurélia* for the Swiss Society for Psychiatry and Psychotherapy. Afterward, he reread and revised his interpretation with extensive handwritten notes, and in the summer of 1945, at seventy years of age and after a long illness, he presented an expanded version of his lecture to the more intimate circle of the Psychological Club in Zurich. World War II had only just ended. In his lecture, Jung introduced listeners to the importance of Nerval's text. Contrasting an orthodox psychoanalytic interpretation with his own synthetic approach to the unconscious, Jung explained why Nerval was not able to make use of his visionary experiences in his own life. At the same time, Jung emphasized the validity of Nerval's visions, differentiating the psychology of a work of art from the psychology of the artist. The lecture suggests how Jung's own experiments with active imagination and the writing of *The Red Book* influenced his reading of Nerval's *Aurélia* as a parallel text to his own *Liber Novus*. Here, then, is a key to understanding Jung's argument about the significance of symbolism in modern thought.

The editors of the Collected Works published only Jung's one-paragraph abstract of the lecture in volume 18. The documents presented here offer a unique window into the stages of Jung's creative process as he responds to an essential Romantic text. They are arranged backwards: from the final, extensively revised 1945 lecture, through the schematic 1942 lecture, to the initial five pages of handwritten notes and Jung's marginalia in his copies of *Aurélia*—that is to say, back to Jung, with pen in hand, reading Nerval.

Gérard de Nerval

NERVAL: THE MAN

Gérard de Nerval was born Gérard Labrunie on May 22, 1808, in Paris. His father, Etienne Labrunie, had run away at the age of sixteen to serve in the revolutionary wars and in 1795 had sustained a crippling injury to his left leg. Undaunted, Etienne studied medicine and reenlisted in Napoleon's Grande Armée in 1806. In 1807, he married Marie-Antoinette-Marguerite Laurent, the daughter of Paris linen merchants. In May 1810, two years after Gérard's birth, Dr. and Mme Labrunie left France for Germany, where Dr. Labrunie would direct military hospitals. One day, after crossing a bridge heaped with cadavers, Mme Labrunie collapsed with a fever; she died and was buried in a local cemetery, in Silesia. Later, during Napoleon's chaotic retreat from Russia, Dr. Labrunie lost all mementos of his wife, including her letters and jewelry.

When Gérard's parents left for Germany, they sent their two-year-old son to live with his mother's uncle, Antoine Boucher, at Mortefontaine, in the Valois region. Boucher was a grocer and tobacco merchant, a warm family man, a free-thinker, and reader of both classical authors and works on the occult. At Clos de Nerval, on the site of an ancient Roman camp, he often looked for coins and pottery shards to add to his antiquarian collection. Gérard was six when his father retired from the army, set up his private practice in Paris, and reclaimed his son. In 1820, when Gérard was twelve, Boucher died. Gérard remained deeply connected imaginatively to this uncle and to the Valois region of his childhood.

A strict father, Labrunie enrolled his son in the prestigious Collège Charlemagne in Paris to study humanities and languages. The boy excelled, particularly in German, which his father spoke fluently. In 1826, finishing his studies at the lycée at the age of eighteen, Gérard published a number of volumes of political verse and, a year later, his French translation of Goethe's *Faust*, part 1.

Figure 1. Portrait of Gérard de Nerval. Nadar, between 1854 and 1855

Goethe praised this translation.[1] Hector Berlioz lifted passages from it for the libretto of his opera *La Damnation de Faust* (1846). Nerval also published translations of works by Friedrich Gottlieb Klopstock, Novalis, and Friedrich von Schiller as well as other works by Goethe. The positive memories of his early childhood inspired several essays on the cultural and political significance of the local legends and ballads of the Valois, and led him to adopt a position much like the folk theory and subjectivism of philosopher and historian Johann Gottfried Herder. Dr. Labrunie did not approve of his son's literary accomplishments, however, and insisted on enrolling him in the medical school at the Clinic de l'Hôtel Dieu; in 1832, Gérard assisted his father during a cholera epidemic. Despite his financial dependence on his father, he increasingly ignored his father's ambitions and persisted with his writing. For the time being, he signed himself simply "Gérard," a nom de plume without a surname.

Figure 2. Mortefontaine, Valois region; Louis-François Casson, 1801

1. "He [Goethe] himself had taken up the latest French translation of his 'Faust,' by Gérard, which he turned over and seemed occasionally to read. 'Some singular thoughts pass through my head,' said he, 'on reflecting that this book is now read in a language over which Voltaire ruled fifty years ago. You cannot understand my thoughts upon this subject, and have no idea of the influence which Voltaire and his great contemporaries had in my youth, and how they governed the whole civilized world. My biography does not clearly show what was the influence of these men in my youth, and what pains it cost me to defend myself against them, and to maintain my own ground in a true relation to nature.' He praised Gérard's translation as very successful, although mostly in prose. 'I do not like,' he said, 'to read my "Faust" any more in German, but in this French translation all seems again fresh, new, and spirited" (Sunday, January 3, 1830). Johann Peter Eckermann, *Conversations of Goethe with Johann Peter Eckermann*, ed. J. K. Moorhead, trans. John Oxenford (New York: Da Capo, 1998), 341.

In 1834, Gérard's maternal grandfather died, and Gérard inherited thirty thousand francs. This windfall enabled him to travel in southern France and Italy, and after returning to Paris, to move out of his father's house and into a flat in the Impasse du Doyenné with a group of young bohemian writer friends. Like many of his companions, he devoted himself to the Paris theater scene, hoping to make a career as a playwright. In this he failed.

Figure 3. Opéra Comique. Paris, 1850–60

Figure 4. Jenny Colon, by Noël Léon Alphonse, 1837

Figure 5. *Le monde dramatique*, volume 1 (frontispiece), by Céléstin Nanteuil, 1835

Gérard chose an actress, Jenny Colon, as the object of what translator Richard Sieburth (1999, xv) describes astutely as "a much-publicized infatuation." Inspired perhaps by this unrequited love, he invested his inheritance in founding a theatrical magazine, *Le monde dramatique*, the first issue of which appeared in May 1835. Gérard also collaborated with Alexandre Dumas on an opera (*Piquillo*, 1836) in which Colon sang the lead soprano role. But by 1838, the magazine had foundered, and Gérard and his friends had to leave their lodgings when the building was condemned and requisitioned. To make things worse, Colon married her tour organizer. Having spent his inheritance, Gérard was increasingly forced to take on work as a drama critic and journalist in order to pay his debts. He joined Dumas in Frankfurt, working for him as a ghostwriter on a number of plays including *L'Alchimiste*; for only one, *Léo Burckhart*, did he receive any credit. In 1840, he began to translate the second part of Goethe's *Faust*. In December, he traveled to Brussels, where Colon was reprising the opera role that he had come to believe he had written for her.

When Gérard returned to Paris, his emotional and financial difficulties overwhelmed him to such an extent that at the age of thirty-three, he experienced his first episode of insanity. He entered the sanitorium of Dr. Esprit

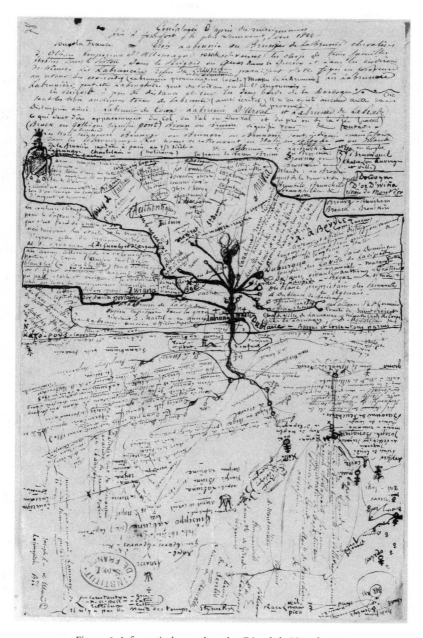

Figure 6. A fantastical genealogy, by Gérard de Nerval, 1841

Blanche in Montmartre, where he resided for nine months; the diagnosis was "*manie aiguë, probablement curable.*" During the time in Blanche's sanitorium, he wrote an imaginary genealogical investigation that replaces his biological father with a mythical line of forebearers, establishing Gérard as the descendant of Napoleon's brother Joseph Bonaparte and of the German knights of Emperor Otto I, founder of the Holy Roman Empire. The diagram silences the father while lending a voice to the son, replacing the conventional paternal line with a deeper continuity. By the time he left the sanitorium, he had emerged from his descent into the underworld of madness with a new aristocratic persona: "Gérard de Nerval." Critics have pointed to possible significances of the name, from the most obvious—an alignment with his mother's uncle and the Clos de Nerval—to an allusion to the Roman emperor Marcus Cocceius Nerva as an imaginary ancestor, and even to an anagram of his mother's maiden name, Laurent.

Jenny Colon died in 1842. Intending to console himself, Nerval left Paris for Alexandria and Cairo. At the time he was reading books on history and ancient religions, and these readings and this journey correlated outwardly with the archetypal universe of dreams that he had discovered during his first descent into insanity. He returned to Paris in 1844.

Over the next eleven years, Nerval alternated between periods of great literary productivity and bouts of madness. He wrote a remarkable introduction to his translations of the poems of Heinrich Heine, who had become a close friend. He coauthored an opera (*Les Monténégrins*, 1849), a Hindu drama (*Le Chariot d'Enfant*, 1850), and his own Faustian play about the invention of printing, *L'Imagier de Haarlem* (1851); none of these stage works met with any success. He also published a brilliantly subversive experimental serial novel (*Les Faux-Saulniers*, 1850/2009) and a moving account of nocturnal wanderings in some of the most squalid neighborhoods of Paris (*Les Nuits d'Octobre*, 1852). During this time, too, he wrote his masterpiece, a novella titled *Sylvie* (1853). But immediately after completing *Sylvie*, he was once more institutionalized, again for nine months, at the rest home of Dr. Émile Blanche, son of Dr. Esprit Blanche, in Passy; the diagnosis this time was "*délire furieux.*" The younger Dr. Blanche recommended that Nerval try writing his way out of his madness.

Thus began the "project" of *Aurélia*. Nerval rallied, and as well as working on *Aurélia*, he started to gather and publish a definitive edition of his works. Released in May 1854 from Blanche's care, Nerval traveled again to Germany, but he had to be readmitted to the Passy clinic in August. In October, against Blanche's wishes, he obtained an official discharge by appealing to friends and the Société des Gens de Lettres, who supported his suggestion that his confinement jeopardized his professional role as a writer. He continued to work on *Aurélia*, no longer for Blanche, but for publication in *La Revue de Paris*. Although Nerval was supposedly in the care of a great-aunt, he led a vagrant and solitary existence.

Figure 7. Antoine-Émile Blanche, 1880

Figure 8. 17 rue d'Ankara, Dr. Blanche's rest home, 1846

Figure 9. Tour Saint-Jacques la Boucherie, 1853

Figure 10. *Death of Gérard de Nerval, rue de la Vieille-Lanterne,* by Gustav Doré, 1855

On January 1, 1855, part I of *Aurélia* was published. Three weeks later, in the early hours of January 26, Nerval was found hanged in the fourth arrondissement of Paris near the fifteenth-century Saint-Jacques Tower, in the Rue de la Vieille-Lanterne. On February 15, *La Revue de Paris* published part II of *Aurélia*.

"AURÉLIA": THE STORY

Aurélia narrates the outer and inner aspects of two phases of the protagonist's madness (see 120). In a city, the protagonist encounters Aurélia, a woman he has loved unrequitedly for a long time. Afterwards, back in Paris, at midnight, he comes across a pale, hollow-eyed woman who resembles Aurélia. They meet in front of a house with the same street number as his own age. In a dream, he witnesses a winged figure falling from above into a shabby Paris courtyard. The next day, as the protagonist awaits the repetition of the fateful hour that he imagines to be the hour of his death, a star leads him through the Paris streets. As he walks, he sheds his clothes, waiting to be separated from his body. Instead, he is arrested by a night patrol and eventually taken to a rest home. He describes a dream in which he visits the house of a maternal great-uncle, where he finds a talking bird that admonishes him for wanting to reside in the underworld. "You still belong to the world above," says the bird. Later, the protagonist dreams that this uncle, as a younger man, guides him in an ascent to a remote mountain village where a Spirit menacingly opposes him. Finally, in a third dream, the protagonist encounters three women at his uncle's house and follows one of them outside. She transforms before his eyes and then disappears, the entire garden taking on her shape and then suddenly turning into a cemetery. Only later, the protagonist learns that Aurélia has died.

The protagonist describes how he is confined to Dr. Esprit Blanche's *maison de santé* in Montmartre (see 143). He recalls that in order to fix his thoughts, he painted the walls of his room with a series of murals in which the figure of Aurélia predominated as a divinity. He also remembers writing down a systematic history of the world—part memory, part dream, part visionary thinking—in which he witnesses creation and the appearance of a radiant goddess who guides the evolution of humankind. This world history includes the emergence of a Promethean half-divine, half-human race of fire, not of clay, and a revolution among the Spirits that causes terrible suffering for humanity. An Eternal Mother goddess weeps and dies repeatedly, while the outlawed race of fire, like a serpent eating its tail, encircles the earth, reconnecting itself into a wholeness that is steeped in human blood.

The protagonist then describes a second phase of suffering in the form of a severe personal relapse (see 151). Two events trigger the relapse. First, he passes a certain house and hears a bird speaking, which reminds him of the earlier dream of his dead uncle. Second, climbing up to a friend's raised terrace, he falls, hurts himself, and faints; returning home, he is gripped by a fever and he associates his falling with having looked out over the Montmartre cemetery where Aurélia is buried.

Now the protagonist reflects on his dreams to understand what attitude he should take towards Aurélia. But instead of seeing her, he encounters the threatening Spirit from before, now in the form of an Oriental prince who is both his double and opponent. In a second dream, he enters a workshop where men are modeling clay into an enormous animal with giant wings. A beam of light pierces the animal's writhing body with purple flames, bringing it to life. In a third dream, the protagonist finds a crowd gathering for a wedding, and fears that Aurélia will appear and marry his rival. He prepares to make a sign that will defeat the rival, but a woman's scream awakes him. Part I ends with the protagonist asking if he should indeed attempt to delve into the mysteries of the universe and question the soul's immortality.

The descent in part I narrates both phases of madness and ends with the scream; part II begins at the bottom, looking upwards for God's pardon (see 160). While the protagonist hopelessly contemplates his death, he recalls that Aurélia died a devout believer in God; she could be his intermediary. He also remembers visiting a close friend who had been ill and spoke of God as consolation. He then reenvisions the bride and bridegroom in a union available only to the devout—a union to which he himself cannot aspire. He finds himself at the Montmartre cemetery, but cannot identify Aurélia's grave. Back home, he looks in a box of her memorabilia to find her last letter and the funeral certificate that would tell him where to find her grave. But then he burns these last documents. He contemplates his formative years—the facts that he never knew his mother and was cared for by his freethinking uncle—and wonders if his liberal education and study of different religions render him now irreconcilable to the Christian God. He listens to a friend of his own age recalling their shared experience of the July Revolution along with their political hopes, skepticism, and consequent social disillusionment. He recounts a series of failed meetings, including one with his father and another with a priest in the street who refuses to hear his confession, and he remarks how the sun is burning itself out and has only enough light to shine for three more days. At the home of a German poet, he tries to set his accounts in order, reimbursing the poet for a translation he hasn't completed, but the poet and his wife send for a cab and have him escorted to a clinic.

During a short period of recovery, the protagonist writes "one of his finest stories," and yet by the end of a month, he finds himself torn between waves of hope and despair. He is confined to the clinic of Dr. Émile Blanche, and begins to understand that this is an ordeal he must undergo as part of a sacred initiation into the mysteries of the goddess Isis, Venus, or even the

Virgin Mary. Blanche introduces him to a young man, a former soldier in Africa, who appears to be blind, deaf, and mute, and refuses to eat. The protagonist attends to this young man in an attempt to help his own recovery, and dreams of climbing up and down within a tower, from the sky to the depths of the earth and back. Suddenly, a side door opens, and a man resembling the soldier says, "Come." A female divinity, who was Aurélia (in part I) and is now Isis/Venus (in part II), encourages him, saying that his vow of faith has been transmitted by this brother, the soldier, to the merciful Virgin Mary.

Next, the protagonist recounts a group of dreams of grace and pardon, gathered under the title "Memorabilia" (see 191): the Messiah appears between him and his beloved; the Icelandic gods Thor, Odin, Hela, and Balder present themselves; and the snake eating its own tail reappears, now in a more positive context. In the final passages, he recounts panoramic dreams that feature Peter the Great and envision France as an arbiter of the conflict between East and West, moving the world towards resolution and peace. Meanwhile, in his daily outer life at the clinic, the protagonist patiently sings his Valois songs to the young soldier, who eventually starts to see and talk. When he asks him why he continues to refuse food, the young man explains that his body is dead and buried, and he is now in purgatory, atoning for his sins. The protagonist recognizes his own self in these "bizarre ideas" and concludes that he is happy with the convictions he has gained from his own ordeals, which are now at an end.

AURÉLIA: COMMENTARY

The shift created by thinkers and artists that later generations came to call Romanticism was a revolt against both an old Christian cosmology and the mechanistic metaphysics that, for a time, replaced it. Christians of the Middle Ages had divided the universe into four strata: at the top, Heaven and the divine; then two middle realms of human nature; and finally, at the bottom, Hell. The upper human realm belonged to the spirit and the lower to the flesh, and sinners could ascend through both realms toward Heaven by mortification of the flesh. As Northrop Frye (2005, 85) astutely observed, the Romantics turned this Christian cosmos on its head. They argued that Reason had seated an imaginary divinity in an empty Heaven and that the true divine force lay in the previously condemned "infernal" world, closely linked to Nature. They still divided the human realm in two, but the upper realm of civilization was a world of artifice close to the empty heavens, and the lower realm of natural wilderness bordered the demonic world, to which humans must have access to reconnect with the life principle.

In the old cosmology, the ordinary or fallen world was imagined as existing beneath an ideal superior one. In the Romantic construct, this ordinary world of experience sat on top of a powerful world to which humans are inescapably connected. Jean-Jacques Rousseau imagined this lower dark world as sympathetic, even benevolently maternal and inherently moral, and "natural man" as shaped by that benevolence and morality, though vulnerable to being misshaped by civilization. The Marquis de Sade portrayed the lower world as dangerous and predatory, and its "natural" laws as violent and deadly. In the generation after Rousseau and Sade, Victor Hugo rejected the one-sided tyranny of the beautiful conceived by the neoclassicists and instead demanded an aesthetic theory that would render legitimate everything the neoclassical era had excluded, particularly "the grotesque."

Nerval looked outside France to the Germans for inspiration. He found that whereas Christianity had rendered the classical theme of descent into the underworld as diabolical, authors such as Goethe strongly privileged the imagination as a way of descending in order to fathom the divine. According to the conventional Christian cosmology, the underworld was where the banished gods presided, and their dwelling place could only be the Inferno; indeed, any human who lived before Christ resided there too. In *The Divine Comedy*, for example, Dante could imagine Virgil as his guide through Hell and part of Purgatory, but from there the ancient poet had to turn back, leaving Dante to journey upwards without him, by God's grace, into Paradise. With the Romantic reimagining of the cosmos came a new valuing of the experience of descent. Now the individual aspired to transcend the limits of what was actual and artificial by descending into the sensual and sublime profundity of nature as well as by intuitively going down, through reverie and dreams, into the ancient and pagan depths of the mind—in Goethe's *Faust*, for instance, to the realm of the "Mothers."

Dante's descent remains framed within a Christian cosmology, even though he rails against the corrupted aspects of its earthly manifestations. The English Romantic William Blake turns Dante's Heaven and Hell upside down to such an extent that in the ironic dialogues in *The Marriage of Heaven and Hell*, only a discerning reader can distinguish between angelic-looking demons aligned with a petrifying God called Urizen and fiery angels inspired by the youthful god Orc. But like Dante, Blake descends and ascends within a firmly framed cosmology, always with reference to "the great code," the Bible. Percy Bysshe Shelley's confrontations with the depths feel far more precarious because Shelley invented his own individual code; he descends without the protection of a communal frame of reference (Woodman 2005, 162). Likewise, at the core of German classical aestheticism, Goethe's cosmology is idiosyncratic and "scholarly"; it is the cosmology of a nonbeliever (Bishop 2008, 20). Nerval's descents, although informed by many precedents, also feel individual—so much so that he fears he cannot claim the consolation offered by the conventional patriarchal Christian Trinity. In Nerval's texts, the dream is the inner gateway to a nonrational life principle that is figured as a goddess, part pagan Isis and part Christian Virgin Mother. When Vyvyan Holland (1933, 12), Oscar Wilde's son, translated *Aurélia* into English, he retained Nerval's original title, *Dreams and Life*, while acknowledging in his introduction that the second title appropriately emphasizes the protagonist's hope that Aurélia, who died a devout Christian, might intervene on his behalf.

Figure 11. "Isis," first century BC, Roman

Even as Nerval directs his attention inwards, he is also a keen observer of the communal and individual outer life. Charles Baudelaire described Nerval as one of the few authors of his age who remained, even in death, "forever lucid."[2] That quality of lucidity informs *Aurélia* to such a degree that the portrayals of outer life match those of dreams and visions in their intensity and clarity. The protagonist travels out of Paris to the Valois in search of the life principle in the same way that he moves down into dreams. And the

2. "And even more recently—just a year ago from today, 26 January, when a writer of admirable honesty, great intelligence, who had been forever lucid, went discretely, without troubling anyone—so discretely that his discretion seemed like disdain—to set his soul free in the gloomiest street he could find—what nauseating homilies! what a refined murder!" (translation mine). Charles Baudelaire, "Edgar Poe, sa vie et ses oeuvres," in *Oeuvres complètes*, ed. Claude Pichois (Paris: Bibliothèque de la Pléiade, 1976), 2:306.

excursions in *Aurélia* become most precarious in the moments when these inner and outer realms begin to spill over into each other in Paris, the city of the poet's birth. In the most terrible instant of the story, overwhelmed by depression and melancholia, the protagonist witnesses a black sun and bloodred orb hovering in the vacant sky over the Tuileries.[3]

If an adjective such as "Nervalian" exists, it should refer not so much to Nerval's lucidity as to his syncretism. Nerval combines elements from different philosophies, religions, and mythologies, so that his use of a single word alludes to centuries of human experience. In a letter to Jenny Colon, he describes this as a curse:

> What a beautiful story I would create for you, if my thoughts were more composed! But too many things present themselves to me at once as I write to you. … There is in my head a storm of thoughts by which I am ceaselessly dazzled and enervated, years of dreams, projects, and anguish that long to be compressed into a phrase, into a single word.[4]

And in part II of *Aurélia*, the protagonist fears that this syncretism, rooted in a liberal education and his knowledge of many religions as well as his study of alchemy and the esoteric sciences, alienates him from the Christian God.

The compression Nerval the man describes as negative also characterizes Nerval the writer's greatest accomplishments as a poet. The compact brilliance of his sonnet series *Les Chimères* (1854) led Antonin Artaud to say that it could only be given diction—that is, not so much interpreted as voiced.[5]

---

3. Jung connects the alchemical figure of the *Sol niger* in masculine psychology with the alter ego and Brother Medardus figure in E.T.A. Hoffman's story *The Devil's Elixir*—a story that Nerval translated. C. G. Jung, *Mysterium Coniunctionis*, vol. 14 of Collected Works (Princeton, NJ: Princeton University Press, 1963), para. 229. With regard to Nerval's "black sun," see Julia Kristeva, "Gerard de Nerval, the Disinherited Poet," in *Black Sun: Depression and Melancholia* (New York: Colombia University, 1989), 139–72.

4. Gérard de Nerval, "Lettres d'amour," in *Oeuvres Complètes*, ed. Jean Guillaume and Claude Pichois (Paris: Bibliothèque de la Pléiade, 1989), 1:721.

5. Artaud writes, "All these verses were written first of all to be heard, embodied by voices, and it is not even that their music illuminates them and that they then can speak by the simple modulations of sound, sound by sound, because it is only off the printed or written page that an authentic verse can acquire meaning, and what is needed is the space of breath between the flight of all the words. The words flee the page and take flight. They flee from the heart of the poet who pushes them with the force of an untranslatable assault and who no longer holds them in his sonnet except by the power of assonance, to sound out in identical guises but on hostile terms. And the syllables of the verses of [Nerval's] 'Chimeras,' so difficult to bring to life, speak, but on condition of their being spat out again at every reading—because only then do their hieroglyphs become clear. And then all the clues to their so-called occultism disappear, rendered useless and noxious in the folds of the brain" (translation mine). Antonin Artaud, "À Georges Le Breton, Rodez, 7 mars 1946," in *Lettres écrites*

In *Aurélia*, the protagonist's dream presents this way of working as traveling up and down in a great tower, like the Tower of Babel, gathering words. Nerval's references from so many contexts crystallize into a personal intertextual mythopoeia. He begins *Aurélia* with Virgil's *Aeneid* (book VI, 893–96) and the two gates of sleep: the gates of horn, through which true shades pass, and the gates of ivory, through which distorted, illusory dreams emerge. These first words introduce Nerval's Romantic dilemma: how best to discern what is vision from what is illusion, what is heaven from what is hell, what is divine sense from what is pathological madness. He also mentions Lucius Apuleius's *The Golden Ass*, in which the lover suffers the humiliation of being changed into an ass and must endure a healing initiation into the mysteries of the goddess Isis. As well as referring to the *Divine Comedy*, Nerval invokes Dante's *Vita Nuova*, in which Dante has a prophetic dream of Beatrice's death. By implication, Aurélia, as the protagonist's Beatrice, promises a path towards a kind of enlightenment different from that of the *philosophes*, culminating in a redemptive vision of love and Goethe's Eternal Feminine. Nerval mentions Emanuel Swedenborg too, whose title *Memorabilia* he will borrow for the penultimate epiphanies of part II.[6] In all these works, listed as precedents in the opening paragraphs of *Aurélia*, Nerval sets up, before beginning his descent, the assurance of his protagonist's subsequent ascent at the end of part II.

At the same time, another, darker Romantic theme runs through the entire text: the tragic double or doppelgänger. Nerval had translated E.T.A. Hoffman's tale *The Devil's Elixir*, and had addressed the theme of the double in his own fiction in "The King of Bedlam" and "The Tale of the Caliph Hakim."[7] In part I of *Aurélia*, the protagonist's friends come to liberate him from prison, but collect the wrong man (see 127); likewise, in his dream the Spirit, who opposes the protagonist and reappears as an Oriental prince, steps malignly into the role of the devout bridegroom of Aurélia (see 152). As much as Nerval structures his text with the promise of reunion with a feminine life principle modeled on Dante's *Commedia* and Francesco Colonna's mythological romance, *Hypnerotomachia Poliphili*, the tragedy of the double subverts the writer's use of these precursors by excluding the protagonist from the sacred marriage.

---

de Rodez (1945-1946): Oeuvres complètes (Paris: Gallimard, 1974), 11:187. See also Richard Sieburth, "Introductory Note to 'The Gramont Manuscript' and 'The Chimeras,'" in *Gérard de Nerval: Selected Writings* (London: Penguin, 1999), 350; Robin Blaser, "Artaud on Nerval," *Pacific Nation* 1 (1968): 69.

6. Emanuel Swedenborg, *The Author's Memorabilia: The Swedenborg Library V10* (Germantown, PA: Swedenborg Publishing Association, 1881).

7. See Gérard de Nerval, "The King of Bedlam," in *Gérard de Nerval: Selected Writings*, trans. Richard Sieburth (London: Penguin, 1999), 6–21; Gérard de Nerval, "The Tale of Caliph Hakim," in *Gérard de Nerval: Selected Writings*, trans. Richard Sieburth (London: Penguin, 1999), 22–58.

Figure 12. "Marriage Scene." Francesco Colonna's *Hypnerotomachia Polophili*, 1499

Commencing part II with the epigraph "Eurydice! Eurydice!" Nerval explicitly frames his second movement in the tragic mode by alluding to Orpheus at the moment when he emerges from his descent into Hell, but fails Eurydice by looking back to her. Nerval's protagonist seeks in dream the world of the dead in order to reunite with Aurélia, and in part II he longs to reconnect with her and reclaim her from the underworld. At the same time, Nerval describes his protagonist destroying the last physical remnants of Aurélia's existence. With this sacrifice, the protagonist hopes to appease an angry patriarchal god, much as Nerval hopes to appease his father and Doctor Blanche by writing this book. The problem for Nerval as a possessed patient is that the doctor as exorcist intends the writing to expel Aurélia as life principle from his body and mind. The problem for Nerval as Orphic poet is that the same words that evoke her presence also objectify her to such an extent that he loses her forever (Butler 2011, 26).

At the time of his death, Nerval the man was regarded as a friend of many writers, but dismissed as a writer himself; he was seen as an emotional and financial failure as well as a madman. Shortly after his death, however, his literary fortune changed, and with the publication of his collected works, Nerval entered the French literary pantheon. Marcel Proust (1927, cited in Rinsler 1973, 140) acknowledged him as the inspiration for his own explorations of time lost and regained. André Breton claimed him as a forerunner of surrealism.[8] Umberto Eco (1994, 11) considers *Sylvie* "one of the greatest books ever written."

8. In *Comoedia*, August 24, 1924, Breton writes, "If we must look for the origin of the word 'surrealism,' we would turn to Nerval, hesitating between 'supernaturalism,' 'surnaturalism' and 'surrealism'" (translation mine). Robert Kopp, *Album André Breton* (Paris: Gallimard, 2008), 99.

AURÉLIA: *AESCLEPIUS VERSUS HIPPOCRATES*

The revolutionary force of Romanticism resided not in its rejection of Reason but rather in relocating the life principle in the depths, in the irrational underworld of the dead. The *Encyclopédie*, compiled by the *philosophes* of the Enlightenment, described dreams as successions of images that represented universal ideas, but that were accessible to the mind only in sleep. For Samuel Formey, author of *Songe: Métaphysique & Physiologie* (1746) and the entry on dreams in the *Encyclopédie*, the absence of reason in dream states rendered them exclusively negative, their idiosyncratic subjectivity constituting mere "anarchy."[9] The Romantic paradigm shifted this formulation by portraying irrational, subjective dreams as a reflective approach to the realm of the dead and the divine.

This Romantic shift coincided with changes in the study of mental alienation and medical management of the insane. In 1792, when Philippe Pinel (1745–1826) became the chief physician at the Bicêtre asylum for men, he began his now-iconic reforms. Inspired by the early Romantic arguments of Rousseau, Pinel emphasized the degree to which mental illnesses were caused by alienating social stresses, even while acknowledging the influence of specific inherited conditions and physiological damage. He eliminated bloodletting, purging, and blistering, and instead favored therapy that was mentally oriented, including close and friendly contact with the patient, discussions of personal difficulties, and programs of purposeful activities within a hospice setting. His assistant Jean-Baptiste Pussin unchained the patients at the Bicêtre, and a few years later followed Pinel to the Hôpital Salpêtrière, where they unchained the female inmates as well.[10] Pinel's disciple, Jean-Étienne-Dominique Esquirol (1772–1840), succeeded him at the Salpêtrière and further developed Pinel's work to achieve a more humane treatment of the mentally ill. Esquirol's book *Des maladies mentales, considérées sous les rapports médical, hygiénique et médico-légal* (1838/1845) is regarded as the first modern treatise on clinical psychiatry.

9. "The imagination of the wakened state is a civilized republic where the voice of the judge puts everything in order; the imagination of dreams is that same republic in a state of anarchy" (translation mine). *Encyclopédie, ou dictionnaire raisonné des sciences, des arts et des métiers, etc.*, ed. Denis Diderot and Jean le Rond d'Alembert (Chicago: University of Chicago, ARTFL Encyclopédie Project, Spring 2013 ed.), ed. Robert Morrissey, http://encyclopedie.uchicago. edu/, 15:355, cols. 1–2.

10. Philippe Pinel, *Traité medico-philosophique sur l'aliénation mentale ou la manie* (Paris: Caille et Ravier, 1800). With regard to the controversy surrounding who precisely unchained the Bicêtre inmates, see Dora Weiner, "Le geste de Pinel: Psychiatric Myth," in *Discovering the History of Psychiatry*, ed. Mark S. Micale and Roy Porter (Oxford: Oxford University Press, 1994), 232–47.

Figure 13. This iconic but incorrect representation, titled *Philippe Pinel Setting Free the Insane at the Bicêtre Asylum*, was painted by Charles Louis Lucien Muller, 1840–50. The artist mistakenly represents Pinel as the protagonist, rather than Jean-Baptiste Pussin, the hospital superintendent.

Figure 14. Jean-Martin Charcot

Figure 15. Drawing by Jean-Martin Charcot, under the influence of hashish, 1853

Esquirol's student Jacques-Joseph Moreau (1845, 31) tried to further the understanding of dreams by studying the dream state induced by hashish, a fairly recent import from India. In the hashish dream state, he said, "I had to admit for delirium in general a psychological nature not only analogous but absolutely identical with dream-states." On at least one occasion, Nerval and other writers were invited to experiment with hashish at a private salon, and without warning found themselves exhibited in their drug-induced state to a group of doctors. In *La psychologie morbide*, published only four years after Nerval's death, Moreau (1859, 223) cited the first phrases of Nerval's *Aurélia* for a medical description of delirium as the overflowing of dream into real life "because from a psychic point of view, dream and delirium are one and the same." Moreau and other sleep and dream researchers such as Alfred Maury worked to identify the laws as well as the logic of dreaming as a means with which to counter the alienating effect of mental illness. Even Jean-Martin Charcot, the neurological pathologist, himself experimented with hashish in 1853 in his investigations of hysteria and hypnosis.[11]

Émile Blanche (1848) earned his medical degree from the Salpêtrière in 1848 with a thesis on how best to keep catatonic and other patients from starving by tube feeding them. For his clinic, Blanche rented l'Hôtel de Lamballe in Passy, the site of an old Turkish embassy, which included a park overlooking the Seine. His rich and famous clientele included Guy de Maupassant, Charles Gounod, Theo van Gogh, and the hypochondriacal

11. Christopher Goetz, Michel Bonduelle, and Toby Gelfand, *Charcot: Constructing Neurology* (Oxford: Oxford University Press, 1995), 25.

countess of Castiglione. Even though the patients were confined, Blanche ran the establishment like a rest home with, for instance, music and nourishing meals, at which he and his wife presided in a familial atmosphere of trust and affection.

When Dr. Blanche proposed to Nerval that he write the text that was to become *Aurélia*, he was applying "*un traitment moral contre une aliénation mentale*." The word "moral" in this context denoted "mental" as opposed to "physical," and only secondarily carried connotations of ethics or just social conduct (Murat, 2001, 36). Blanche recommended that Nerval the man engage Nerval the author to undertake a literary exercise that could lead him out of his alienating madness. Because *Aurélia* was written in response to Blanche's prescription as a therapeutic exercise, it became for Nerval a demonstration that he was mentally competent and in control of his irrationality. He made this explicit in a letter to his father, Dr. Labrunie: "I am engaged in writing down and recording all the impressions occasioned by my illness. This will be a study not without utility for science and first-hand observation"[12] The next day, Nerval also defined the study in precisely these terms in a note to Blanche:

> I can resign myself to rarely receiving visitors, but the sight of my father would give me the energy to continue a project which, I believe, can only be of great use and honour to your establishment and which is allowing me to rid my head of all those visions that had so long inhabited it. These sickly fantasmagorias will be succeeded by healthier notions, and I will be able to make my reappearance in the world living proof of your medical care and talents. It is above all morally that you will have healed me and you will have reintegrated into society a writer who can still be of some service; in me you have above all conquered a friend and an admirer.[13]

The passage draws attention to the difficult power dynamic operating in what we would now call the "transference" between patient and doctor. Nerval the author appreciated and complied with Blanche's moral treatment, but Nerval the man railed against it and worked to subvert it. Nerval both acknowledged the value of Blanche's treatment and, at the same time, feared it would sever him from the possibility of rejuvenation or rebirth. In another letter to his father after a relapse, Nerval writes, "At any rate, let's

12. Gérard de Nerval, "À son père," December 2, 1853, in *Oeuvres Complètes*, ed. Jean Guillaume and Claude Pichois (Paris: Bibliothèque de la Pléiade, 1993), 3:832; Gérard de Nerval, *Gérard de Nerval: Selected Works*, trans. Richard Sieburth (London: Penguin, 1999), 338.
13. Gérard de Nerval, "Au Docteur Émile Blanche," December 3, 1853, in *Oeuvres Complètes*, ed. Jean Guillaume and Claude Pichois (Paris: Bibliothèque de la Pléiade, 1993), 3:833; Gérard de Nerval, *Gérard de Nerval: Selected Works*, trans. Richard Sieburth (London: Penguin, 1999), 339.

hope that Asclepius will save us from Hippocrates."[14] Pitting the ancient Greek god-doctor who healed the sick through incubated dreams against the classical Greek doctor whose name still defines the mandate of scientific medicine, Nerval made explicit his concern that Blanche's treatment left out something that ought not to have been left out.

Nerval the author realized to what extent the psychiatric strategies relegated Nerval the man's imagination, steeped in religious visions, to a kind of scientific purgatory, with the irony that he would only be permitted release from the *maison de santé* through a psychiatric-sanctioned version of confession. The problem had already presented itself during his first long hospitalization. In 1841, Nerval had written a letter to Alexandre Dumas's wife, a well-known actress who was also a friend, in which he presented his predicament as a patient:

> Seeing as how there are doctors and police inspectors here whose business it is to keep the field of poetry from invading public thoroughfares, I was only allowed to be released and to mingle among reasonable folk once I had formally admitted that I had *been sick* which costs a lot to my self-esteem and my honesty. Confess! Confess! They shrieked at me, as they used to do to sorcerers and heretics, and to settle the matter, I allowed myself to be classified as afflicted with a malady defined by doctors and variously labelled Theomania or Demonomania in the medical dictionaries. ... But I resign myself to my fate, and if I do not fulfil my predestination, I will accuse Doctor [Esprit] Blanche of having spirited away the divine Spirit.[15]

The medical dictionaries referred to by Nerval would have included the *Dictionnaire des sciences medicales* (1812–22) in which Esquirol repositioned diagnoses such as theomania and demonomania, replete as they were with religious connotations, within the contexts of civil law and medical illness.[16] In his letter, Nerval picked up this diagnostic language and cleverly pitted its religious etymology against its use by his doctors. He characterized the elder Doctor Blanche, whose first name was Esprit, as a medieval inquisitor trying to "spirit away" the divine in Nerval the man's experiences of

14. Gérard de Nerval, "À son père," October 21, 1853, in *Oeuvres Complètes*, ed. Jean Guillaume and Claude Pichois (Paris: Bibliothèque de la Pléiade, 1993), 3:817; Gérard de Nerval, *Gérard de Nerval: Selected Works*, trans. Richard Sieburth (London: Penguin, 1999), 336.

15. Gérard de Nerval, "À Mme Alexandre Dumas," November 9, 1841, in *Oeuvres Complètes*, ed. Jean Guillaume and Claude Pichois (Paris: Bibliothèque de la Pléiade, 1989), 1:1383; Gérard de Nerval, *Gérard de Nerval: Selected Works*, trans. Richard Sieburth (London: Penguin, 1999), 330–31.

16. In English, see theomania (under "Monomania") and demonomania in Jean-Étienne-Dominique Esquirol, *Mental Maladies: Treatise on Insanity*, trans. E. K. Hunt (Philadelphia: Lea and Blanchard, 1845), 319–76, 235–52.

the irrational; Blanche imprisoned and tortured his patient like a medieval exorcist attempting to expel a demon. The implication is that in casting out demons, science risked banishing the entire irrational realm, including an understanding of the life principle of rebirth and its potential for psychological healing.

Around the same time, in a letter to a friend, Nerval described his lucid madness in a more direct, honest, and less ironic manner:

> O my dear [Victor] Loubens, how surprised you must have been by the sorry commotion I made several months ago. But imagine my own surprise when I suddenly awoke from a dream of several weeks that was as bizarre as it was unexpected. I had been mad, that much is certain, that is, if one can apply the sorry term "madness" to my condition, given the fact that my memory remained entirely intact and that not for a single moment did I lose my reasoning powers. For my doctors it was indeed a case of madness, even though they tried to dress it up for me in polite synonyms; and for my friends as well there was no doubt but that this was the case; for me alone it was merely a kind of transfiguration of my habitual thoughts, a waking dream, a series of grotesque or sublime illusions which held so many charms that all I wished to do was to immerse myself in them forever. ... I thought I myself was God, and I merely considered myself trapped in some sorry incarnation.[17]

This letter brings to mind the winged figure in *Aurélia* that the protagonist witnesses crashing down into the sordid courtyard—a god image trapped in the squalid lowlife of Paris. The emotional candor in this second letter is terrifying when compared to the irony in the first.

During Nerval's 1853 hospitalization, his relationship with his father may have exacerbated the problem of his ambivalence toward Dr. Émile Blanche. When Nerval was a young man, the more the cold father exercised his authority, insisting that his brilliant young son complete his medical studies, the more the son identified with his bohemian friends and a life connected to the theater. Only much later did he begin to recuperate the positive memories of his experiences as a medical student. In a letter he wrote to his father while under Blanche's care, he recalled, "I am a little bit of a doctor, having followed two years of courses at the École and the Hôtel-Dieu clinic."[18] It was just such a shift that Blanche apparently sought to promote when he introduced him as lay healer to

17. Gérard de Nerval, "Fin de 1841," in *Oeuvres Complètes*, ed. Jean Guillaume and Claude Pichois (Paris: Bibliothèque de la Pléiade, 1993), 3:1487–8; Gérard de Nerval, *Gérard de Nerval: Selected Works*, trans. Richard Sieburth (London: Penguin, 1999), 331–32.
18. Nerval, "À son père," 3:816.

a fellow inmate. Bearing witness to the delusions of the soldier provoked not only Nerval's compassion but also a gradual identification with that part of himself that had taken care of cholera victims alongside his father long ago.

Thus, one problem in *Aurélia* is the ambiguous way the medical definitions insinuate themselves into the text, in which Nerval the writer admits the pathological nature of the experiences that Nerval the man recounted for Blanche. If the text narrates a pathological descent in part I into the Paris night and into dreams, then is the confinement to the asylum and its Hippocratic language the key to the ascent and cure with which part II concludes? This would render *Aurélia* the emblematic psychiatric tale of the successful resolution of a moral treatment, with Blanche's therapeutic writing project even reconciling the protagonist with the doctor/father. But in such a strict reading, the hermeneutical loss would be too great. Nerval the writer claims a positive potential in locating his text in a Romantic narrative of descent into death and life, a rejuvenation in the protagonist's journey back to the nurturing childhood setting of the Valois, and finally a reimagining of the psychiatric confinement as an ordeal imposed not so much by Blanche as by the divine feminine figure of Isis/Venus/Mary. He casts Aurélia herself as the protagonist's lost star, his Beatrice intervening on his behalf. And he takes up the language of prophecy and vision in the passages of part II identified as "Memorabilia."

Aurélia portrays the tension between the doctors (including the young doctor incarnated in the protagonist himself) who use discursive words to exorcise and "spirit away the Spirit," and the Romantic poet who forges a metaphoric language with which to engage with the dead and the divine. At the end of part II, Nerval asserts that the protagonist has taken up a more active attitude, not simply submitting to his dreams and visions, but working to render them meaningful. He concludes *Aurélia* with these words:

> The treatments I had received had already returned me to the renewed affection of my family and friends, and I now had a healthier view of the world of illusions in which I had for some time lived. All the same, I am happy with the convictions I have acquired, and I compare this series of ordeals I have undergone to what, in the eyes of the ancients, was represented by the idea of a descent into Hell.[19]

Nerval's text ends, then, with "happy" assurances to Blanche, but also with the counterrational phrase "all the same." These last sentences maintain

19. Gérard de Nerval, *Aurélia*, in *Oeuvres Complètes*, ed. Jean Guillaume and Claude Pichois (Paris: Bibliothèque de la Pléiade, 1993), 3:750. See 196.

the powerful contradiction between what the Hippocratic would call "illusions" and what the Asclepian might call "convictions."

Of course, the history of *Aurélia*'s publication skews its reception. Readers of *La Revue de Paris* could read part I simply, but part II was published only after the announcement of the author's death. Has any modern reader not read *Aurélia* as a psychobiographical story? Is it possible to read Nerval's textual assurances at the closing of part II without bringing to bear what is known about his terrible last days? Because of this history, we have come to read *Aurélia* as a cautionary tale, and assess Nerval's Romanticism and possibly also Blanche's treatment as a tragic scientific experiment.

Jung and "Aurélia"

JUNG AND THE FRENCH

In January 1854, at the Hôpital Salpêtrière in Paris, Jules Baillarger (1854) presented his hypothesis of a double-form madness, characterized by alternating poles of depression and mania. Jean-Pierre Falret (1864) challenged this diagnostic innovation with a prior scientific claim, based on work undertaken in 1850. This work had identified a circular madness that moved through three stages: mania, melancholy, and lucidity. The German psychiatrist Emil Kraepelin didn't identify manic-depressive psychosis until 1899, and Eugen Bleuler created the diagnostic category of schizophrenia only in 1908. Even so, the double- or triple-form controversy informed debate in Paris at the time of Nerval's last hospitalizations. When Charcot and Émile Blanche both died in mid-August 1893, the world-famous neurologist was eulogized for his cutting-edge clinical brilliance yet also disparaged for his Napoleonesque theatricality, while the old-school doctor, son of the mental alienist, was remembered not for theoretical innovation but instead as a generous and compassionate practitioner (Murat 2001, 132, 354).

In 1902, Jung quit the Burghölzli sanitorium in Zurich and attended lectures by Pierre Janet in Paris at the Collège de France.[20] From Janet's famous cases of Lucie, Marcelle, and Justine, Jung acquired the notion of charting a divided self into numbered mental states. For example, Janet (1907, 89) described an *abaissement du niveau mental* in which the conscious interests of Marcelle's no. 2 state diminished, and the inferior parts of her mental

20. Pierre Janet, "1902–1903, Les émotions et les oscillations du niveau mental," in *Leçons au Collège de France, 1895-1934* (Paris: l'Harmattan, 2004), 37–41. For contemporaneous lectures in English, see Pierre Janet, *The Majors Symptoms of Hysteria: Fifteen Lectures Given in the Medical School of Harvard University* (New York: Macmillan, 1907).

Figure 16. Pierre Janet

functions, the no. 1 or instinctual side of the personality, prevailed over the ethical—the infantile over the mature. Jung reworked this eventually into his theory of autonomous unconscious complexes that acquire energy withdrawn from the conscious personality (designating ego consciousness as no. 1 and the "Other" or Self as no. 2).[21] Jung also found Janet (1907, 35), like his predecessor Charcot, employing the analogy of the religious concept of possession to portray the mental suffering caused by a fixed idea tyrannizing the brain: "To make yourself heard, you must dream with the patient and speak to him only words in accordance with his delirium. As the patient perceives nothing except the idea he is possessed of, he remembers nothing except that one idea."

21. "How does an autonomous complex arise? For reasons which we cannot go into here, a hitherto unconscious portion of the psyche is thrown into activity, and gains ground by activating the adjacent areas of association. The energy needed for this is naturally drawn from consciousness—unless the latter happens to identify with the complex. ... The intensity of conscious interests and activities gradually diminishes, leading either to apathy—a condition very common with artists—or to a regressive development of the conscious functions, that is, they revert to an infantile and archaic level and undergo something like a degeneration. The 'inferior parts of the functions,' as Janet calls them, push to the fore. ... This too is something we see in the lives of many artists. The autonomous complex thus develops by using the energy that has been withdrawn from the conscious control of the personality." C. G. Jung, "On the Relation of Analytical Psychology to Poetry," in *The Spirit in Man, Art, and Literature*, vol. 15 of Collected Works (1922/1931; repr., Princeton, NJ: Princeton University Press, 1966), para. 123.

Figure 17. C. G. Jung in front of the Burghözli sanitorium

Jung came to evaluate Janet's position as too rationalistic, and he cred-
ited Sigmund Freud and Josef Breuer with the first attempts to abreact the
blocked affect and integrate the repressed contents into consciousness,
rather than working merely to excise or exorcise symptoms from the unconscious sufferer.[22] Still, Jung identified his work with Janet's theorizing of
dissociation as the psychological norm, with the self defined as a wished-for
unity between consciousness and a protean-like multiplicity of unconscious
mental processes. In hysteria, such a synthesis is undermined. For the insane
in general, the *abaissement* into myriad infantile and instinctual functions
happens involuntarily. With artists, such a dissolution of consciousness is
the result of deliberate training.[23] Freudian psychoanalysis ultimately rejected Janet's dissociationism, but according to John Haule, Jung countered
with an archetypal form of dissociationism in which analysts deliberately
use their own dissociability and the possibility of archetypes to forge connections within the disconnectedness of the patient.[24]

22. "The medieval theory of possession (toned down by Janet to 'obsession') was thus taken
over by Breuer and Freud in a more positive form." C. G. Jung, "In Memory of Sigmund
Freud," in *The Spirit in Man, Art, and Literature*, vol. 15 of Collected Works (1939; repr., Princeton, NJ: Princeton University Press, 1966), para. 62.
23. "In Janet's psychology this phenomenon is known as *abaissement du niveau mental*.
Among the insane it happens involuntarily, but with [James] Joyce it is the result of deliberate
training." C. W. Jung, "*Ulysses*: A Monologue," in *The Spirit in Man, Art, and Literature*, vol. 15 of
Collected Works (1934/1952; repr., Princeton, NJ: Princeton University Press, 1966), para. 166.
24. John Haule, "From Somnambulism to the Archetypes: The French Roots of Jung's Split
with Freud," *Psychoanalytic Review* 71, no. 4 (1984): 635–59, in *Carl Gustav Jung: Critical Assess-*

Jung's 1902 trip to Paris was one of the happiest times of his life in terms of free inquiry. For the most part, he frequented both the museums and Paris slums, absorbing the dichotomies between the opulence of the collections at the Louvre and misery such as he had never before witnessed clinging about the neighborhoods north of Les Halles. And he read French novels "in order to approach closer to the French spirit, outwardly so foreign, inwardly so familiar to me."[25] Nerval, the poet/playwright/translator and editor of *le monde dramatique* as well as the disinherited mad wanderer, would have been the perfect companion to both sides of Paris. It is not known if Jung ever discussed Nerval with Janet or Théodore Flournoy, the Geneva specialist in the paranormal whom Jung cited in his medical dissertation and with whom he maintained a positive exchange of ideas until Flournoy's death in 1920; their correspondence is lost. Emma Jung-Rauschenbach, who was far better read in French history and literature than her husband, may have encouraged Jung in his reading of Nerval, although there is no reference to Nerval in the letters they exchanged while Jung stayed in Paris.[26]

In the last of his many revisions of "On the Psychology of the Unconscious," Jung ([1917/1926/1943] 1953/1966, para. 122) introduces Nerval's *Aurélia* into the text to illustrate a discussion of his synthetic or constructive method, showing how a reductive analytic approach breaks down symbolic material into its components:

> The process of coming to terms with the unconscious is a true labour, a work which involves both action and suffering. It has been named the "transcendent function" because it represents a function based on real and "imaginary" or rational and irrational data, thus bridging the yawning gulf between conscious and unconscious. It is a natural process, a manifestation of the energy that springs from the tension of opposites, and it consists in a series of fantasy-occurrences which appear spontaneously in dreams and visions. . . . A classical account of such a proceeding is to be found, for example, in Gérard de Nerval's autobiographical fragment, *Aurélia*.

In this essay, Jung explores the problem of when and how to work psychotherapeutically with archetypal material from the unconscious without breaking it down and translating it directly into consciousness. He acknowledges that many individuals may lack the mental and spiritual

---

ments, ed. Renos Papadopoulos (London: Routledge, 1992), 238–60. On Janet's importance to Jung, see also Sonu Shamdasani, "From Geneva to Zürich: Jung and French Switzerland," *Journal of Analytical Psychology* 43, no. 1 (January 1998): 115–26.

25. Carl Gustav Jung, English translation of draft of *Memories, Dreams, Reflections*, Countway Library of Medicine, Boston, 183.

26. Andreas Jung, personal correspondence, December 24, 2012; Thomas Fischer, personal correspondence, February 8, 2012.

capacities to master the psychological events taking place within them, and thus will require medical help.

With regard to medical psychology, in his *General Psychopathology* Karl Jaspers (1997, 27), taking up Wilhelm Dilthey's terminology, distinguished between Kraepelin's "explanations" (*Erklären*), which worked to discern natural laws acting impersonally through causal connections to produce mental disorders, and "understanding" (*Verstehen*), the "meaningful connections" which worked to demonstrate that mental disorders emerged because of individual and social conflicts. Jaspers articulated the critical epistemological divide between these two methods to which psychiatrists were disposed as well as the danger of mistaking one for the other. For his psychopathology, Jaspers looked to Nerval's *Aurélia* for subjective phenomenological descriptions of crystal clear insight and inflated feelings of possessing strength or power along with a demonstration that the experience of psychosis is not necessarily unpleasant. Jaspers (ibid., 115, 120, 423) considered Nerval to have been schizophrenic or perhaps schizoaffective—or in any case, someone within the schizophrenia diagnostic spectrum.

Jung became convinced that psychiatry functioned at its best in a middle ground between science and history, in service of the whole human being.[27] Mental disorders originated in brain disease, he thought, but also emerge as consequences of conflict between an individual's desires and life circumstances. Jung came to articulate an interpretative pole almost exclusively because he regarded contemporary psychiatric practice as overidentified with brain science; if the conflict between empirical and interpretative psychiatry were more balanced, he said, he would not have felt obliged to take such a strong position. The result of his choice was to identify his psychotherapeutic work with the dynamic interpretative epistemology of understanding rather than with explanations. And the best way to understand was to employ a deliberately equivocal language of psychopathology, describing mental suffering as caused by autonomous complexes that were simultaneously spirits or gods. Unfortunately, as a

---

27. "It will assuredly be a long time before the physiology and pathology of the brain and the psychology of the unconscious are able to join hands. Till then they must go their separate ways. But psychiatry, whose concern is the total man, is forced by its task of understanding and treating the sick to consider both sides, regardless of the gulf that yawns between the two aspects of the psychic phenomenon. Even if it is not yet granted to our present insight to discover the bridges that connect the visible and tangible nature of the brain with the apparent insubstantiality of psychic forms, the unerring certainty of their presence nevertheless remains. May this certainty safeguard investigators from the impatient error of neglecting one side in favor of the other, and, still worse, of wishing to replace one by the other." C. G. Jung, "Schizophrenia," in *The Psychogenesis of Mental Disease*, vol. 3 of Collected Works (1958; repr., Princeton, NJ: Princeton University Press, 1960), para. 584.

result, thinkers such as Jaspers dismissed Jung as either a reductionist or demonologist, respectively.[28]

In his early work at the Burghölzli sanitorium, Jung worked with psychotics, and as late as 1956, lectured to psychiatrists on schizophrenia. In 1945, he used diagnostic terms to describe Nerval in the discussion following the lecture (see 83), and argued that Nerval was unable to handle the psychological events taking place and needed medical containment. At the same time, Jung took up an interpretative position like that of the French psychiatrist and neurologist Jean Delay, who wrote that "a diagnosis … explains nothing about the genius of Nerval and leaves intact the mystery of *Aurélia.*"[29]

JUNG AND ALFRED KUBIN'S ILLUSTRATIONS FOR AURÉLIA

Alfred Kubin was born April 10, 1877, in northern Bohemia. His father was an officer in the Imperial Army of the Austro-Hungarian Empire. When Kubin was only ten years old, his mother died, and he may have tried to commit suicide at her grave. As a child, Kubin was fascinated with the fantastic and drew what he refers to in his autobiography as "psychologically morbid images." When he grew up, he began a military career, but soon suffered another loss: the sudden death of his divisional commander. This loss provoked a psychological crisis for which Kubin was hospitalized for three months. At the age of twenty-five, he proposed to a young woman, but she too died suddenly; her death plunged him into another crisis. A few years later, after he had married and settled into adult life as a professional artist, the death of his father occasioned a fourth crisis. He felt flooded with images that he could not draw. Instead, for an intense period of twelve weeks, Kubin (1967) wrote the novel *Die andere Seite* (*The Other Side*). When he finished it, he worked equally intensely for a period of four weeks drawing illustrations to accompany the text. Kubin (ibid., lxxv) reflected:

> The book was written when I was thirty years old, out of an inner compulsion and psychological necessity. I am more interested in the illustrations than in the text, which I wrote down in an extraordinary state of mind that was literally comparable to intoxication. I felt as though actually possessed of true clairvoyance. My proce-

28. See "3. Jaspers' Attack on Demonology," from "The Pandaemonium of Images," in James Hillman, *Healing Fiction* (Dallas: Spring Publications, 1983), 63–70.

29. Jean Delay, "Autour d'Aurélia," *Les Nouvelles littéraires*, May 29, 1958, cited in Laure Murat, *La jdu docteur Blanche: Historie d'un asile et de ses pensionnaires de Nerval à Maupassant* (Paris: Edition J. C. Lattés, 2001), 110 (translation mine).

dure for the fifty-one drawings was, as usual, a carefully considered one.

Reimagining the text of *The Other Side* as pictures, Kubin (ibid., xxxix) gave up shading and coloring, and devoted himself exclusively to pen-and-ink line drawings, the better to depict the whole imaginary structure of his fantasy. Discovering a métier as an illustrator of text rather than as a painter, he considered his novel a turning point in his spiritual development and art. When he had finished his own book, Kubin began interpreting through images the works of Romantic writers such as Edgar Allan Poe, Fyodor Dostoyevsky, and E.T.A Hoffman. In 1910, his wife, Hedwig Kubin, translated Nerval's *Aurélia* into German, and he illustrated her translation. The book was published by Georg Müller in Munich, under the title *Aurélia oder De Traum und Das Leben*.

Figure 18. Alfred and Hedwig Kubin, 1904

In his autobiography, Kubin (ibid., xl) described his inner creative process as a divided psychological state:

> My fantasy plunges me into a tormenting chaos, and I can regain some measure of calm thought from [philosophy]'s icy thoughts— a seeming paradox that will have to be accepted as fact. I read philosophy with passionate curiosity, the way one reads novels, eager each time to find out "how it will turn out." Nevertheless for years my essential attitude has been one of profound resignation.

In *Psychological Types*, Jung ([1921] 1964, para. 630–31) characterizes the relative strengths and weaknesses of a superior thinking function, and identifies Kubin's "personal equation" as a superior introverted thinking type with intuition:

The extraordinary impoverishment of introverted thinking is compensated by a wealth of unconscious facts. The more consciousness is impelled by the thinking function to confine itself within the smallest and emptiest circle—which seems, however, to contain all the riches of the gods—the more the unconscious fantasies will be enriched by a multitude of archaic contents, a veritable "pandaemonium" of irrational and magical figures, whose physiognomy will accord with the nature of the function that will supersede the thinking function as the vehicle of life. If it should be the intuitive function, then the "other side" will be viewed through the eyes of a Kubin.

The implication here seems to be that Kubin's psychological crises in response to the deaths of his mother, his military commandant, his fiancée, and his father showed deeply dissociative splitting. His ego consciousness, so strongly identified with a superior introverted thinking function, was repeatedly overwhelmed by grief through imagistic intuitions of wounding and abandonment to a morbid world, just on the "other side" of everyday psychological experience.

Jung judged Kubin's *The Other Side* as a richly recorded account of the artist's fantasy life with which the man perhaps had not engaged consciously enough; Kubin had not rendered the fantasies meaningful. Jung ([1928/1935] 1953/1966, para. 342) writes:

Alfred Kubin has given a very good description of the unconscious in his book *Die andere Seite*; that is, he has described what he, as an artist, experienced of the unconscious. It is an artistic experience which, in the deeper meaning of human experience, is incomplete. I would like to recommend an attentive reading of this book to everybody who is interested in these questions. He will then discover the incompleteness I speak of: the vision is experienced artistically, but not humanly. By "human" experience I mean that the person of the author should not just be included passively in the vision, but that he should face the figures of the vision actively and reactively, with full consciousness. ... [A] real settlement with the unconscious demands a firmly opposed conscious standpoint.

Jung depicts the artist as inclined to be satisfied with the aesthetic formulation of the experience of the unconscious, but the person may not understand the formulation enough to act on its moral demands. In his essay "The Transcendent Function," Jung ([1916/1958] 1960/1969, para. 177) argues that the corollary is also true: someone who is inclined to render comprehensible the secrets of the unconscious may need to learn how to suspend judgment, to simply engage with unconscious images in active imagination and thus experience their autonomy.

Jung's path crossed with Kubin's twice in 1932. Jung ([1932] 1976, para. 1716n1) had written a foreword to Oskar A. H. Schmitz's *Märchen aus dem Unbewussten* (1932), illustrated by Kubin. Then, towards the end of that year, Jung answered a letter from Kubin in which he qualifies a comment in his review of James Joyce's *Ulysses*. In that review, Jung referred to *The Other Side* as "a country-cousin of the metropolitan *Ulysses*," and in his letter he praises the rural directness of Kubin's perceptions of unconscious processes, contrasting it to the more labyrinthine quality of Joyce's urbanity.[30]

JUNG ON KUBIN AND NERVAL

Jung's assessment of Kubin is important, particularly because Jung read and imagined *Aurélia* through Kubin's illustrations. Did this incline Jung to group Nerval and Kubin together, as artists who engaged too passively with the unconscious? I suspect Jung differentiated between the two. In writing about artistic creation, Jung often differentiated between psychological and visionary modes. He would have classified *The Other Side* as "visionary," but only in a "restricted and succinct form"; it can be read more fittingly as an ironic allegory in which Kubin's Dream City in central Asia comes to stand for certain shadow aspects of Western civilization. Kubin's (1967, 55) Claus Patera builds his Dream City in central Asia, yet it consists entirely of European buildings and is peopled with the stratifications of Austrian society, with German speakers on top and a shady French quarter populated by "disreputable" Romanians, Slavs, and Jews. Asians reside on the other side of the river (the other side of the other side, as it were) and remain, as in the cliché, inscrutably silent. In a seminar in 1934, Jung (1997, 1308) praised Kubin's Dream City without irony: "It is seen as an artist would see it, who was properly trained not to think about the things he sees in order not to disturb the absolute form and surface of the object; he saw the surface of the collective unconscious most accurately." But in a 1938 seminar, Jung (2008, 214) could downplay *The Other Side* as "actually quite silly": "It was written by a modern artist keen not to think anything, in contrast with the artists of the Renaissance. He gives a description of the unconscious *tel quel* [as it is], pure raw material, a reproduction."

Although Nerval's *Aurélia* also narrates a psychological process, the personal account and settings shift repeatedly into modes that correspond pre-

---

30. See Jung, "*Ulysses*: A Monologue," para. 163–203; see also Carl Gustav Jung, "19 November 1932," in *Letters*, ed. Gerhard Adler and Aniela Jaffé, trans. R.F.C. Hull (Princeton, NJ: Princeton University Press, 1973), 2:104

cisely to the kind of artistic creation that Jung ([1922/1931] 1966, para. 141) considered distinctly visionary:

> This disturbing spectacle of some tremendous process that in every way transcends our human feeling and understanding makes quite other demands upon the powers of the artist than do the experiences of the foreground of life. These never rend the curtain that veils the cosmos; they do not exceed the bounds of our human capacities, and for this reason they are more readily shaped to the demands of art, however shattering they may be for the individual. But the primordial experiences rend from top to bottom the curtain upon which is painted the picture of an ordered world, and allow a glimpse into the unfathomable abyss of the unborn and of things yet to be.

The visionary passages in *Aurélia* depict the protagonist witnessing creation and the evolution of life on earth, as if he has descended dangerously into what Jung (ibid., para. 141) characterizes as "the abyss of prehuman ages, or … a superhuman world of contrasting light and darkness … a primordial experience which surpasses man's understanding and to which in his weakness he may easily succumb."

Nerval's text is explicitly visionary in Jung's sense. Certainly, in both *Aurélia* and *The Other Side*, psychological and archetypal readings are possible, but Nerval's text demands a deeper and more expansive reading than Kubin's. Nerval's protagonist, for instance, identifies a contradiction at the collective heart of mid-nineteenth-century French society, but by the end of the text, "France" accumulates a symbolic significance not unlike "England's green and pleasant land" for Blake. In a dreamlike lysis, Nerval witnesses the possible emergence of "France" as a New Jerusalem, a possible unifier of East and West. In other words, Nerval (1993, 3:722–23) imaginatively sees the possibility of a personal healing of his split consciousness as the resolution of collective political or nationalistic dilemmas:

> When the soul hovers uncertainly between life and dream, between mental disarray and the reappearance of cold reflection, it is in religious belief that one must seek solace. I have never been able to find relief in that school of philosophy which merely supplies us with maxims of self-interest or, at the most, of reciprocity, leaving us nothing but empty experience and bitter doubts. Such a philosophy combats our moral sufferings by deadening our sensibility; like the surgeon, it knows only how to cut out the organ which is causing the pain. But for us, born in an age of revolutions and upheavals which shattered all beliefs, raised at best to practice a vague religion based on a few outward observances and whose lukewarm devotion

is perhaps more sinful than impiety or heresy, for us things become quite difficult whenever we feel the need to reconstruct that mystic temple whose edifice the pure and simple of spirit accept fully traced in their hearts. "The Tree of Knowledge is not that of Life!" And yet can we rid our mind of all the good or evil implanted in it by so many intelligent generations? Ignorance cannot be learned.

I have higher hopes in the goodness of God: we may well be approaching that era when science, as predicted, having accomplished its entire cycle of synthesis and analysis, of belief and negation, will now be able to purify itself and usher forth the miraculous city from chaos and ruin. (see 160)

Identifying a catastrophic split in contemporary consciousness, Nerval employs the Romantic conventions of going down and going back—down into collective memory and back to Clos de Nerval in the Valois where he had collected Roman shards with his great-uncle—all in order to leap forward into the future. Similarly, Jung often used the French colloquial phrase *reculer pour mieux sauter* (to draw back, the better to leap forward) to describe the positive potential in psychological regression. Nerval's protagonist finds within these conventions and dynamics a way to express hope for a new religious attitude and for a science that would correct itself for the benefit of humankind.

Jung demonstrates how one can read Kubin's and Nerval's texts psychologically. However, unlike Kubin, Nerval strips *Aurélia* of proper nouns, deleting names of friends and city streets, deliberately pushing the narrative into a nameless realm. More important, Jung finds that while Kubin is a passive witness in a strange land, Nerval's protagonist begins to "oppose" his dreams and visions. First, his opposition is inward: in the dream, the protagonist attempts to confront and depose his shadowy rival, the Oriental prince. Second, his opposition is outward: he opposes his own attitude toward his confinement in the hospice, which he comes to regard as an ordeal of healing imposed not by Dr. Blanche but instead by a feminine principle to which he must subject himself. Later still, he takes steps towards integrating a Hippocratic stance by trying to heal the soldier and differentiating himself from this soldier's woundedness. Most crucial, Nerval the writer took up Blanche's "moral" project, and chose to portray his protagonist studying his fantasies for their significance and attempting to communicate his way out of his mental alienation. Ironically, at the same time, Nerval increasingly opposed Blanche by actively petitioning for release against the doctor's wishes.

The German poet Heine, who counted Nerval as the only one of his Paris friends with whom he experienced any genuine emotional kinship and the only successful translator of his work from German into any language, described Nerval as "pure soul rather than man, the soul of an angel" (cited in Pawel 1995, 99). When Nerval left the clinic at Passy for the last time, he slipped out of the therapeutic communal frame constructed by Blanche and dropped tragically alone into the shadow side of the so-called City of Light. Jung interprets the numinous figure falling in the squalid Paris courtyard in *Aurélia* as a dream symbol of Nerval's no. 2 personality (1993, 3:698):

> A creature of disproportionate size—man or woman, I do not know—was fluttering about with great difficulty overhead and seemed to be floundering in the thick clouds. In the end, out of breath and energy, it plummeted into the centre of the dark court-yard, snagging and bruising its wings on the roofs and balustrades as it fell. I was able to get a brief look at it. It was tinged with rosy hues and its wings shimmered with countless changing reflections. Draped in a long robe falling into classical folds, it resembled the Angel of Melancholy by Albrecht Dürer. I could not stifle my shrieks of terror, which woke me with a start. (see 123)

Jung himself had wrestled with just such a winged figure during his own psychological crisis, also objectifying it in images and words, and eventually naming it Philemon.

Figure 19. *Melancholia*, by Albrecht Dürer, 1514

Figure 20. *Jacob Wrestling the Angel* (detail), by Eugène Delacroix, 1853–61

Figure 21. "Philemon," by C. G. Jung, *The Red Book: Liber Novus*

NERVAL AND JUNG'S "RED BOOK"

Nerval's "autobiographical fragments" provide a clue for understanding Jung's *Red Book*, about which Jung himself was reticent to speak publicly even late in his life. In fact, *Aurélia* can be regarded as a precursor of *The Red Book*. Both *Aurélia* and *The Red Book* are literary vehicles written for a psychological purpose. In an attempt to heal Nerval the man, Dr. Blanche recommended that Nerval the writer narrate the experiences of a protagonist named "I," a man in love with the figure of Aurélia. Ross Woodman (2005, 159) describes this as learning to "inhabit oneself as a fiction," and differentiates between the English Romantic poets, such as William Wordsworth, who failed in this regard, with negative consequences for their art and lives, and those who accomplished it, such as Blake. In the same way but with an important psychological difference, Dr. Jung advises Jung the writer that to heal Jung the man from a potential psychosis, he should narrate the visions of a protagonist named "I." In this way, he can signify his way out of madness. The result was *The Red Book*. It is particularly moving to consider Jung playing all four roles: doctor, writer, man, and fictional protagonist. One could argue that herein resides one source of Jung's notion of images of the Self as emerging from the complexity of the personality—something irreducible and greater than the sum of its many parts.

Jung recorded his inner life in a series of notebooks known as the *Black Books*. He transferred and transformed some of this material into a more formal presentation that became *The Red Book: Liber Novus*. As the text and images evolved, Jung the writer, like Nerval, took up the symbols and literary conventions of Virgil's *Aeneid*, Dante's *Divine Comedy*, Colonna's *Hypnerotomachia Poliphili*, and Goethe's *Faust*. He portrayed his protagonist's inner states metaphorically and commented on them allegorically, even "scrutinizing" them, and thereby produced what Sonu Shamdasani calls "a work of psychology in a literary form," (cited in Jung 2009, 194), an individual and prophetic work with implications for the split in Western collective consciousness. Jung the writer attempted to formulate the text as Romantic revelation in service of the survival of Eros, a connecting principle; at the same time, he wrote in the language of Jung the psychiatrist, examining the protagonist's insights and trying to draw conclusions. Jung locates his protagonist precisely in this epistemological chasm that Nerval identified between the Asclepian and the Hippocratic. The Romantic approach to such a tension was to seek connections with a time that is both past and future—an imaginal time when the split did not and will not exist. At the end of *Aurélia*, Nerval records Swedenborgian visions of France mediating a transformative reunificiation of East and West.

The 1959 calligraphic transcription of *The Red Book* breaks off with Jung acknowledging that he left his protagonist and his book in order to study the imaginal inherent in alchemy.[31] This strategic leap resembles the double-edged ending of *Aurélia*.[32] Jung's move to investigate alchemy as premodern art/science before its separation into rhetoric versus chemistry was an effort to imagine a possible reunion or, at least, reclassification of art and science. At the time of its publication in English, Jung's *Psychology and Alchemy* was praised as both an important explanation of the practice of psychotherapy and a lexicon of symbolism that is a key to Western culture and language (Frye [1954] 2006). Jung grounded the argument of that book in a psychological analysis of the dreams of the physicist Wolfgang Pauli. In their correspondence, these two thinkers explore the symbolism of fourfold cosmologies in search of a unifying principle. For Pauli, in addition to physics, psychology, and a neutral language, the fourth element to be introduced would be Eros as a connecting principle. For Jung (2001, 110, 128), in addition to the triad of classical physics—space, time, and causality—there would be synchronicity (see also Zabriskie 2001; Cambray 2014). Together, they searched symbolic experiences of the sublime for ways to purify science of its subject-object dualism and value-laden dogmatism. Their findings, in Nerval's terms, are like doors that could liberate one from merely climbing up and down forever in the tower of knowledge.

What better guide for Jung in these explorations than Nerval, with his medical history of psychotic episodes and his lucid, syncretic art? Except, of course, that Nerval did not survive his descent into Hell (see Jung [1918] 1964/1970, para. 24). This difference underlies the psychoanalytic readings of *Aurélia* as cautionary autobiography. Still, Jung distinguishes between a psychological reading of the artist's life and a psychological reading of the art. The autobiographical context may be intriguing for the reader, but Jung ([1922/1931] 1966, para. 147) wants to concentrate instead on the psychology of the art:

---

31. "1959: I worked on this book for 16 years. My acquaintance with alchemy in 1930 took me away from it. The beginning of the end came in 1928, when Wilhelm sent me the text of the 'Golden Flower,' an alchemical treatise. There the contents of this book found their way into actuality and I could no longer continue working on it. To the superficial observer, it will appear like madness. It would also have developed into one, had I not been able to absorb the overpowering force of the original experiences. With the help of alchemy, I could finally arrange them into a whole. I always knew that these experiences contained something precious, and therefore I knew of nothing better than to write them down in a 'precious,' that is to say, costly book and to paint the images that emerged through reliving it all—as well as I could. I knew how frightfully inadequate this undertaking was, but despite much work and many distractions I remained true to it, even if another/possibility never. ... " Carl Gustav Jung, *Liber Novus* [*The Red Book*] (New York: W. W. Norton, 2009), 360.

32. For Jung's interest in the symbolic method of Swedenborg's spiritual hermeneutics, see Eugene Taylor, "Jung on Swedenborg, Redivivus," *Jung History* 2, no. 2 (2007): 27–31.

We should do well, I think, to bear clearly in mind the full consequences of this reduction of art to personal factors, and see where it leads. The truth is that it deflects our attention from the psychology of the work of art and focuses it on the psychology of the artist. The latter presents a problem that cannot be denied, but the work of art exists in its own right and cannot be got rid of by changing it into a personal complex.

Of course, as Jung (ibid., para. 162) makes clear, this position contradicts Freud's important essay on Leonardo da Vinci as well as an entire school of critical interpretation that employs the works to interpret the life of the artist and vice versa:

> Every great work of art is objective and impersonal, and yet profoundly moving. And that is also why the personal life of the artist is at most a help or a hindrance, but is never essential to his creative task. He may go the way of the Philistine, a good citizen, a fool, or a criminal. His personal career may be interesting and inevitable, but it does not explain his art.

That said, it is interesting to chart the extent to which Jung's lecture on *Aurélia* alternates between these two possible readings: the psychology of Nerval's life and that of Nerval's art. It is also intriguing to see how much Jung glosses over Nerval's text rather than analyzing it. In his opening comments Jung (51) warns his audience, "I shall have to leave much for discussion. I can only imply things, because the material is of extraordinary magnitude, and mainly I would like to let the material speak for itself first, while keeping my own interpretations in the background." As much as he theorizes and argues an interpretation, Jung privileges presenting the text. For the most part, he chose simply to read the story aloud (in French) to his audience, to give it voice.[33] Artaud would have approved.

Oddly, Jung ends his lecture not with the psychology of the art but rather with the psychology of Nerval, "a personality that never understood how to prize open the narrow circle of the personal 'I' or to grant admission to the forbidden shadow of another order of things." Perhaps Jung did this under the influence of Kubin's last illustration of *Aurélia*: a picture of an event that is not in the text—its author's death. To what degree, then, did Jung's edition of *Aurélia* with Kubin's illustrations color his reading of Nerval's text?

---

33. "He didn't have a manuscript. He had a few notes and some pictures and the book. He started his lecture by giving a biography of Gérard de Nerval and then to read from the book, the original, in French. His French was very good. Suddenly, he got so much into the story and into the language that he gave the whole lecture in French. ... [H]e so completely entered into the spirit of the book." Marie-Jeanne Schmid interview with Gene Nameche, Jung biographical archive, Countway Library of Medicine, Boston, 60–61.

Or was he inclined to reemphasize Nerval's suffering and leave the audience to confront a dilemma?

As John MacGregor (1989, 81–84) emphasizes, Nerval's contribution to the art of the insane consists not only in writing but also in ink sketches on paper. Like his protagonist, he too painted murals on the walls of the *maison de santé* at Montmartre and also Passy. Observers responded to Nerval's wall paintings (which no longer exist) with astonishment, demanding to know how he could have suddenly intuited artistic techniques that he had never studied and that artists would embrace only a generation later. In *Les maisons de fous*, Alphonse Esquiros wrote, "Illness had developed in him a new talent which had not existed in his state of sanity, or which had, at least, prior to this time, played a scarcely significant role" (1843–44, cited in MacGregor 1989, 82). Statements such as these situate Nerval's paintings as precursors of *art brut* (outsider art), as defined in the studies of the spontaneous art of psychotic patients by Hans Prinzhorn and Jean Dubuffet. Nerval's surviving drawings—the small vignette illustrations, fantastic genealogical charts, and sketches of butterflies and queens—are impossible to date. They are not identifiable with the artist's autobiography and therefore not reducible to the psychological.

The art in Jung's *Red Book* is carefully executed; truly, the book may be called an illuminated text. Jung would no doubt have studied Nerval's artwork assiduously, had he had access to it. Nerval's sketch "Political Assembly for Catherine de Medici" (figure 22) offers a visual assertion to accompany and counterbalance the biographical slant of the last Kubin illustration to *Aurélia*. It corresponds to what Jung calls the movingly impersonal and objective aspect of Nerval's last work, expressed in its closing phrase: "I am happy with the convictions I have acquired, and I compare this series of ordeals I have undergone to what, in the eyes of the ancients, was represented by the idea of a descent into Hell."[34]

Like all literary concepts, the Romantic fell into disfavor. Modernists working between the world wars, however, eventually revived Nerval's reputation. They recognized the prophetic and visionary quality of his art, and celebrated him as a precursor of their own aesthetic. Equally enthusiastic postmodernists claimed Nerval as a pioneer in blurring the boundaries between outer and inner worlds, fact and fiction.

34. One can, with a comparative eye, examine Kubin's rubrics and illustrations in Jung's copy of the Georg Müller edition of Nerval's text, *Aurélia oder De Traum und Das Leben*, reproduced herein (120–96), and Jung's artwork in the *Red Book*.

Figure 22. "Political Assembly for Catherine de Medici." Gérard de Nerval, 1854–55

As for Jung, Frye considered him to be the most comprehensive guide not to Romanticism as a movement but instead to the myth of romance itself (Dolzani 2004, lvii). The often-stated opposition between Freud and Jung renders this distinction explicit. One of the great writers of descent, Freud focused on falling: the metamorphic fall of the gods into humankind, of humanity into the reality principle, of life into dead matter, of tragedy and Thanatos. Jung, on the other hand, articulated descent and the possibility of ascent, the goal being to create a genuinely human community grounded in Eros. This notion highlights Jung's ideas about the dangerous creative possibilities that are born when endogamic psychic energy flows back into the unconscious. He identifies this energy historically with the revolutionary spirit in Romanticism that contradicted Enlightenment assumptions that all genuine questions can be answered, that all answers are knowable, that virtue consists ultimately in knowledge accessible to reason, and that all virtues are compatible (see his comments on Philipp Lersch's *Des Traum in der deutschen Romantik*, cited in Jung 2014, 74–81). As Isaiah Berlin observed, the Romantic movement throughout Europe clustered around two obsessive feelings associated with regressive descent, both articulated in *Aurélia*: nostalgia, the sense of having lost an eternal home with the concomitant agony of feeling driven to describe what is irretrievable and inexpressible; and paranoia, the terrifying sensation of floating like Arthur Schopenhauer's tiny boat on a vast and fathomless ocean, an overwhelming intuition that tips easily into fearful delusions and eventually ends in death by water. Jung, as psychologist, looks for the unifying impulse of romance residing behind these apparently irreconcilable clusters of images and feelings, something akin to the hazardous wish to break up the nature of the given (Berlin 1999, 104).

It is the individual's conscious relationship with the symbol of rebirth and restorative healing, not only historically Romantic, but also inherent in the romantic mode at any time, that Jung clearly wants to honor in Nerval and preserve for collective consciousness in the future. In this regard, in the minutes of the discussion that followed the 1945 lecture, Jung points specifically to Nerval's mysterious and painful image of the forging of a winged animal in a beam of light and purple flames, his fallen daemon or genius writhing back into life. Inspired by Heine's doppelgänger and Hoffman, Jung portrays the divided self as necessarily locked in conflictual interplay. He characterizes those who excel in human endeavor—including patients like Nerval and doctors like Émile Blanche, artists like James Joyce and Alfred Kubin, and scientists like Wolfgang Pauli—as sick human beings who nevertheless bring to bear upon history the weight of their consciousness and creative integrity. In any culture, the boundaries that define the disciplines of art and science constantly shift, but artists and scientists all attempt to evoke the inexpressible vision of that unceasing activity that is life. And in romance as a mode, the only way to understand reality without killing it in the process is by creating myths and symbols.

In a late short story (1854), Nerval describes the stone inscriptions famously known as the Enigma of Bologna, which he encountered during his travels in Italy. He cites the palindromic riddle AELIA LAELIA and the Latin epitaphs carved into the stone—the first being *nec vir, nec mulier, nec androgyna, nec puella, nec iuvenis, nec anus, nec casta, nec meretrix, nec pudica, sed omnia* [neither male nor female, nor androgyne, nor maiden, nor young, nor old, nor chaste, nor mad, nor modest, but all this together]—and what comes to his mind from this little collection of paradoxes is a sequence of mythologized memories. Nerval writes a text about a character in contemporary Vienna, identifying himself with Prometheus, who is tortured by a sweet and seductive Pandora with her box of woes.[35]

Figure 23. *Eva Prima Pandora*, (oil on canvas), by Jean Cousin the Elder, 1549–50

In his late work, *Mysterium Coniunctionis*, Jung also looks into the nature of the Enigma of Bologna. Jung ([1963] 1970, para. 52) writes that the epitaphs are sheer nonsense, a joke that inspired two centuries of commentaries, "a flypaper for every conceivable projection that buzzed in the human mind," but he is intrigued by the psychological fact of all that buzzing just outside the definition of what is rational. As a psychologist, Jung (ibid.,

35. Gérard de Nerval, "Pandora," in *Oeuvres Complètes*, ed. Jean Guillaume and Claude Pichois (Paris: Bibliothèque de la Pléiade, 1993), 3:655–63; Gérard de Nerval, *Gérard de Nerval: Selected Works*, trans. Richard Sieburth (London: Penguin, 1999), 245–53. See also Knapp 1980.

(para. 52) explains that often when a logical argument is at its most stupid, its content is at its most significant: "Sometimes a differential diagnosis as between tomfoolery and creativity is difficult to make, and it happens again and again that the two are confused." That is, whenever socially sanctioned knowledge has petrified into dogma, unconscious projections onto paradoxes and other puzzles merit investigating. In that inferior matter may be a nugget of truth cast on to the cultural scrap heap. Jung emphasizes that in any myth of rebirth, the scrap heap outside the city walls contains the possibilities for a society's future survival. Reexamining the stone of Bologna, Jung sifts through numerous nonsensical Renaissance alchemical interpretations and proposes that there is one that merits rescuing. The singular interpretation describes the Enigma of Bologna as the complex product of a number of things: a fictitious woman; an imagined shadowy genius in female form; an ungodly spirit that mythical Jupiter employs to contradict the hubris of the Promethean impulse, an anima enclosed within a tomb that is also a boxlike container that is also a living oak; and a precarious beloved (*incertissima amasia*) who is also an *inspiratrice*. In passing, Jung notes that in 1588, the alchemist H. Reusner identifies this torchbearing tree-woman, this philosophical tree personified in its feminine numen, as Pandora. All this is to say, a century apart, Nerval and Jung read the same enigmatic text, and from the scrap heap, they each retrieve the same name (see Panofsky and Panofsky 1965).

When Jung gave his 1945 lecture in Zurich, the amorality and shadow possibilities in historic Romanticism, with its roots in the darkness, had been terrifyingly concretized in the distorted nationalistic irrationalism of Nazi Germany. Ninety years earlier, Nerval, citing the myth of Orpheus, cast his Asclepian convictions in a tragic mode: the severed sections of the uroboric snake that encircles the earth rejoin in a demonic parody of wholeness, sealed by the blood of humankind. (In the discussion that followed Jung's lecture, Linda Fierz pointed to the depiction of youths in *Aurélia* as prophetically similar to the German youths in Ernst Jünger's *On the Marble Cliffs*; see 85). At the same time, Nerval subverted what he discerned as the dangerous hubris in Dr. Blanche's Hippocratic outlook by submitting the manuscript of *Aurélia* to his publisher rather than to his doctor. Jung likewise resisted calling his visionary experiences "art," and thereby rendering them either inflationary and egoistic or deflationary and merely personal.[36] And at the same time, he emphasized the extent to which individual neuroses and collective manias like nationalism are caused by one-sided rationalism and a poverty of symbols, so that our divided selves fail to connect one

36. For an argument about Jung's distinction between art and nature, and its origins in Jung's discussions with Maria Moltzer, see Sonu Shamdasani 1995, 115–37; 1998a, 56–75.

experience to another and we become possessed by the few symbols that we can call our own (see Auden 2002, 242).

Jung's lecture on *Aurélia* rewards study now for what it argues about Nerval as visionary artist and what it reveals about *The Red Book* as Jung's articulation of the symbolic in modern thought. Here in this only reading by Jung of a Romantic text, we find both a cautionary psychological tale and a validation of Nerval's visionary experience as genuine encounter.[37] Jung reasserts the extraordinary magnitude of Nerval's argument for renewing science as it becomes increasingly doctrinaire and grounding humanity's hopes for the future in a connection with the dead.

Editor's Note

The documents in this volume are presented in reverse chronological order:
- Jung's handwritten abstract of his lecture—the only document about Nerval included by the editors in Jung's Collected Works. Translated transcription.
- The revised 1945 lecture (with alchemical illustrations) that Jung presented at the Psychological Club in Zurich, translated into English.
- In a letter dated September 11, 1956, to Marie-Louise von Franz (now in the ETH-Bibliothek collections), Aniela Jaffé acknowledges having found in a cabinet a copy of the 1945 lecture, apparently drawn up by Jung's secretary, Marie-Jeanne Schmid, as well as the minutes of the discussion that followed that lecture. Included here are, in English translation, these minutes of the discussion that followed the 1945 lecture, which convey more of Jung's ironic conversational tone and Swiss colloquialisms than do the lecture notes themselves.
- In English translation, the notes of the 1942 lecture to the Swiss Society for Psychiatry and Psychotherapy, showing Jung's extensive revisions (many handwritten on the backs of the pages).
- Five pages of Jung's handwritten notes. Translated transcription and five holographs.
- Richard Sieburth's translation into English of the entire text of Nerval's *Aurélia*, presented with Kubin's illustrations and Jung's marginalia. The library of Jung's home at Seestrasse 228, Küsnacht,

---

37. "It is of course ironical that I, a psychiatrist, should at almost every step of my experiment have run into the same psychic material which is the stuff of psychosis and is found in the insane. This is the fund of unconscious images which fatally confuse the mental patient. But it is also the matrix of a mythopoeic imagination which has vanished from our rational age." Carl Gustav Jung, *Memories, Dreams, Reflections* (New York: Random House, 1962) 188.

Switzerland, holds three copies of *Aurélia* (listed here in order by the cataloging system): BF20, a version in the original French, published in 1927 in the Editions de la Pléiade series by Gauthier-Ferrières, with an introduction by Jean Giraudoux; BF21, a Swiss edition of *Aurélia* in German translation, published by Verlag Benna Schwabe and Company in Klosterberg, Basel, in 1943; and most important, BF22, *Aurélia oder De Traum und Das Leben*, the translation into German by Hedwig Kubin, with Alfred Kubin's illustrations, published in 1910 by Georg Müller of Munich.

Jung's Abstract on Nerval from
The Symbolic Life
(Collected Works, Volume 18)

GÉRARD DE NERVAL (PSEUDONYM OF GÉRARD LABRUNIE, 1808–1853) WAS A lyric poet and translator of Goethe and Heine. He is best known by his posthumously published novel *Aurélia*, in which he relates the history of his anima and at the same time of his psychosis. The dream at the beginning, of a vast edifice and the fatal fall of a winged daemon, deserves special attention. The dream has no lysis. The daemon represents the self, which no longer has any room to unfold its wings. The disastrous event preceding the dream is the projection of the anima upon *"une personne ordinaire de notre siècle,"* with whom the poet was unable to work on the *mysterium* and in consequence jilted Aurélia. Thus he lost his *"pied à terre"* and the collective unconscious could break in. His psychotic experiences are largely descriptions of archetypal figures. During his psychosis the real Aurélia appears to have died, so that his last chance of connecting the unconscious with reality, and of assimilating its archetypal contents, vanished. The poet ended by suicide. The MS of *Aurélia* was found on his body.

Published in the Psychological Club's *Jahresbericht*, 1945–46.

Translated by R.F.C. Hull, in C. G. Jung, "Gérard de Nerval," *The Symbolic Life*, vol.18 of Collected Works (1945; repr., Princeton, NJ: Princeton University Press, 1976), para. 1748.

THREE

Lecture on Gérard de Nerval
by C. G. Jung

Lecture
delivered at the
Psychological Club
9 June 1945

LADIES AND GENTLEMEN.

The reason why of all things I want to speak about Gérard de Nerval lies in the fact that there is a posthumous text of his titled *Aurélia* whose content I would like to make accessible to you. Unfortunately, I cannot do this in a way that would illuminate it down to its darkest corner. I shall have to leave much to discussion. I can only imply things, because the material is of extraordinary magnitude, and mainly I would like to let the material speak for itself first, while keeping my own interpretations in the background.

Gérard de Nerval is the pseudonym of Gérard Labrunie, born 23 May 1808, died 25 January 1853. He published some beautiful lyric poems, the so-called *Vers dorés* [Golden Verses]; as well, he translated many poems by Klopstock, Goethe, and Heine. Also, in 1828, he published a translation of *Faust* that he presented to the still-living Goethe, from whom he received a flattering response. From what I've read of this translation, I am a little doubtful about the sincerity of the complements that Goethe bestowed upon him. Later he published two further texts, *Lorely: Souvenirs d'Allemagne* [Lorelei: Memories of Germany] and *Carnet de Voyage en Orient* [Voyage to the Orient] (1848–50).[1] He traveled a lot in the Orient and also in Germany, mainly under unusual psychological circumstances. We will come back to that.

---

1. Gérard de Nerval's *Voyage to the Orient*, in English translation by Conrad Elphinstone (originally published in two volumes as *Women of Cairo: Scenes of Life in the Orient*), has been recently republished, in 2012, by Antipodes Press.

With regard to [secondary] literature about Gérard de Nerval, I will be able to give you details later.[2]

The text *Aurélia* opens with the following sentence: "Dream is a second life."[3] And from here, the author immediately goes on to speak of what nowadays we call the unconscious: "Little by little, the dim cavern is suffused with light and, emerging from its shadowy depths, the pale figures who dwell in limbo come into view, solemn and still. Then the tableau takes on shape, a new clarity illuminates these bizarre apparitions and sets them in motion—the spirit world opens for us."[4]

Then he begins to describe his experiences and adventures and says the following: "I shall attempt to transcribe the impressions of a lengthy illness that took place entirely within the mysteries of my own mind—although I do not know why I use the term illness here, for so far as I am concerned, I never felt more fit. At times I believed my strength and energy had redoubled; I seemed to know everything, understand everything; my imagination afforded me infinite delights. Having recovered what men call reason, must I lament the loss of such joys?..."[5]

He calls this state a "*Vita nuova*," following the example of Dante, as you will already have noticed.[6] Of it, he says: "This *Vita nuova* was divided into two phases in my case. Here are the notes relating to the first of these.

"A woman I had long loved and whom I shall call Aurélia was lost to me. The circumstances of this event which was to have such a major influence on my life do not really matter. Anybody can search his memories for the emotion which proved the most devastating or for the cruelest blow of fate; the only decision in these cases is whether to die or go on living—later I shall explain why I did not choose death. Condemned by the woman I loved, guilty of an offense for which I no longer hoped to be forgiven, my only course was to plunge myself into vulgar intoxications; I affected a gay, carefree air, I traveled the world, entranced by its diversity and un-

---

2. Jung's 1942 and 1945 lecture notes cite the following secondary sources: "Gauthier-Ferrières: *Gérard de Nerval. La Vie et l'Oeuvre, 1808-1855*, Paris, 1906. Julia Cartier: *Un Intermédiaire entre la France et l'Allemagne. Gérard de Nerval*. Genève 1904. R. Bizet: *La double vie de Gérard de Nerval*. 1928."

3. 1945 lecture footnote: "1852–1853" [*sic*]. Much of the text was probably composed beginning in 1853, although some portions, especially part II, may well be as late as December 1854. See Nerval's letter to Dr. Blanche, December 3, 1853, and his letter to his father, December 2, 1853, explaining his intentions, in Gérard de Nerval, *Oeuvres Complètes*, ed. Jean Guillaume and Claude Pichois (Paris: Bibliothèque de la Pléiade, 1993), 3:832–33.

4. 1945 lecture footnote: "Gérard de Nerval: Aurélia. Collection des Écrits Intimes, Editions de la Pléiade, Paris, 1927, p. 25."

5. 1945 lecture footnote: "l.c. p. 26."

6. Dante's first book, titled literally "The New Life," is composed of a selection of his early poems accompanied by a commentary in prose. See Dante, *Vita Nuova*, trans. Barbara Reynolds (London: Penguin Classics, 2004).

predictability; the bizarre costumes and customs of distant lands especially appealed to me, for it seemed to me that I was thereby relocating the conditions of good and evil, the outer limits, as it were, of what we French define as *feelings*. What madness, I told myself, to go on platonically loving a woman who no longer loves you. The trouble is I have read too much; I have taken the inventions of the poets too seriously and have made a Laura or Beatrice out of an ordinary woman of our century."[7]

At this point we must ask: Who was this Aurélia? Unfortunately, very little is known about her. We know that she was a minor actress and that the two of them met, but we do not know at all what kind of relationship they had. Still, from what I have just read to you, you will be able to gather what is remarkable about it. Namely, that he had taken this relationship to be an entirely ordinary attachment, which is apparent from his down-to-earth phrase: "She is a little woman!" It was only belatedly, so to speak, that he became aware of somehow having done something wrong. That is, it seemed to him that he had taken the "inventions of the poets too seriously" and cobbled together a Beatrice for himself out of an "ordinary woman of our century." He viewed this as "madness." You can see where it comes from: he had read too much. In books, you speak like that; it's the kind of thing you do in books. In his self-absorption and literary delusion, he thought he had manufactured a case out of sheer literary tradition.[8] And he was unable to reconcile what had so portentously crept out from within, with this "ordinary woman of our century." No wonder he escaped and tried to forget, as one gets over a little love story by taking up a distraction.

Then, in Italy he was lucky to enjoy a little *intermezzo amoroso*. He was able to feel genuine emotion again. But oh horror! in the decisive moment his libido let him down (as we say in our technical jargon). Abruptly he was disillusioned and realized that he had no relationship with this lady at all. Still, she cared for him in a friendly way and apparently—according to his description—even arranged a meeting with Aurélia. Now we have to bear in mind that Gérard de Nerval believed something terrible had happened. He believes he had somehow committed a wrong, suffered a loss that he was apparently unable to explain. And so in this state he meets her again at a party. About this meeting he says: "As a result, finding myself one day at a gathering at which she was also present, I saw her come in my direction and extend her hand. How to interpret this gesture and the deep, mournful glance she cast in greeting me? I took it to be forgiveness for the past; the simple phrases she addressed to me, graced by the divine accent of pity, acquired a value beyond words; it was as if something religious had infused itself into a love heretofore profane and imprinted it with the seal of eternity."

---

7. 1945 lecture footnote: "l.c. p. 26 ff."
8. Self-absorption, in German, is literally *Ichbefangenheit*. See 86, 90.

In spite of this impression, the meeting didn't lead to a reconciliation or a renewal of the relationship. Shortly afterwards he has to return to Paris, but with the intention of seeing there again these two ladies, "*ses deux amies.*" However, back in Paris something altogether different happens: "One evening, around midnight, as I was making my way back to my lodgings, I raised my eyes by chance and noticed a house number lit up by a street lamp. It was the same number as my age. Then, lowering my eyes, I saw before me a woman with hollow eyes and a pallid face whose features seemed to be those of Aurélia. I said to myself: this must be an omen of her death or mine!"

So, instead of meeting Aurélia in reality, he has this strange experience from which—as you have heard—he infers either her death or his own. Gradually it becomes clear to him that it is he who is going to die; in fact, on the very next day at the same time: "That night I had a dream which confirmed this idea. I was wandering through an immense building made up of several rooms, some being used as study halls, others devoted to conversation or philosophic debate. Out of curiosity, I stopped in one of the former rooms, where I thought I recognized my old teachers and schoolmates. The lessons dealing with Greek and Roman authors droned on, their monotonous hum resembling some prayer to the goddess Mnemosyne. I passed on to another room where philosophical discussions were taking place. I took part in these for a while, then left to find myself a room in a hostelry with huge staircases and bustling with travelers.

"I lost my way several times in the long corridors, and as I was crossing one of the central galleries, I was struck by a strange scene. A creature of disproportionate size—man or woman, I do not know—was fluttering about with great difficulty overhead and seemed to be floundering in the thick clouds. In the end, out of breath and energy, it plummeted into the center of the dark courtyard, snagging and bruising its wings on the roofs and balustrades as it fell. I was able to get a brief look at it. It was tinged with rosy hues and its wings shimmered with countless changing reflections. Draped in a long robe falling in classical folds, it resembled the Angel of Melancholy by Albrecht Dürer. I could not stifle my shrieks of terror, which woke me with a start."

The exposition of this dream shows the past and present life of the dreamer in confrontation and discussion—his philosophical and scientific-historic interests and so on. The complication, that is to say, the development, consists of the fact that throughout all these activities, he is looking for a room, his room, which apparently he does not know. And for that reason he gets lost. Up until this moment, he had been going through life without having a room of his own. His individual existence appears to have been a mere assumption and not yet a fact. Hence his search for his room. The climax of the dream, its peripeteia, is in this case also the catastrophe.

This is the fall of the daemon or genius into the inner court of the building. It is noteworthy that this dream has no lysis. From my experience, dreams without lysis are extremely rare, and I have reached the assumption—which I am not proclaiming as a universal truth—that there is something fatal about such dreams.[9]

The daemon's "rosy hues" indicate a fiery quality.[10] The wings of a thousand colors evoke the alchemical idea of *cauda pavonis*, which for its part, represents a colorful unfolding, a breaking open.[11] The same idea appears in Goethe: "In colorful refraction, we find life."[12] This superhuman daemonic being appears to be something like *his* daemon. If we want to translate this into modern vocabulary, we would have to say: It represents the Self. That is why it is related to the inner court of the huge building. But there is something peculiar about this collapse, this fall of the daemon into the inner courtyard. Obviously this does not mean that the winged being would have taken up lasting residence in the inner court; more to the point, it would hover over the court—otherwise, it would have no need of wings. This being, with its thousand colors, with its obviously lavish play of colors, represents a complete unfolding, because the Self wishes to realize itself, namely, in the abundance of its qualities and its colors. It can only do so when the man, the human being, gives it actions to perform. Without such actions the Self cannot unfold, since the Self appears only in what we do. If we give it nothing to do, or nothing more to do, then the Self remains invisible, imprisoned inside itself and robbed of its impetus. It cannot unfold anymore, as we have withdrawn the necessary basis, and as a consequence it turns into the Angel of Melancholy. Melancholy supplies a striking image for this condition.[13] She is indeed a depression, a weighing down, and to be

9. With regard to the form of Nerval's dreams, already in his handwritten notes (108), Jung structures his interpretations into four parts: the exposition or statement of place, the development (literally, in German, the tying of the knot), the culmination or peripeteia, and the lysis—a solution or result. He outlines this interpretative structure in C. G. Jung, "On the Nature of Dreams," in *The Structure and Dynamics of the Psyche*, vol. 8 of Collected Works (1945/1948; repr., Princeton, NJ: Princeton University Press, 1960/1969), para. 561–64.

10. 1942 lecture: "The daemon's 'rosy hues' ('*teintes vermeilles*') indicate Eros or fire." See 92.

11. *Cauda pavonis*: "The 'Peacock's Tail' is a significant moment in alchemical work when the material in the vessel changes into many colors, the play of colors leading back to the one white color that contains all colors and to the creation of the Philosopher's Stone." C. G. Jung, *Mysterium Coniunctionis*, vol. 14 of Collected Works (1963; repr., Princeton, NJ: Princeton University Press, 1970), para. 388.

12. Translator's note: "*Am farbigen Abglanz haben wir das Leben*," Goethe, Faust II, line 4727. *Abglanz* can mean both reflection and refraction, but of the two, the more Goethean expression would seem to refer to refraction, also used in his "*Farbenlehre*."

13. "Thus an old alchemist—and a cleric!—prays: '*Horridas nostrae mentis purge tenebras, accende lumen sensibus!*' (Purge the horrible darkness of our mind, light a light for our senses!) The author of this sentence must have been undergoing the experience of the *nigredo*, the first stage of the work, which was felt as 'melancholia' in alchemy and corresponds to the

even more precise, from the head to the deeper regions of the body. All life, so to speak, pulls itself back into the depths of the body. Externally all that remains are inhibitions, actually the inhibition of all vital activities, and nothing happens anymore—with the one exception of suicide.

At this point the question naturally arises: What is the source of this strange situation? What are its causes? But of course we have already heard. The poet has somehow withdrawn from the reality in which he might have been able to develop. Something has come upon him in the form of his Aurélia that he is wholly unable to associate with an "ordinary person of our century." He has evaded reality, and it has gradually dawned on him, as I have already pointed out, that something really special had happened. He discovered that he had made a Beatrice out of this person. And it is precisely in this perception that he has become entrapped, unable to develop any further. He withdraws the power of his actions from the Self, and the Self can no longer manifest. It crashes down.[14]

The author then continues his description: "The next day I was in a hurry to see all my friends. I was mentally saying good-bye to them, and without letting them know what was on my mind, I launched into passionate disquisitions on mystical topics; I astonished them by my peculiar eloquence; it seemed to me that I understood everything, that the mysteries of the world were being revealed to me in these final hours." This peculiar mood is like a launching out, but a launching out before retreating.

Once again, this swells up in him, but then only to bid farewell to his friends. And significantly he devotes himself to "mystical topics," to the "mysteries of the world" that begin to obtrude whenever this figure that is Aurélia appears on the scene.

"That evening, as the fatal hour seemed to be drawing near [—precisely that hour in which he expected to die—], I was at a club, sitting at table with two friends, holding forth on painting and music, defining my views on the generation of colors and the meaning of numbers. One of them, by the name of Paul ***, wanted to accompany me back to my lodgings, but I told him I was not going home. 'Where are you going?' he asked. 'To the Orient!'" [—said he]. Now, the Orient is the territory in which he had traveled. But the East also includes Germany to which he tended to return whenever he was feeling deranged, as it was there that he felt at his best in these moments.

"And as he walked by my side, I began to scan the sky for a certain star I thought I knew, as if it had some influence over my fate. Having located it, I continued on my way, following the streets where I could see it ahead of

---

encounter with the shadow in psychology." C. G. Jung, *Psychology and Alchemy*, vol. 12 of Collected Works (1953; repr., Princeton: Princeton University Press, 1968), para. 42.

14. In the 1942 lecture, Jung formulates this differently: "The Angel of Melancholy is the mental alienation that drops on him." See 92.

me, forging onwards, as it were, towards my destiny and wanting to keep the star in view until the moment death was to strike. But having reached the intersection of three streets, I refused to go any further. My friend seemed to be exerting superhuman strength to get me to move on; he was growing ever larger in my eyes and taking on the features of an apostle. The spot on which we stood appeared to rise up, losing all its urban features—on a hilltop surrounded by vast expanses of emptiness, this scene had now become a battle between two spirits, a kind of biblical temptation. "'No!' I said. 'I do not belong to your heaven. Those who await me are in that star. They predate the revelation that you have announced. Let me rejoin them, for the one I love is among them, waiting for us to meet again.'"

The idea of the dream, that he is searching for his room, recurs here as a living vision, in a sort of delirious condition. Now it has become a star with which his fate is linked, and he resolves to go to this star or at least to travel in its direction—while believing that he will die on the way. But where the three roads converge, he feels his journey has been halted. Well, these three roads form a three-way crossroad and, as you know, that is always an uncanny place. Hecate is the Trivia.[15] This is a legacy from antiquity (we shall encounter antiquity also in another form). Here it suddenly becomes clear to him that he stands in contradiction to his Christian world. His friend takes on the features of an apostle and steps in his way, trying to drive him away from the place. But he cries out that he does not belong in his friend's [Christian] heaven. Those who were waiting for him on that star, they were older than the Christian revelation. It was with *them* he sought reunion, because Aurélia belongs to them. Here you can see how the anima is linked to antiquity. I want to refrain from further amplifications, which you yourselves can imagine anyhow.[16]

---

15. "The triadic character is an attribute of the gods of the underworld, as for instance the three-bodied Typhon, three-bodied and three-faced Hecate, and the 'ancestors' with their serpent bodies." C. G. Jung, "The Spirit Mercurius," *Alchemical Studies*, vol. 13 of Collected Works (1943/1948; repr., Princeton, NJ: Princeton University Press, 1968), para. 270.

16. Here, as explained in his opening words, Jung deliberately privileges Nerval's material itself and refrains from presenting the following amplifications from his 1942 lecture (93): "Cf.: ROSENCREUTZ: Aegean Festival and the hierosgamos. FAUST: Walpurgis Night. ... TANNHAEUSER: The mountain of Venus." Respectively: (1) Christian Rosencreutz is the pseudonym of the alchemical author Johann Valentin Andreae, whose works include *The Chymical Wedding*. Jung writes: "An essential feature of the royal marriage is therefore the sea-journey, as described by Christian Rosencreutz. This alchemical motif was taken up by Goethe in *Faust II*, where it underlies the meaning of the Aegean Festival." Jung, *Mysterium Coniunctionis*, para. 658. (2) Jung also notes that Faust only just survives gazing on the spooks and bogeys of Walpurgis Night (April 30) because of Mephistopheles's helpful matter-of-fact point of view. Jung, *Psychology and Alchemy*, para. 119. (3) Tannhäuser is the legendary knight who found and eventually never returned from the subterranean realm of Venus. With regard to this group of citations, in his essay "The Visions of Zosimos," Jung writes, "It is evident that some alchemists passed through this process of realization to the point where only a

This enormous "elevation," this being lifted up into the realm of the gigantic, stems from the approach of the unconscious, representing a powerful world that, as you know, is capable of bringing about monstrous inflations. For Gérard, the Orient is the Land of the Unconscious (as we would say), the land of the inner life. He especially associates a lot of mystical ideas with the Orient. One might say that his goal seems first to join antiquity, which is why he sojourns at Hecate's crossroads. You know, of course, that Aurélia is in good company here. For instance, the "She" in Rider Haggard's book also had a previous life in antiquity.[17] You know the Helen story in *Faust*, you know the legend of Orpheus who had to seek his Euridyce in the underworld. In this connection I would also like to quote Faust, who says:

> Mephisto, do you see
> off there, alone, dead-pale, a lovely girl?
> Now she is slowly moving away,
> dragging her feet as if they were in fetters.
> I have to say I can't help thinking
> that she looks like my own dear Gretchen.
> …
> I know those are the eyes of someone dead,
> eyes that no loving hand has closed.
> That is the breast which Gretchen let me press,
> that the sweet body which gave me joy.
> …
> What ecstasy, and yet what pain!
> I cannot bear to let this vision go.

---

thin wall separated them from psychological self-awareness. Christian Rosencreutz is still this side of the dividing line, but with Faust, Goethe came out on the other side and was able to describe the psychological problem which arises when the inner man, or greater personality that before had lain hidden in the homunculus, emerges into the light of consciousness and confronts the erstwhile ego, the animal man… [Rosencreutz] was wise enough to stay outside the magic circle, living as he did within the confines of tradition. Goethe was more modern and therefore more incautious. He never really understood how dreadful was the Walpurgisnacht of the mind against which the Christian dogma offered protection, even though his own masterpiece spread out this underworld before his eyes in two versions." C. G. Jung, "The Visions of Zosimos," in *Alchemical Studies*, vol. 13 of Collected Works (1938/1954; repr., Princeton, NJ: Princeton University Press, 1968), para. 120.

17.   Jung refers often to Haggard's fictional anima figure "She-who-must-be-obeyed," such as in the essay "Marriage as a Psychological Relationship," where he observes, "Rider Haggard's *She* gives some indication of the curious world of ideas that underlies the anima projection. They are in essence spiritual contents, often in erotic disguise, obvious fragments of a primitive mythological mentality that consists of archetypes, and whose totality constitutes the collective unconscious." C. G. Jung, "Marriage as a Psychological Relationship," in *The Development of Personality*, vol. 17 of Collected Works (1925/1931; repr., Princeton, NJ: Princeton University Press, 1954), para. 341.

How strange that on that lovely neck
there is an ornament a single scarlet thread
no thicker than a knife!

Mephisto: You're right, I see it too.
She also can transport her head beneath her arm,
thanks to the fact that Perseus lopped it off.[18] *(—the Gorgon!)*

Hecate is also the Gorgon, and that indicates the other aspect of the meeting at the Trivia: namely, the petrification, the imprisonment and torpidity in schizophrenia. So, like Lot's wife and Eurydice, the author begins to look back and to go back. He does not go forward as life does, because he has indeed rejected life. He goes backwards out of life—he goes back into history. For this reason he also says: "Here began for me what I shall call the overflow of dream into real life." The dreamworld begins to replace his real world.

Now he goes on alone—having parted from his friend—heading farther towards the star, while singing a mysterious hymn about which he says: "Finding myself alone, I struggled to my feet and again set off in the direction of the star, not letting it stray from my sight for one moment. As I walked along, I chanted a mysterious hymn which I thought I remembered having heard in some other life and which filled me with a joy beyond words."—But do not forget that he is, of course, always in the face of death, and this extraordinary mysterious joy that fills him brings Nietzsche to mind:

Golden Serenity, come!
You, most secret, sweetest
anticipation of the pleasure of death![19]

While singing this hymn he takes off his clothes—meaning symbolically that he discards his body.

"The route appeared to lead ever upwards as the star grew ever larger. Then, standing there with my arms outstretched, I awaited the moment at which my soul would separate from my body, magnetically attracted into

---

18. Johann Wolfgang von Goethe, *Faust I* and *II*, trans. Stuart Atkins (Princeton, NJ: Princeton University Press, 1984), part I, lines 4184–208. The handwritten note in the 1945 lecture (punctuated with an exclamation mark) emphasizes Mephisto's matter-of-fact point about who Faust sees.
19. Nietzsche's *"Die Sonne sinkt"* [The Sun Sets] (1888) is one of six poems titled *Dionysos-Dithyramben* [*Dionysian Dithyrambs*] that were published in the 1891 edition of *Also Sprache Zarathustra*. See Friedrich Nietzsche, *Dithyrambs of Dionysus*, trans. R. J. Hollingdale (Greenwich, UK: Anvil Press Poetry, 2004).

the ray of the star. Then I felt a shudder go through me; my heart was seized with regrets for the earth and those I loved, and so fervently did I inwardly beseech the Spirit who was drawing me upwards that it seemed I was now redescending among humankind. I was surrounded by a night patrol. I was under the impression that I had grown quite tall and that, flooded as I was with electrical forces, I was sure to knock down anybody who approached me." Now the police arrive. He tries to be as restrained as possible, so as not to assault all these policemen and immediately beat them to death. But the result is that he is taken to the guard post and locked up.

"Stretched out on a camp bed, I thought I saw the sky lift its veil and open out on to a thousand vistas of unsuspected magnificence. It seemed that the fate of the Soul after its deliverance was being revealed to me, as if to fill me with remorse for having so single-mindedly wished to set foot back on the very earth I was about to leave. … Immense circles traced their way through infinity, like the rings touched off in water by a falling body; peopled by radiant figures, each region in its turn took on color and movement and then dissolved; a divinity, always the same, smiled as she cast off the fleeting masks of her various incarnations, and then took refuge, out of grasp, in the mystical splendors or the sky of Asia."

"The idea has often occurred to me that at certain crucial junctures in life, this or that Spirit from the external world suddenly takes on the bodily shape of an ordinary person [Aurélia!] and then acts or attempts to act on us without that person ever having been aware of it or remembering it."[20] Here the illumination comes to him as to the actual meaning of the experience, constructed out of literature and then forestalled.

He continues his account: "This heavenly vision, by a phenomenon everyone has experienced in certain dreams, did not leave me oblivious to what was going on around me. Lying on the camp bed, I overheard the soldiers discuss some nameless person who, like me, had been arrested and whose voice had echoed through the same room. By an odd effect of vibration, it seemed to me that this voice was resonating in my own chest and that my soul was, so to speak, dividing into two—distinctly split between vision and reality. For a second, I thought I might make the effort to turn towards the individual in question, then I shuddered as I remembered that according to a tradition well known in Germany, every man has a double and that when he sees him, death is near.

"I closed my eyes and lapsed into a confused state of mind in which the figures around me, whether real or fantastic, proceeded to shatter into a thousand evanescent guises. At one point, I saw two friends of mine who had come looking for me; the soldiers pointed me out to them; then the door opened and someone of my own height whose face I could not see

20. Here Jung inserts Nerval's sentence beginning "The idea has often occurred to me…" from a different paragraph, see 125.

left with my friends. I called after them in vain. 'But there's been a mistake!' I shouted. 'It's me they came to get but it's somebody else who's leaving!' I made such a commotion that they clapped me into a cell.

"There I remained for several hours in a kind of stupor; in the end, the two friends I thought I had already seen came to fetch me in a carriage. I told them what had occurred, but they denied they had come by that night." What has happened here is an act of foreseeing that is unlikely to be doubted. Such things are apt to happen when one approaches the unconscious, or when the unconscious itself draws near. For on such occasions time becomes uncertain, and then something can be seen that does not yet exist but that lies just around the corner. I am mentioning this instance as it characterizes the situation quite well.—"I dined with them calmly enough, but as night approached, I thought I had reason to fear that very hour which had nearly proved fatal to me the day before. I asked one of them for the Oriental ring he was wearing on his finger and which I regarded as an ancient talisman; I slipped a scarf through it, which I knotted around my neck, taking care to turn the stone—a turquoise—so that it pressed against a point in my nape where I felt pain. I imagined that it was from this point that my soul would exit when the star I had seen the previous night eventually reached its zenith and touched me with a certain ray. Either by sheer coincidence or owing to the intensity of the preoccupation to which I was prey, I was struck down as if by lightning at the same hour as the night before."

Thus, at the same hour he suffers another loss of consciousness. Immediately after, he is taken into a mental home, a sanitorium, where he passes the first days in an almost-unconscious condition. But in this condition he experiences visions. He narrates: "One evening I was convinced I had been carried off to the banks of the Rhine." [Now comes Germany!] "I found myself in front of menacing crags whose outlines were sketched out in the shadows." [At this point, I want to recall a similar vision D. H. Lawrence had, when he saw the Black Forest from a distance—Acheron-like as well.][21] "I entered a cheerful cottage; a last ray of sun was playing through the green shutters wreathed with grape-vines. It seemed to me I had found my way back to some familiar dwelling, the home of one of my maternal uncles, a Flemish painter, dead for over a century. Unfinished canvases hung about the place; one of them depicted the celebrated fairy of this river [this is the Lorelei]. An ancient servant, whom I called Marguerite [this is Gretchen]

21. "Immediately you are over the Rhine, the spirit of the place has changed. ... And there stand the heavy, ponderous, round hills of the Black Forest, black with an inky blackness of Germanic trees, and patched with a whiteness of snow. They are like a series of huge, involved black mounds, obstructing the vision eastwards. You look at them from the Rhine plain, and know that you stand on an actual border, up against something." D. H. Lawrence, "A Letter from Germany," in *Phoenix: The Posthumous Papers of D. H. Lawrence*, ed. Edward D. McDonald (1936; repr., New York: Viking Press, 1968), 107–10.

and whom it seemed I had known since childhood, said to me: 'Why don't you go and lie down? You have traveled a great distance and your uncle won't be back until late; we'll wake you for supper.' I stretched out on a four-poster bed whose chintz canopy was printed with large red flowers. Facing me on the wall was a rustic clock, and on this clock sat a bird, who proceeded to talk like a human [this is obviously a cuckoo clock]. To my mind, the soul of my ancestor was in this bird; but I was no less astonished by its speech and shape than I was to find myself carried a century or so back in time. Referring to them as if they all existed simultaneously, the bird spoke to me about members of my family who were still alive or had died at different times, adding: 'You see, your uncle took care to paint *her* portrait in advance … Now *she* is with us.' I directed my gaze towards a canvas representing a woman dressed in old-fashioned German costume, leaning over the river's edge, her eyes drawn to a cluster of forget-me-nots."

What is happening here is that he is accessing the room of his unconscious. He does not find the grandfather there but—following the matriarchal rule—the granduncle, the "maternal uncle." Lorelei is depicted only as an image, but a living maiden with the ominous name of Marguerite is also present.[22] On the wall are the clock, the circle, and the bird that actually represents the soul of the ancestor or the matriarchal uncle. The dreamer is displaced in time; he has entered the time of Alcheringa (as expressed by Australian aboriginals), the time of Heroes.[23] And now the bird, which immediately brings to mind *avis Hermetis*, the prophet bird, speaks to him: "You see, your uncle took care to paint *her* portrait in advance."[24] That is, the

22.   Of course, Jung refers here not to "die Lorelei," the rock on the eastern bank of the Rhine, but rather to Lorelei, the river maiden or water spirit, best known in Heine's poem (1824) and to which Nerval alludes in the title of his travel book *Lorely: Souvenirs d'Allemagne* [*Lorelei: Memories of Germany*] (1852).

23.   Jung defines alcheringa time in Australian aboriginal culture as the primeval time of the world of the ancestors and the world of dreams. Jung, "The Visions of Zosimos," para. 130n15. He refers to aboriginal restitution ceremonies as analogous to the therapeutic method of complex psychology, making as fully conscious as possible the constellated unconscious contents and then synthetizing them with consciousness through the act of recognition. C. G. Jung, "Archetypes of the Collective Unconscious," in *The Archetypes and the Collective Unconscious*, vol. 9i of Collected Works (1935/1954; repr., Princeton, NJ: Princeton University Press, 1959/1968), para. 84. See also Carl Gustav Jung, *Dream Interpretation Ancient and Modern, Notes from the Seminar Given in 1936–1941*, ed. John Peck, Lorenz Jung, and Maria Meyer-Grass (Princeton, NJ: Princeton University Press, 2014), 147–48, 152.

24.   "The bird of Hermes [*avis Hermetis*] is an alchemical term for a moment in the process associated with the bitterness of salt: 'As regards the origin and meaning of the *avis Hermetis*, I would like to mention the report of Aelian that the ibis is "dear to Hermes, father of words, since in its form it resembles the nature of the Logos."'" Jung, *Mysterium Coniunctionis*, para. 250. In his handwritten revisions of the 1942 lecture, Jung notes the illustration of the dove as *avis Hermetis* from *Musaeum Hermeticum* (1678), similar to the image that he reproduced in *Psychology and Alchemy*, para. 442, fig. 178.

uncle has established the identity of the anima. "Now *she* is with us." From which we can also say that Gretchen is with us, Marguerite is with us, is also there. The uncle's transformation into a bird, or the uncle's soul as a bird, is once again a very primitive notion, with the souls of the dead appearing in various animal bodies.[25]

The vision continues: "I thought I was sinking into an abyss which cut through the globe. I felt myself being buoyed along by a current of molten metal; a thousand similar streams whose hues varied with their chemical composition were criss-crossing the earth like vessels or veins that wind through the lobes of the brain. From the pulse and flux of their circulation, I gathered these streams were made up of living beings in a molecular state, which only the speed at which I was traveling made it impossible to distinguish. A whitish light was filtering into these channels, and at last I saw a new horizon open up like a huge dome dotted with islands washed by luminous waves. I found myself on a coast lit by a light not of the sun and saw an old man who was cultivating the soil. I recognized him as the same man who had spoken to me through the voice of the bird, and whether it was his words or my inner intuition of them, it became evident to me that our ancestors assumed the shape of certain animals in order to visit us on earth and take part in the various phases of our existence as silent observers."

In other words, the ancestors are present in animal shape, in the components of our animal soul. This plunging into the earth represents a dive into the deeper, more primitive levels of the collective unconscious. The stream of metal in which he finds himself readily brings to mind the curious alchemical identification of metal and spirit. It is an intellectual and psychological stream, and a truly alchemical spirit with metallic characteristics. There is an old Persian legend of Gayomard that tells of his [Gayomard's] blood pouring forth into the earth as seven metals.[26] But [to Nerval], this

25. Already in *Psychology of the Unconscious: A Study of the Transformations and Symbolisms of the Libido*, Jung describes a psychotic patient "who began to understand the language of the birds." C. G. Jung, *Psychology of the Unconscious: A Study of the Transformations and Symbolisms of the Libido*, in vol. 5, sup. vol. B of Collected Works (1912; repr., Princeton, NJ: Princeton University Press, 1991), para. 645n3. And in *The Red Book: Liber Novus*, Jung describes his own protagonist in dialogue with his bird/soul as well as with the raven. In this regard, consider also the motif of understanding animal languages in fairy tales such as the Brothers Grimm's "The Three Languages."

26. For Jung, "Gayomart" in the *Bundahish* is an inner primordial image of the Anthropos: "In Persia, he is Gayomart (*gayo-maretan*, 'mortal life'), a youth of dazzling whiteness, as is also said of the alchemical Mercurius." Jung, "The Visions of Zosimos," 132, para. 168. "The heavy darkness of earth, metal, has a secret relationship to the Anthropos. That is obvious in alchemy, but occurs also in the history of religion, where the metals grow from Gayomart's blood. This curious relationship is explained by the identity of the lowest, most material thing with the highest and most spiritual, which we have already met in the interpretation of the serpent as a chthonic and at the same time the 'most spiritual' animal." C. G. Jung, "The Phenomenology of the Spirit in Fairy Tales," in *The Archetypes and the Collective Unconscious*,

fall into the earth seems a descent into the matter of the brain. This is well worth noting.[27] And to him the rivers are composed of living souls. The idea of the island that emerges here is indeed the idea of the "blessed isle"—that isle of peace that exists somewhere amid the monstrous chaos of movement. The isle of which Mörike sings:

> You are Orplid, my country!
> in the distance gleaming;[28]

It is a strange fact that in the case of someone like Gérard de Nerval, who knew nothing of alchemy, an idea emerges that is connected to the old man whom we have already compared to Hermes: namely, the idea that he was a husbandman or a gardener.[29] We find this idea as early as in the magical papyruses in which Agathos Daimon, often identified with Hermes, appears as a farmer: "Come to me, you good husbandman"; or "I call to you, Dame Isis, and he who comes with you, Agathos Daimon, who dwells in total darkness."[30] As I can only briefly explain, this darkness is the blackness in the eye's pupil; it is also the black Egyptian earth and the black Isis. Which is why this idea appears among the Egyptians. The hymn to the first days of autumn says: "The day on which the goddess's left eye became ready for the arrival of the god." The blackness is the black earth in which the god is buried, in which he achieves rest, and with which he is united. In the writings of the alchemist Olympiodor, we find also this passage: "He came to Achaab, the husbandman, and will learn how he who sows the grain also engenders it."[31] In alchemy, Saturn is the gardener, while the black earth and *prima materia* is lead.

---

vol. 9i of Collected Works (1945/1948; repr., Princeton, NJ: Princeton University Press, 1959/1968), para. 389.

27. Jung makes this point even more emphatically in the 1942 lecture. See 97.

28. Eduard Mörike's "Gesang Weylas" [Weyla's Song] (1831) was one of Jung's favorite German poems. See Sonu Shamdasani, C. G. Jung: A Biography in Books (New York: W. W. Norton, 2012), 12.

29. Jung is misinformed in this regard. Nerval read widely in alchemy, writing a play based on the life of Nicolas Flamel (1831) and coauthoring another with Dumas titled L'Alchimiste (1839).

30. On the magical papyruses, from the 1942 lecture: "For the old man [= aïeul] as a tiller of the soil ἧκέ μοι ἀγαθὲ γεωργέ = ἀγαθὸς δαίμων compare the Berliner Zauber-Papyrus." See 98. In his handwritten 1942 notes (110), Jung quotes the original Greek from the Greek Magical Papyrus 7, lines 493–94. See also "Agathos Daimon," in Hans Dieter Betz, ed., The Greek Magical Papyri in Translation (Chicago: University of Chicago Press, 1985), 331. Jung writes, "This spirit is the snake-like Nous or Agathodaimon, which in Hellenistic syncretism merges together with Hermes." Jung, Mysterium Coniunctionis, para. 251.

31. In his handwritten notes (110), Jung quotes the original Greek from Olympiodorus, in Marcellin Berthelot, Collection des anciens alchimistes grecs (Paris: G. Steinheil), 2, 4:32. See 115.

EMBLEMA VI. *De secretis Naturæ.* 33

Seminate aurum vestrum in terram albam foliatam.

EPIGRAMMA VI.

R Uricolæ pingui mandant sua semina terræ,
    Cùm fuerit rastris hæc foliata suis.
Philosophi niveos aurum docuêre per agros
    Spargere, qui folii se levis instar habent :
Hoc ut agas, illud bene respice, namque quod aurum
    Germinet, ex tritico videris ut speculo.

                E   P LATO

Figure 24. "Sow your gold in the white foliate earth," from *De Secretis Naturae*, 1617

AVREAE MENSAE. LIB. XII. 555

SATVRNVS HVMECTAT TERRAM
portantem Solis flores & Lunæ.

Nonymi Sarmatæ, (cui quidam hoc testimo-
rium perhibet, quod sit Heliocatharus Borea-
lis, cuius tincturæ admirabilem potentiam
in diuersa metalla proiectæ ipse viderit suis
oculis, eorumq; in aurum optimū cōuersi-
onē) aut vitam & mores, aut scripta velle e-
uoluere, cum & ipse & eius tractatus habeantur & tam
mente quam oculis à plurimis obseruentur, nobis hic non
fore necessarium arbitramur; De iis, qui in locum, omni-
Aaaa 2   bus

M. 8.
Of. Cr.
Heliocan-
tharus Bo-
realis à
Crollio di-
ctus, .

Figure 25. "Saturn waters the earth that bears the Sun and Moon flowers,"
from *Symbola aureae mensae duodecim nationum*, 1617

The vision continues. "The old man left off working and accompanied me to a house which stood near by. The local landscape reminded me of a region of French Flanders where ancestors of mine had lived and which now held their tombs: the field ringed with thickets at the forest's edge, the neighboring lake, the river with its washerwomen, the village with its sloping street, the dark sandstone hills with their tufts of broom and heather—a rejuvenated image of the places I had loved. But the house I was now entering was unfamiliar to me [this is the unknown room]. I gathered that it had existed at some moment or other in time and that this world I was now visiting included the ghosts of things as well as of bodies.

"I entered a huge hall where many persons were assembled. I recognized familiar faces everywhere. The features of relatives whose deaths I had mourned were reproduced in the faces of other ancestors who, dressed in more ancient garb, greeted me with the same fatherly warmth. They seemed to have gathered for a family banquet. One of them came towards me and embraced me tenderly. He was wearing an old-fashioned outfit whose colors seemed to have faded, and beneath his powdered hair, his smiling face bore a certain resemblance to mine. He seemed more distinctly alive than the others and, as it were, in more deliberate sympathy with my own mind. It was my uncle. He seated me by his side, and a kind of communication sprang up between us; for I cannot say I heard his voice, but the moment my thoughts turned to a particular question, the explanation immediately became clear and the images were as sharp to my eyes as paintings that had come to life.

"'So it's true!' I exclaimed with elation. 'We are immortal and retain the images of the world in which we once lived. What a joy to realize that everything we have loved will always exist around us! ... I was tired of living!!'

"'Don't be so quick to rejoice,' he said, 'for you still belong to the world above and still have years of severe trials ahead of you. This dwelling place which so enchants you also has its sorrows, its struggles, and its dangers. The earth on which we formerly lived remains the theater in which our fates are played out; we are the rays of the fire which lies at the core of the earth and which gives it life, dimming all the while.'

"'You mean the earth could die and all of us be swallowed into the void?'

"'The void,' he said, 'does not exist in the usual sense of the term; but the earth is itself a material body whose soul is made up of the sum total of minds. Matter can no more die than can the mind, but it can be modified for good or evil. Our past and our future are intertwined. We live in our race, and our race lives in us.'

"This notion immediately became tangible to me, and as if the walls of the hall had opened out on to infinite vistas, I thought I saw an unbroken chain of men and women to whom I belonged and yet all of whom were myself; the costumes of every nation, the images of every land appeared distinctly and simultaneously, as if my powers of attention had been multiplied without losing their sense of detail, by a spatial phenomenon analogous to the temporal concentration of an entire century of action into a single moment of a dream. My astonishment grew when I realized that this immense proliferation of beings was composed solely of those persons gathered in the hall and whose images I had seen divide and recombine into countless fleeting features.

"'We are seven,' I said to my uncle.

"'The very number,' he replied, 'typical of every human family, and by extension, seven times seven and so on down the line.' I cannot hope to make his answer understood, for it still remains quite obscure to me."

He makes a further comment on the number seven: "But how to go about establishing the individual centers that emanate from these [the seven persons]—or from which they emanate—like some collective anima figure whose permutations would at once be finite and unlimited?" The number seven invites us to remember the seven gods. Our beautiful German name, Elisabeth, derives from the language of Babylon: *Eli si beti* = our God is Seven (Father, Mother = Sun and Moon and the five planetary children).[32] Gérard de Nerval adds: "You might as well query a flower about the number of its petals or the divisions of its corolla."

Further in the course of the dream vision, the old man transforms into a youth, which again raises alchemical parallels with Hermes, who appears both as Senex and Juvenis. It is no longer the old man who brings him revelation and enlightenment, but the youth who receives ideas from him, the dreamer. They are on a pilgrimage and arrive in a large town, of whose inhabitants he says: "They had managed to maintain their fierce individuality amid the mixed and undistinguished population of this enormous city." So they meet these people who have managed to remain themselves. The town lies in the form of terraces along a mountain slope, with one terrace of houses above the other, almost piled over each other. First they climb an endless flight of steps up through the town until they reach the ornamental garden at its lovely summit: "Amid this unsuspected solitude, the noisy hubbub of the city below was little more than a murmur." And he describes the people he meets there: "A fortunate race of men had created this sanctuary for itself, a place favored by birds, flowers, clear air, and light. These are the ancient inhabitants of this mountain, which dominates the city we are now visiting." So above the town is the mountain and the mountain people; down below are the common people.

---

32.   Translator's note: In Hebrew, Elisheva (Élischeba; Élisabeth; אֱלִישֶׁבַע in Hebrew) was Aaron's wife. Eli means "my God." *Sheva* in Hebrew can be understood as "oath" or "subsistence, being satisfied." So the name Elisheva could signify both "My God is my oath" and "My God is my subsistence/satiety." And *sheva* also means "seven," referring to perfection, as in the seven days of the week or Creation.

(371)

Hic Pater & Filius in unum funt copulati,
Ut fimul in æternum manent.

DECIMAQVINTA FIGVRA.

Aaa 2   TRIPUS

Figure 26. "Mercurius in the form of the god of revelation [a winged old man],
who is identical with Hermes Trismegistus and, together with the King and the King's
Son, forms the alchemical trinity," from *Decimaquinta Figura*, 1677

From above, they climb down into one of these houses, that is to say, they descend down through the house. "It seemed as if my feet were sinking into the successive strata of buildings of different eras." And this could be like an excavation, going deeper layer by layer. Finally at the lowest level they reach a chamber, and there again is an old man. However, this old man, sitting by his work, is no longer a husbandman but a kind of craftsman. The dreamer walks in, but a man dressed in white threatens him and tries to prevent him from penetrating any further into the mystery of the place. The mystery is in fact that this place represents the isle of bliss. Then they meet an old woman [Marguerite again] and then a child [a new arrival]. And then he sees young people, of whom he says: "Fending off the flood of new races which threatened to invade them, it was here that they had gone about their lives, simple in their customs, loving and just, steadfast, ingenious and astute—peacefully triumphing over those blind masses who had so repeatedly encroached upon their heritage. And lo and behold, they were neither corrupted nor destroyed nor enslaved; having conquered ignorance, they still remained pure; having prospered, they still held to the virtues of poverty. I cannot convey what it felt like to find myself among these charming creatures whom I adored without knowing who they were. They were like some primordial heavenly family, their smiling eyes seeking out mine with gentle compassion."

Here Gérard de Nerval actually describes an essential attitude—namely, that of truthfulness to oneself and to one's own simplicity. He describes a human race that is as it really ought to be, how he himself should have been. These young people wish to keep him in this happy place. But suddenly everything dissolves and vanishes, and he now returns to consciousness.

After a while, still in the sanitorium, he has the following dream: "A subsequent dream confirmed my views [namely, the idea of the immortality of his friends]. I found myself all of a sudden in a room of my ancestor's house, except that the room had grown in size. The ancient furniture gleamed with a wondrous sheen, the carpets and curtains seemed refurbished, a light three times brighter than day streamed through the window and door, and the fresh scent of an early spring morning wafted through the air. Three women were at work in this room, and without exactly resembling them, they represented various female family members and friends of my childhood. Each of the three women seemed to possess various characteristics of these childhood figures. Their profiles flickered like the flame of a lamp, one person's features continually migrating into another's. Smile, voice, color of eyes or hair, posture, habitual gesture—all these traits shifted back and forth between them as if they were sharing in a single life, and each was a composite image of all the others, like those ideal types fashioned by painters after several different models so as to capture the complete range of beauty. The oldest of the three addressed me in a melodious voice whose trill I recognized from my childhood, although I do not know what it was she said that struck me as so profoundly accurate. But she managed to draw my attention back to myself, and I saw I was wearing a small, brown, old-fashioned suit of clothes with gossamer needlework as fine as a spider's web. The little outfit was stylish in cut and gently perfumed. Clad in these clothes which had sprung from their fairy fingers, I felt young and spry again and I thanked them, blushing like a little boy in the presence of beautiful ladies. Then one of them got up and proceeded towards the garden." He is enmeshed by the spinners, the three Fates, who are only one. It is always the one and the same.

"As everybody knows, one never sees the sun in one's dreams, even though one is often aware of a light far more luminous. Objects and bodies have a radiance all their own. I saw myself in a small park with a long row of arbors, whose arches were heavy with bunches of white and black grapes; as the lady who was guiding me moved beneath these bowers, the latticed shadows cast by the trellises again caused her body and garments to fluctuate before my eyes. She at last emerged from under the arbors, and we found ourselves in an open area where one could still see the faint traces of the ancient lanes that had once cut through here crosswise. The grounds had not been tended for many years, and fresh growth of clematis, hop, honeysuckle, jasmine, ivy, and yellow creeper had sprouted all over the place, looping their fast-growing vines around the trees. Branches loaded with fruit brushed the ground and several garden flowers, having reverted to the wild, were blooming amid clumps of weeds.

"Stands of poplar, acacia, and pine rose here and there, and within their groves were glimpses of statues blackened by time. I saw before me a mound of ivy-covered rock from which a freshwater spring gushed, its pretty splash echoing off a pool of still water half veiled by large water lilies.

"The lady I was following, her slender figure advancing at a rhythm that caused the folds of her shot taffeta dress to shimmer, twined her bare arm around a long stalk of hollyhock; then, in a shaft of light, she began to grow so gigantic that the entire garden took on her shape; the flowers and the trees became the rosettes and flounces of her dress, while her face and arms imprinted their outlines on the purple clouds of the sky. I lost sight of her as she went through this transfiguration, for she seemed to be vanishing into her own immensity.

"'No! Don't disappear!' I shouted after her. 'All of nature is dying with you.'

"As I uttered these words, I fought my way through the bramble, as if in pursuit of the expanding shade who was eluding my grasp, but I stumbled against a crumbling wall, at the foot of which lay the sculpted bust of a woman. Picking it up, I was convinced it was hers ... I recognized the features I adored, and as I glanced around me, I saw that the garden now looked like a graveyard. Voices were saying:

"'The Universe lies in night!'"

The exposition of this dream shows again the room and the house of the Old One, the Ancestor, where the three Parcae dwell.[33] The development shows the dreamer in a spider's-web costume. He now wanders into the garden with the lady and finds the ancient shape of a cross. Everything has returned to its natural state again, overgrown with wild flowers. Even the cultivated flowers have returned to their original wild condition. This is the culmination of the dream, its peripeteia. It now becomes apparent that the lady "in her shot taffeta dress" (which is her secret connection with the daemon) is herself the garden. She becomes the garden, but he only has a vision of what she stands for as *mater natura*. In her own significance, she escapes him—which is why he exclaims: "Don't disappear! All of nature is dying with you." This means that for him, the world will die if she transforms herself back into her original state. He can no longer grasp the figure and finds only the shattered bust of his beloved Aurélia. Of which the author says: "This dream, which had started out so happily, caused me no end of perplexity. What did it mean? Only later did I find out. Aurélia had died." She really had died; this is a historical fact, and maybe even just at that moment. However, he says: "Besides, she belonged to me far more in her death than in her life ... A selfish thought for which my reason would later pay with bitter regrets."

In the ensuing deliria [he is still in the asylum], he constantly draws charcoal pictures of Aurélia on the wall [this really happened].[34]

[*Note*: References to pictures of Husbandman (figures 24–26), Hermaphrodite. Anima on the ball—an alchemical idea, meaning the Anima of the globe, the Anima of the earth (figures 27–30).]

33.   The Parcae are the Fates in Roman mythology. See the image of a "maternal figure presiding over the goddesses of fate" from Thenaud's "*Traité de la cabale*" that Jung reproduced in the first pages of "Individual Dream Symbolism in Relation to Alchemy," in Jung, *Psychology and Alchemy*, paras. 48–50, fig. 6.

34.   1942 lecture: "In the ensuing deliria *in a sanitorium*, ~~he sees~~ *he draws* Aurélia *with charcoal on the wall* 'drawn with divine features, ... a turning wheel under her feet' *and the Gods made her cortege* (cf. dream symbols of the process of individuation: woman on the globe, *anima mundi*)." See 103. Concerning Nerval's wall paintings, see the citation from *Les maisons de fous* by Alphonse Esquiros (1843–44) on 42.

Figure 27. "The Virgin is Mercurius who, owing to the presence of sulphur, the active masculine principle, is hermaphroditic," from *Turba Philosophorum*

Figure 28. "Conjoining of Sun and Moon," from *Splendor Solis*, 1582

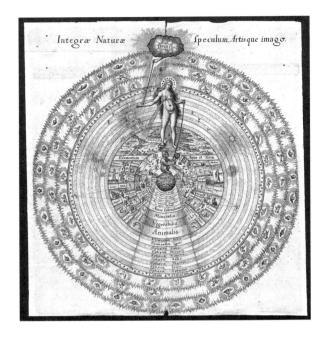

Figure 29. "The anima mundi, guide of mankind, herself guided by God,"
by Robert Fludd, 1617

Figure 30. "Mercurius as the Sun-Moon hermaphrodite (rebis)
standing on the (round) chaos," by Stiocio de Stolcenberg, 1624

At this time, he has many visions, which lead him to the story of Creation. Functionally the story of Creation signifies the process of his recovery. Then he is finally discharged, and for a longer period he does quite well.

But one day he sees a bird that starts speaking. This reminds him of his earlier vision of the great-uncle bird. And on the same day he falls down a flight of stairs. He becomes ill, and his deliria begin anew. He says: "As I thought back on the location where my fall had taken place, I remembered that the vista I had so admired overlooked a cemetery, the very cemetery which contained Aurélia's grave ... Initially, all I had were disjointed dreams, a jumble of bloody scenes. It seemed as if an entire race of malignant creatures had been unleashed on that ideal world I had formerly glimpsed, a world of which she was the queen."

This relates once again to the isle of bliss where those beautiful people live and where Aurélia is Queen. The lower and common people have again become outraged and apparently invaded the island. In his vision he now sees a young man who is dressed in white like the island's inhabitants, and he recognizes him as the one who tried to prevent him from exploring the island's mysteries. At the same time he appears to him as the "Prince of the Orient." We hear that Aurélia is the Queen of this island and the young man is now the "Prince of the Orient." And now he suddenly realizes that he himself looks like this young man. At this very important point, he says: "I lunged towards him, threatening him, but he turned towards me serenely. O horror, O rage! It was my very face, my very body, enlarged and idealized." This is the one who also had been released before him from the police station. This is the "Other." And he knows that the Other is his enemy. But he asks himself doubtingly which of these two he may be and cannot decide. "A fatal flash of lightning suddenly tore through these uncertainties ... Aurélia was no longer mine! ... I thought I heard talk of a ceremony that was to take place elsewhere and that preparations were being made for a mystical wedding which was mine, but at which *the other* was going to benefit from the mistake of my friends and of Aurélia herself."

The subsequent visions lead him once again into the great town on the mountain, and into a workshop where the workers are constructing a gigantic animal—a winged llama. "A beam of fire seemed to be shooting through this monster and slowly bringing it to life; it twisted this way and that, penetrated by the countless purple shafts of flame." He is told that this fire was originally the central fire that had once reached up to the surface of the earth. "Its wellsprings have dried up." He thinks that "the primordial fires which animated the first created beings" contributes to the making of this creature. This creature is evidently a double of the genius, namely, the genius restored to its animal level—but "the wellsprings have dried up."[35] It remains at a trial stage.

And this trial is not carried out. Because he becomes gripped by something else. Once again he hears talk of "marriage" and that Aurélia will celebrate her wedding with the "Other." "I was immediately gripped by an insane fit of rage. I imagined the bridegroom they were all awaiting was my double who was due to marry Aurélia." He himself is then attacked by enemies, who assault his head with a red-hot ball.[36] These people force him into a great hall, towards the center where a throne stands. This is where the "mystical marriage" shall be celebrated. And he knows that a magical sign must be given to initiate the ceremony. He himself wants to give this sign, which should be given by the bridegroom. But at this moment he hears the cry of a woman and knows it is Aurélia. And he realizes: "Lost, a second time! Everything is over, everything is past! It is now my turn to die, and to die without hope!"

This ends the first part of the book. The second part begins with the author's reflections on the past events and depictions, and here he says something very peculiar: "We may well be approaching that era when science, as predicted, having accomplished its entire cycle of synthesis and analysis, of belief and negation, will now be able to purify itself and usher forth the miraculous city of the future from chaos and ruin." And this is again his dream city, this *"cité merveilleuse."* "God will no doubt appreciate the purity of these intentions; what father relishes the sight of his son abdicating all reason and pride in his presence? The apostle who needed to touch in order to believe was not cursed for having doubts!" And then he adds: "What have I just written? Blasphemies. This is not the way Christian humility is permitted to speak. Ideas of this sort are hardly calculated to mellow the soul. They wear the proud lightning bolts of Satan's crown on their brow. A pact with God himself? ... O science! O vanity!"

With regard to what follows, I would like to mention just one more dream that Gérard de Nerval recounts. He heard it at the deathbed of one of his friends. He says: "A sublime dream in the shadowy realms of infinity, a conversation with a being at once distinct from and identical to himself, and of whom he asked, believing himself dead, the whereabouts of God.

35. Jung refers here to the daemon or genius that collapsed into the Paris inner courtyard in the earlier dream. See 123. See also Jung's explanation of this daemon-genius restored only to its animal level in the minutes of the discussion, 81.

36. 1942 lecture: "He himself is threatened by a red-hot bullet against his head (cf. dream symbols: billiard ball that dashes the navigation instruments)." *"En ce moment un des ouvriers de l'atelier que j'avais visité en entrant parut tenant une longue barre, dont l'extrémité se composait d'une boule rougie au feu. Je voulus m'élancer sur lui, mais la boule qu'il tenait en arrêt menaçait ma tête."* Aurélia, in Nerval, *Oeuvres complètes*, 3:720. From French into English, Sieburth translates "boule" as the red-hot "knob" on the end of a bar. From French into German, Kubin translates it as *"die Kugel,"* hence Jung's reference to either "bullet" or "ball."

'But God is everywhere, his spirit answered. 'He is in you, he is in everyone. He judges you, he listens to you, he counsels you. He is us, you and I, as we think and dream in unison—we have never parted, we are eternal!'" The author says: "God is with him but he is no longer with me! What a disaster! I have cursed him, I have threatened him, I have disowned him! It was he, that mystic brother who had been drawing further and further away from my soul and sending me warnings in vain! Favored bridegroom and king of glory, it is he who is now judging and condemning me; it is he who is now carrying off to his heaven that bride that he might have bestowed on me, a bride of whom I am no longer worthy!"

After this he recounts yet another of his own dreams. He heard from an innkeeper about the suicide of a friend. In the dream he was speaking to this friend, and at the same time he saw a large mirror behind them. He believed he saw Aurélia in it. "She seemed sad and pensive; but suddenly, whether it was because she had stepped out of the mirror or because she had been reflected in it a moment earlier as she crossed the room, this tender figure was standing by my side. She extended her hand to me and, casting me a mournful glance, said: 'We shall meet again later … at your friend's house.'

"And it came to me in a flash—her marriage, the curse that was keeping us apart. I said to myself: Is it possible? Will she ever come back to me?' In tears, I asked: 'Have you forgiven me?' But everything had vanished.

"She is lost, I cried out, but why? … Now I understand, she made one last effort to save me—but I missed that final crucial moment at which forgiveness was still possible. She could have interceded on my behalf with the divine Bridegroom in the heavens above. … But does my salvation even matter? She has been snatched into the abyss, lost to me, lost to all!"

The manuscript of *Aurélia* was found on the author's corpse. On a cold January night he was wandering the streets of Paris and around three in the morning arrived at an alleyway in the Tour Saint-Jacques district.[37] There was an antique shop that displayed a mummy in the window. Presumably it was this that had drawn him to the little street. Previously it had been known as "Rue de la Tuerie," because of an abattoir that had once stood there. It led to the Seine, where a sewer discharged into the river. The sewer was covered with a grille, and on this grille Gérard de Nerval hanged himself with a corset string.[38]

37. The fifteenth-century Saint-Jacques Tower is located in the fourth arrondissement of Paris, at 39 Rue de Rivoli and Rue Nicolas Flamel. See note 37, figure 9.
38. Differing accounts of how Nerval died (i.e., the cord tied to a lamppost, window grille, or sewer grate) were published. Alexandre Dumas (not the most reliable journalist) described the setting a number of times—the earliest version in *Le Mousquetaire*, January 30, 1855: "In the darkness at the far end of this covered passage, you will find a window framed with iron bars similar to those that close off prison windows. Go down five steps, stop at the last, lift your arms up to the metal crossbar. You have arrived: this is the crossbar to which the

This was the end of a personality who had never understood how to prize open the narrow circle of the personal "I" and grant admission to the shadow, that ambiguous herald of yet another order of things.

cord was attached. A white cord, like those used to make apron strings. In front of you is an open sewer, covered by a metal grille. This place, as I told you, is sinister. Facing you runs the little street of the Vieille-Lanterne that goes up to the Rue Saint-Martin. In this street, to the right, a cheap lodging house, something filthy that must be seen to be imagined, with a lamp, on the glass of which is written: 'Lodgings for the night. Café à l'eau.' Opposite these lodgings are mews that during the long frozen nights that we've gone through, were left open in order to lend refuge to those too poor to claim a place at the lodgings. You've reached the last step, haven't you? Well, there, with his feet barely two inches above that step, on Friday morning at 7:03, the body of Gérard was found, still warm and with his hat on his head" (translation mine). Dumas revised this in *Nouveaux Mémoires: Sur Gérard de Nerval* (1866). For a different account, see Théophile Gautier, "Portraits et souvenirs littéraires: Gérard de Nerval," in *L'univers illustré* (1867). All these are quoted in Claude Pichois and Michel Brix, *Gérard de Nerval* (Paris: Fayard, 1995), 366–68. For the official police report, see http://www.paperblog.fr/4028005/sur-la-mort-de-gerard-de-nerval-rue-de-la-vieille-lanterne/#QPSqKcoMxQJqXM2x.99 (accessed December 2, 2014).

FOUR

Minutes of the Discussion following the 1945 Lecture

Participants (in chronological order, according to their contribution to the discussion): Marie-Louise von Franz, Linda Fierz, Carl Alfred Meier, Rivkah Schärf, Tina Keller, Jolande Jacobi, Roland Cahen, Gertrud Gilli, Aniela Jaffé, Liliane Frey, and Una Thomas.

MARIE-LOUISE VON FRANZ: WHILE [THERE IS] NO LYSIS IN THE FIRST DREAM, there are in the later dreams more and more motives that appear remarkably positive. How might one understand that, on the one hand, Nerval's fate already seems sealed and then, on the other hand, a possibility of rescue seems to exist repeatedly?[1]

Carl Gustav Jung: This is precisely the confusing aspect in this case. One has to weigh the symbolism most carefully. To imagine always precisely from which level, out of which situation, the dream is dreamed. In the first

---

1. Marie-Louise von Franz on Nerval: "Gérard de Nerval consciously had a Parisian-French mentality which was too small and rationalistic and could well be compared to a hotel backyard [translation correction: courtyard]. It was not up to the inner experience and that brought about his schizophrenic explosion. As Jung says, if the conscious mind or heart is not up to a tremendous inner experience it leads to schizophrenia, for the invasion of the unconscious then explodes the conscious personality... He could not bear it that this woman should mean so much to him... He therefore kicked her away and then fell into his first episode, after which he tried to have a reconciliation. But he could not get on with her because of the terrific tension of seeing clearly that she was an ordinary human being and experiencing her as a goddess and not being able to hold these two paradoxical things together. He could not see that that was the paradox of love, which is a divine mystery and at the same time a very ordinary, if not anthropoid, affair. The dream shows the drowning of the Self, its descent into the narrowness of the human realm. In Gérard de Nerval's case, ego conception was too narrow and the Self exploded it, and Nerval hung himself in the most horrible way. But even if the Self approaches human consciousness in a normal case there is the drowning, the falling down process, so that it can be said that for the Self, for the greater part of the inner personality, it is agony to be imprisoned in the confines of consciousness." Marie-Louise von Franz, *Individuation in Fairy Tales* (Dallas: Spring, 1977), 104.

dream, for example, the level is still the normal one, isn't it[.] This is why the dream appears quite disastrous. And this dream of an absolutely unfavorable omen is after all human, but then later, dreams come that look much more pleasant, that are almost cozy. But these are dreamed from an entirely different level; that is to say, there he has already descended into the underworld, and so the underworld is rendered acceptable to him. And this leads into going even deeper. There the dreams become positive, because they extend into the other land. There is a turning point towards which the catastrophe is heading, but once you are past this point, the positive dreams come. But these lead beyond this life. These dreams have a very positive character. You will see, it's true, if you follow this line, that seen from the position of a living person, these dreams are much more sinister than madness[,] they are "more than dead."

Linda Fierz: Comparing Poliphilo [to Nerval's protagonist]: Has the French mentality not changed since the Renaissance, or why [has it] remained the same.[2] But then [there is this] difference: [for Poliphilo, the] anima is always clearly visible, and such a figure is not available here [in the Nerval]. Marguerite = Venus[,] because she is old and belongs to the world of the ancestors. Polia [is] always [Polophilo's] anima. This [is] the more positive [aspect], this is why it never comes to a complete break. I wonder if the sense of guilt [in *Aurélia*] derives from the fact that he has given the anima the boot. [A] completely separate idea is the motif of the llama. The great Nietzsche called his sister "llama."[3]

Jung: I can only agree about the similarity of the symbolism and dramatis personae, the accessories, the incredible resemblance to the *Poliphili*. But then again it is altogether dissimilar. Nothing of the tragedy that is played out here, can be found throughout the entire *Poliphili*. There, it is about quite an ordinary person who describes an anima experience, whereas here it is a very great and strange tragedy, namely, of a missed experience. That is his great fault. He did not notice. Only when it [was] too late. This *"personne ordinaire de notre siècle"* just went off with her umbrella, and he has [words missing]. Isn't it so[,] that this tragedy is strange, that it would not belong

2.   Linda Fierz-David, *The Dream of Poliphilo*, related and interpreted Linda Fierz-David, trans. Mary Hottinger (New York: Bollingen Series XXV, 1950). In *Hypnerotomachia Poliphili, ubi humana Omnia non nisi somnium esse docet* (*The Strife of Love in a Dream*), an allegorical and mythological romance attributed to Francesco Colonna, first published in Venice by Aldus Manutius in 1499, Poliphilo ("friend of many things") pursues his love Polia ("many things") through a dreamlike landscape and is seemingly at least reconciled with her by the Fountain of Venus. For the only translation into English of the entire text, see Francesco Colonna, *Hypnerotomachia Poliphili: The Strife of Love in a Dream*, trans. Joscelyn Godwin (New York: Thames and Hudson, 1999).

3.   Nietzsche called his sister llama, a nickname that according to her, derived from a description in a natural history book. See Carol Diethe, *Nietzsche's Sister and the Will to Power: A Biography of Elisabeth Förster-Nietzsche* (Champaign: University of Illinois Press, 2007).

to the fifteenth century. Only in modern times can one so miss the anima, formerly not. Not due to sheer unconsciousness.

Carl Alfred Meier: It is a peculiar fact that ancient examples have such essential significance. With regard to the winged llama, there is [a] parallel, namely, to the decapitation of the Gorgon by Paris [sic] and the winged animal that emerges, Pegasus.[4] This certainly has to do with his poetic genius. The question is whether this peculiar animal has to do with the fact that he has not cut off the Gorgon's head. Doesn't the breakdown of the situation have to do with the fact that he skipped the problem of the shadow, which would have to have been solved before [the problem of the anima]?

Jung: [This is a] With regard to the Gorgon and Pegasus, a deeper correlation actually exists. It was rather wicked of me to use the passage from *Faust* and thereby to lead the discussion astray.[5] However, it just had to be like that. The other aspect of Gretchen is the Gorgon[,] and whoever is able to cut her head off, can release Pegasus from it. This means, if the unconscious has already adopted the aspect of the Gorgon, then you can only liberate the genius when you cut off the Gorgon's head. Then it springs forth again. This dream of Nerval's vision of the llama means that in the depths of the soul, things are already being produced again. The deeper we dig beneath the mental illness, [the more] we get into those layers where restoration is constantly at work. Life never goes under. It is never lost. In the dreams, one finds quite normal processes taking place. Among the voices are normal voices. The normal truth is spoken. So also in Gérard de Nerval, even during the time of his severe illness, a process of restoration is at work. But it is always at work. The genius can only acquire the divine shape from the animal shape in the unconscious if the head of the Gorgon has been cut off. But precisely this he cannot do. This was actually the question, because when the Gorgon rose, Aurélia had long since disappeared from the horizon; because "*une personne ordinaire de notre siècle*" is not a Gorgon. She is much more genteel, she is literary. She has nothing to do with a dangerous person at all. It is a typical aesthetic misunderstanding. He thought that one thing is literature, the other is reality. In fact there are only "*petites femmes*"[;] what is in literary history certainly has nothing to do with life. That is just the megalomania of the man of letters who thinks he writes the books. Well, when he writes them, they are, all and sundry, bad[.] If they are written for him, they can be good. If he thinks he has done it, he becomes inflated.

---

4.   Meier on Pegasus: "[Poseidon] is highly emotional and has tempestuous love affairs with Gorgo, the Furies, Demeter, and many others, apart from Amphitrite. A product of his union with Gorgo is Medusa, who in turn produces the horses Chrysaor and Pegasos." C. A. Meier, *The Meaning and Significance of Dreams*, trans. David Roscoe (Boston: Sigo Press, 1987), 10.

5.   Johann Wolfgang von Goethe, *Faust I* and *Faust II*, ed. and trans. Stuart Atkins (Princeton, NJ: Princeton University Press, 1984), part I, lines 4184–208. See Jung's lecture, 58.

If he is a genius, he knows that he has not done it. Of course, there are also pathological geniuses.

[With respect to] the shadow: When this problem of the anima arises, it can be regarded only as a problem. [Then one] can take a firm position only when one has accepted the shadow beforehand. Only then can one take on the anima problem. The shadow that arises is swollen by the anima and by whatever else comes from behind, whatever the anima brings with it. Therefore it is absolutely necessary that the shadow be accepted if one wants to cope with the unconscious. Otherwise the shadow runs away with the anima, and the two form an unholy conspiracy against the one. Then it is two against one. Then usually the person needs an analyst, so that it can be two against two.

Rivkah Schärf: In that vision at the beginning, the friend of Nerval who wanted to hold him back appeared as a Christian apostle. And you mentioned that he conflicts with antiquity. In a later dream, Mary appears in a very positive light. She tells [Nerval] that he has passed his test, which hints at Isis, who is incidentally also mentioned once. Am I to understand now, that Christianity beyond real life (in the postmortal state, so to speak) again appears as positive?

Jung: The conflict with the apostle occurs at Hecate's three-way (the Trivia), [with] the friend as apostle who wants to edge him away from that place. There indeed comes the statement, "I do not belong to your heaven. Those who await me are in that star. They predate the revelation that you have announced"; that is to say, I belong to antiquity. Now, later, when he has this dream about Isis, he is already on his way to the underworld, and this is one of those positive dreams. He has now, to some extent, passed the test. He has shed his body[,] waived his life[,] and now he can approach the Great Mother. And this way goes down now, through prehistory. This way out of life goes down through prehistory. And finally he lands at the Great Mother. With the Great Mother of the Gods there the heroes were buried in a grave in a circular tumulus, which represented the body of the Mother of the Gods, like the Dea Matuta, the Etruscan goddess.[6]

Christianity has first [a] negative aspect in the walking to the star, and this walking leads him out of life. [There beckons] The last motif, which could prevent him from coming out of this existence, is Christianity. For this is moralizing Christian doubt, a decision, and behind that decision is the primeval world proffering itself.

---

6. Tumulus is an archaeological term for a burial mound of earth and stones over a grave or graves, also known as a barrow or kurgan; it is from the Latin *tumere*, "to swell up." With regard to the goddess Matuta, see C. G. Jung, *Symbols of Transformation*, vol. 5 of Collected Works (Princeton, NJ: Princeton University Press, 1956/1967), para. 536.

Tina Keller: It was said that man must provide deeds for the Self, otherwise it cannot realize itself. Mustn't the personal be exploded in such acts? That is to say, [mustn't] the shadow be involved?

Jung: There isn't much else one can say generally. One would have to talk specifically about what the whole of man wants, and in the whole of man there is the shadow. Otherwise one is only two-dimensional. One doesn't cast shadows. Of course, when I say man "acts," I mean the man as a whole acts. This is what the Self wants and needs to express. Otherwise there is no development. Two-dimensional, a man remains only a drawing on the wall.

Jolande Jacobi: Should he have had [to deal] with this woman?

Jung: He should have reconciled himself with the fact that she messes with literary history in an unorthodox way. Then one cannot say, this comes only from literary history. That is cheap. Anyone can say that. Besides, he wasn't even a professor of literary history.

Roland Cahen: The question of aesthetic misunderstanding is incredibly tragic in France. We suffer from it to outrageous extents, and I would like to [verb missing: ask?] Professor Jung whether he is optimistic in this respect.

Jung: Aestheticism is the literary original sin. One doesn't let the whole person speak, one doesn't participate, one shoves it away. Thus everything is only aesthetic. Gérard de Nerval just makes literary history out of it, makes poems about it, as if it were nothing else. Here what was meant was his life, the anima, which is the archetype of life. He who shoves life away, gets into trouble with the anima. The anima becomes venomous and dangerous. One can't push it aside with an "-ism." There is no case of schizophrenia where there is not a narrowness.[7] An agonizing tightness, and this narrowness strangles life. Somehow or other. And this has a shattering effect. Life itself shatters the shell. If one cannot shatter one's "I," then one will be shattered. Either physically or morally. If one has it in oneself[;] there are people who have no dynamite, who have only carrot juice in their veins.

Gertrud Gilli: How should we understand the idealized image of the man who is hostile to him?

Jung: That is his shadow. He believed that it was hostile to him. Yes, of course, he has not accepted it. The unconscious always shows the ugly face that we affix to it. If you show it your teeth, it does that too, only it can do it much better.

Jacobi: Could we say that the fatal outcome of this daemon only wants to show him [words missing] ...

Jung: This image, as it appears in Gérard de Nerval, is a product of nature, it is not an artificial or philosophical image. This is a real birth of the unconscious. Therefore it is difficult to compare such a thing to philosophical

7. See C. G. Jung, "Schizophrenia," in *The Psychogenesis of Mental Disease*, vol. 3 of Collected Works (1958; repr., Princeton, NJ: Princeton University Press, 1960), 256–72.

creations. But, of course, if I just call this daemon the Self, then the whole residual range of symbols of the Self certainly comes with it. Naturally this shape of the daemon is by definition a timeless figure. Something that towers over man. And consequently towers over him in time, too. At all events, one can say, it is his immortal aspect that couldn't find its full unfolding because of the unfavorable conditions. Namely, as a result of what preceded. Of this guilt, he is conscious. He knows that he has left behind a guilt, namely, that he has missed life. The opportunity in his life to deal with a problem that was unknown to him. How could he have known it[?] He knew it only as a literary problem. This was proscriptive. One can dismiss a thing by saying, now this is this and that. There are people who use psychology only to get a label to attach to things. Then they are done. Then it just belongs to psychology. One must never forget, psychology is only a stammering stopgap measure, so that one is able to talk about life at all.

von Franz: The thing is that these positive images that emerge later on are positive because they already usher him on the way to death. But there are still catastrophes after all. Could someone with a wasted life stay with the old man and the youths? And I wonder, does he really have to atone for that forever. Because he cannot change it anymore. Does this state go on ad infinitum?

Jung: Right, it is implied in the text: the old man says to him, "Don't be so quick to rejoice, you aren't dead yet, you ought to return to life '*en haut*' again. You're not quite in the underworld. You still belong to life." These moments when he is thrown out of the sphere of Hades, are the moments in which he recovers consciousness again. This is not to be understood as life after death, but what is happening to him now. As to the old man, it is stated that [Nerval] must not imagine that there is a state of constant bliss. There are all kinds of conflicts that are indicated by [words missing] of those blissful people. And there is the threat of the blind masses. So don't you agree, we cannot speculate about this point, we simply must listen to it and wait until we get other cases that also have such experiences. And further clarify this question, what does this actually mean. There are more things here, about which Gérard de Nerval speaks, than are dreamt of in our philosophy.[8] There are important things behind this. Therefore, not everything can be elucidated.

Meier: [A] question emerges, what role does Gérard de Nerval's peculiar preference for Germany play in this disease process?

Jung: This is really a problem. I explain it to myself this way: The relationship between Germany and France is like conscious and unconscious. For the French, Germany is the country of the unconscious. That's why he

8. "There are more things in heaven and earth, Horatio/Than are dreamt of in your philosophy." William Shakespeare, *Hamlet*, act I, scene v, 167–68.

doesn't understand it. Of course, this has led [Nerval] also to the Orient, into another nationhood in which he also somehow found his other side. It allows for a certain experience, but it wasn't conscious enough.

Meier: Is it an escape then[?]

Jung: Yes, but an escape into himself. The Germany of that time consisted of many ministates [*Stäätchen* (*sic*)] and minitowns. And the originals … [words missing].

Rivkah Schärf: Gérard de Nerval hasn't given dignity to the anima [problem], he trivializes the relationship to Aurélia. But isn't it often the other way round, that there is the reverse danger of not seeing the reality of a person but of identifying her with the anima or, respectively, the animus? Which can lead out of life just as much.

Jung: One can't simply say that the opposite would be true. But then the question arises, how would it have been if [Nerval] had given an astonished "Oh!" … [words missing]. Well, then the whole problem would have started from the fact that the "*personne ordinaire*" has a meaning that is just as real, and that nevertheless is not real. And if it works as with Faust and Gretchen, then of course it all backfires again. The principle of the solution is always, "Don't overdo. Don't overdo, not too much." This is, of course, quite a different problem. Gérard de Nerval was confronted with the fact that he had missed the unique chance of his life, and he felt enormously guilty. There is guilt in the fact of living. One cannot say: someone didn't know, so he is not to blame. Life has no mercy. Water has no mercy, whether or not someone didn't know that it has typhus bacilli. He wasn't asked the question.[9]

Fierz: The city with the dangerous masses of people and the youths reminds me of *Marmorklippen* by Jünger.[10] [I] find it astonishing that this future Germany could already be in the psychic background.

Jung: This was already alive in Germany at that time. Think of the Rosicrucian poem "*Geheimnisse*" ["The Mysteries"] by Goethe.[11] These youths are there.

[missing words]

Aniela Jaffé: Gérard de Nerval says in a certain passage that he had lost A[urélia] for a second time, and shortly before there is talk of Aurélia's marriage with the doppelgänger.[12] [The] question [is] whether the sense of guilt

9. With regard to guilt and typhus-infected water, see the case described in C. G. Jung, *Memories, Dreams, Reflections* (New York: Random House, 1962), 115–17.

10. Ernst Jünger, *On the Marble Cliffs*, trans. Stuart Hood (1939; repr., New York: Penguin Books, 1970).

11. In *Psychological Types*, Jung also refers to Goethe's "*Geheimnisse*": "Here the Rosicrucian solution is attempted: the union of Dionysus and Christ, rose and cross. The poem leaves one cold. One cannot pour new wine into old bottles." C. G. Jung, *Psychological Types*, vol. 6 of Collected Works (1921; repr., Princeton, NJ: Princeton University Press, 1964), para. 314n31.

12. A doppelgänger is an uncanny double of a living person, from the German *Doppelgänger*, literally "double goer."

isn't connected with that [as well]. The first guilt was because he missed the opportunity to come to terms with the anima. Here is the second guilt: this misunderstanding.

Jung: That's right. It is a second guilt. He does what Faust did, doesn't he? [Faust] put himself immediately in the place of Paris and took Helen for himself. This, Gérard de Nerval also wants to do here. He, his "I," this certain Gérard Labrunie, wants to incorporate Aurélia completely and cannot stand that someone else snatches her from under his nose. This someone else is really him. He simply can't bear himself as the other. He cannot see himself as such a person. And this other, the one who lives on the mountain, Aurélia is destined for this person, and not for him. And so he simply commits this transgression, mistakenly, which is understandable. As in the beginning, he declares the matter a literary [~~invention~~] sensation. In the first place it isn't a true sensation, and, if it should be true, the sensation belongs to me.[13] Here, he commits again this sin of self-absorption.[14]

Liliane Frey: Is the fact that in the room there are seven persons but Gérard de Nerval sees seven × seven and even many more figures, is this the phenomenon of multiplication?

Jung: Yes, it is, the endless splitting of the one character or of a few characters. So, for instance, the fragmentation of the family of seven into an infinite number that have all the qualities of the seven. A character that is split into infinite facets.

Frey: Does the seven mean a basic tendency of man, and then each of these individual characteristics includes a splitting in the unconscious?

Jung: No. There is here a reduction of the infinite manifoldness of human characters to a few types. *One* family of seven. This belongs to the anima problem. The anima figure is the [feminine] *one* of the many. As the animus is the [masculine] *one* of the many. And a figure that, as he says himself, contains the paradox of being indeed one, but being everywhere. [~~Much more could be said about this.~~]

Una Thomas: Which is the illness that he finds "beautiful"? Is this his madness?

But this feels uncanny.

Jung: It is a proper schizophrenia, viewed clinically, medically; but, you see, if he is in there, for these people [*sic*] it is of course different. We believe that many mentally ill persons are unhappy. Not at all! They don't want to get out at all. I once treated someone, she was in it, too. I got her out using

---

13. In this sentence, Jung speaks (countertransferentially) from the point of view of Nerval. To paraphrase: "This is nothing but *my* sensation."

14. Literally, *Ichbefangenheit*. One can translate this as "self-absorption" or "egocentricism," except that Jung adds here to this denotation the special connotation of sinfulness, suggesting a negative kind of "self-consciousness" that is a corollary to the sin of pride. See 1945 lecture, 53, 90.

all the tricks of the trade. She explained to me: Now you've got me out of there into this filthy world. I don't want to be here[.] Now I can't get back. You see, I had locked the door behind her. But she would much rather have been insane.[15]

Jacobi: When he met Aurélia in Italy again, there was a sign in her look that she had forgiven him, which he could have understood.

Jung: But this is precisely what he did not understand. He noticed it, and then the "*personne ordinaire*" just gets in the way. That doesn't go together. You may also interpret that as French rationalism. But it is an "-ism" in any case.

15. "Thus I was automatically threatened with death, as was everyone who might have persuaded her to return to normal human life. By telling me her story she had in a sense betrayed the demon and attached herself to an earthly human being." See Jung's explanation of this case of the woman who lived on the Moon, in Jung, *Memories, Dreams, Reflections*, 130.

FIVE

Jung's Notes to the 1942 Lecture
Gérard de Nerval's *Aurélia*

by C. G. Jung

Notes and extracts of the
lecture delivered at the
General Meeting of the S.G.P.P. [Swiss Society for Psychiatry and Psychotherapy]
21 March 1942.

Gérard de Nerval is the pseudonym of Gérard Labrunie, born 23.5.1808, died 25.1.1853. His writings are *Vers dorés* [Golden Verses] (beautiful lyric poems), translations of poems by Klopstock, Goethe, and Heine, a translation of *Faust* (1828), *Lorely, souvenirs d'Allemagne* [Lorelei: Recollections of Germany], *Scènes de la vie Orientale* (1848–50) [Journey to the Orient (1851)], *Le rêve et la vie* (postum) and finally *Aurélia* (1852–53.).

Biographical data about him are provided by: Gauthier-Ferrères: *Gérard de Nerval. La Vie et l'Oeuvre. 1805–1855.* Paris 1906, and Julia Cartier: *Un Intermédiaire entre la France et l'Allemagne. Gérard de Nerval.* Genève 1904.[+]

> [+] *R. Bizet: La double vie de Gér. de Nerval. 1928*
> *(Aurélia, a young actress, quick acquaintance.*
> *Contrast between reality and dream. Later gradual*
> *realization.)*

The manuscript of *Aurélia* was found on the corpse of the author who had, on a cold January night, committed suicide by hanging himself with a corset-string on a sewer grating on the bank of the Seine. The grating was at the exit of a small lane, originally named "rue de la Tuerie." At the head of the lane was an antique shop with a mummy displayed in the window.

Aurélia opens with the following sentence: "*Le rêve est une seconde vie—* Dream is a second life." And then the author says about the unconscious: "Little by little, the dim cavern is suffused with light and, emerging from its shadowy depths, the pale figures who dwell in limbo come into view, solemn and still …—the spirit world opens for us." He then begins to describe his experiences and adventures and says the following:

"I shall attempt to transcribe the impressions of a lengthy illness that took place entirely within the mysteries of my own mind—although I do not know why I use the term illness here, for so far as I am concerned, I never felt better. At times I believed my strength and energy had redoubled; I seemed to know everything, understand everything; my imagination afforded me infinite delights. Having recovered what men call reason, must I lament the loss of such joys? …

This *Vita nuova* was divided into two phases in my case. Here are the notes relating to the first of these."+

+*Example of Dante*

"A woman I had long loved and whom I shall call Aurélia was lost to me. The circumstances of this event that was to have such a major influence on my life do not really matter. Anyone can search his memories for the emotion that proved the most devastating or for the cruelest blow of fate; the only decision in these cases is whether to die or go on living—later I shall explain why I did not choose death. Condemned by the woman I loved, guilty of an offense for which I no longer hoped to be forgiven, my only course was to plunge myself into vulgar intoxications; I affected a gay, carefree air, I traveled the world, entranced by its diversity and unpredictability; the bizarre costumes and customs of distant lands especially appealed to me, for it seemed to me that I was thereby relocating the conditions of good and evil, the terms, as it were, of what we French define as *feelings*. What madness, I told myself, to go on platonically loving a woman who no longer loves you. The trouble is I have read too much; I have taken the inventions of the poets too seriously and have made a Laura or Beatrice out of an ordinary woman of our century … " +

+*Who was Aurélia?*
His perception: madness, believes he had created a Beatrice
for himself! Self-absorption. Writer's mania.

He then mentions a little intermezzo *amoroso* in Italy, (where he falls in love with another woman,) which is followed by a sudden withdrawal of libido. But through this woman he meets Aurélia again:

"As a result, finding myself one day at a gathering at which she was also present, I saw her come in my direction and extend her hand. How to interpret this gesture and the deep, mournful glance she cast in greeting me? I took it to be forgiveness for the past; the simple phrases she addressed to me, graced by the divine accent of pity, acquired a value beyond words; it was as if something religious had infused itself into a love heretofore profane and imprinted it with the <u>seal of eternity</u>."

He has to return to Paris, but with the intention of seeing "*ses deux amies*" again. However:

"One evening, around midnight, as I was making my way back to my lodgings, I raised my eyes by chance and noticed a house number lit up by a streetlamp. It was the same number as my age. Then, lowering my eyes, I saw before me a woman with hollow eyes and a pallid face whose features seemed to be those of Aurélia. I said to myself: this must be an omen of *her* death or mine!"

He supposes that it is he who is to die; in fact, on the next day at the same time:

"That night I had a dream that confirmed this idea. I was wandering through an immense building made up of several rooms, some being used <u>as study halls</u>, others devoted to <u>conversation</u> or <u>philosophic debate</u>. Out of curiosity, I stopped in one of the former rooms, where I thought I recognized my old teachers and schoolmates. The lessons dealing with Greek and Roman authors droned on, their monotonous hum resembling some prayer to the goddess Mnemosyne. I passed on to another room where philosophic discussions were taking place. I took part in these for a while, then left to <u>find myself a room</u> in <u>a hostelry with huge staircases</u> and bustling with travelers.

"<u>I lost my way several times in the long corridors,</u> and as I was crossing one of the <u>central galleries,</u> I was struck by a strange scene. A <u>creature of disproportionate size—man or woman,</u> I do not know—was fluttering about with great difficulty overhead and seemed to be floundering in the thick clouds. In the end, out of breath and energy, <u>it plummeted into the center of the dark courtyard,</u> snagging and bruising its wings on the roofs and balustrades as it fell. I was able to get a brief look at it. It was <u>tinged with rosy hues</u> and <u>its wings shimmered with countless changing reflections.</u> Draped in a long robe falling in classical folds, it resembled <u>the Angel of Melancholy</u> by Albrecht Dürer. [See figure 19.] I could not stifle my shrieks of terror, which woke me with a start."

The exposition of this dream shows the past and present life of the dreamer. The development would be that he is looking for <u>his</u> room, but in the process gets lost.[+]

> [+]*Up until this moment, he had been going through his life without having a room of his own. His individual existence was a mere assumption, not yet a fact.*

The fall of the <u>daemon</u> into the inner courtyard ("*galéries centrales*") brings the peripeteia ~~or~~ ^{and the} catastrophe. The essential thing is that this dream has <u>no lysis</u>.

The daemon's "rosy hues" ("*teintes vermeilles*") indicate Eros or fire. The wings of a thousand colors evoke the "*cauda pavonis*" (*continet omnes colores*).⁺

> ⁺*Colorful unfolding!*
> *"In colorful refraction we find life." Goethe:*
> *only in our actions do we appear. The Self wishes to realize itself*
> *in the abundance of its colors, which is*
> *only possible if we lend it actions. If this does not happen*
> *or no longer happens the Self remains imprisoned within us*
> *and it turns into the Angel of Melancholy. In melancholy nothing*
> *happens anymore—with the exception of suicide, concentration*
> *in the stomach, inhibition of all life procedures.*

As a <u>superhumanly great</u> being he is the <u>Self</u> that contains himself.

The dreamer <u>withdraws from his life</u>; ^{*thinks of his death. Has rejected the anima, the archetype of life*} that is a <u>catastrophe</u> also for the Self, which ~~is~~ remains captured in the "inner court." It cannot unfold anymore like the *causa pavonis*.—The Angel of Melancholy is the mental alienation that drops on him.

The author then continues his description:

"The next day I hurried <u>to see all my friends</u>. I was mentally saying <u>good-bye</u> to them, and without letting them know what was on my mind, I launched into passionate disquisitions on <u>mystical topics</u>; I astonished them by my <u>peculiar eloquence</u>; it seemed to me that I <u>understood every-thing</u>,⁺

> ⁺*approach of the Unconscious—and of death*

that <u>the mysteries of the world</u> were being revealed to me in these final hours.

"That evening, as the fatal hour seemed to be drawing near, I was at a club, sitting at a table with two friends, holding forth on painting and music, defining my views on the generation of colors and the meaning of numbers. One of them, by the name of Paul ***, wanted to accompany me back to my lodgings, but I told him I was not going home. 'Where are you going?' he asked. '<u>To the Orient!</u>' ^{*his room*} "And as he walked by my side, I began to scan the sky for <u>a certain star</u> I thought I knew, as if it had some influence over my fate. Having located it, I continued on my way, following the streets where I could see it ahead of me, forging onwards, as it were, towards my destiny and wanting to keep the star in view until the moment death was to strike. But having reached <u>the intersection of three streets,</u> I refused to go any further. My friend seemed to be exerting superhuman strength to get me to move on; he was growing ever larger in my eyes and taking on <u>the features of an apostle.</u> The spot on which we stood seemed to rise up, losing all its urban appearance—on a hilltop surrounded by vast expanses of emptiness, this scene had now become a battle between two spirits, a kind of biblical temptation. 'No!' I cried. '<u>I do not belong to your heaven.</u> Those who await me are in that star. They predate the revelation that you have announced. Let me rejoin them, for <u>the one I love is among them,</u> waiting for us to meet again.'"

Herein the depicted elevation stems from the approach of the unconscious. The "Orient" refers to Germany, where the author had actually traveled now and then, when he was somewhat deranged. Germany is ^{to him} the Land of the Unconscious. The "star" of his fate is both fixed point and goal. The halt at the <u>three-way crossroad</u> is reminiscent of the mythologem of <u>Hecate.</u> He does not aim further, remaining in antiquity. Therefore his friend suddenly appears as an <u>apostle.</u> So it is about a clash with Christianity, in which the author takes the heathen standpoint: "I do not belong to your heaven. Those who await me are in that star. They predate the revelation."

The Unconscious is all that ever was.

And so his goal is the <u>ancient world.</u> (Cf.: ROSENCREUTZ: Aegeisches Fest und Hieros Gamos. FAUST: Klassische Walpurgisnacht. POLIPHILO: court of Venus. TANNHAEUSER: Venusberg. ALCHEMY: 7 planetary gods.) [See figure 29.]—There he also hopes to find Aurélia. The anima announces the antique world. <u>SHE</u> shows the <u>ancient past life</u> of the hero. ORPHEUS seeks his Eurydice in the underworld. FAUST seeks Gretchen:

> Mephisto, do you see
> off there, alone, dead-pale, a lovely girl?
> Now she is slowly moving away,
> dragging her feet as if they were in fetters.
> I have to say I can't help thinking
> That she looks like my own dear Gretchen.
> ...
> I know those are the eyes of someone dead,
> eyes that no loving hand has closed.
> That is the breast which Gretchen let me press,
> that the sweet body which gave me joy.
> ...

What ecstasy, and yet what pain!
I cannot bear to let this vision go.
How strange that on that lovely neck
there is an ornament a single scarlet thread
no thicker than a knife!
…
Mephisto: You're right, I see it too.
She also can transport her head beneath her arm,
thanks to the fact that Perseus lopped it off.

Hecate at the three-way crossroad is also the Gorgon. This relates to <u>the petrification, the imprisonment, and the torpidity</u> of schizophrenia. So like Lot's wife and Eurydice, the author <u>looks</u> back. He does not go forward into life, but backward out of life. He withdraws from reality. "Here began for me … the overflow of dream into real life."

He continues his way <u>toward the star, singing a mysterious hymn</u> ~~from another existence, 'which filled me with a joy beyond words.~~" *Nietzsche:+*

> *+"Finding myself alone, I struggled to my feet and again set off in the direction of the star, not letting it stray from my sight for one moment. As I walked along, I chanted a mysterious hymn that I thought I remembered having heard in some other life and that filled me with a joy beyond words.*

Golden serenity, come!
You, most secret, sweetest
anticipation of the pleasure of death.

The author continues his account: While singing this hymn he takes off his clothes. (Discards his body).+

> *+"The route appeared to lead ever upwards as the star grew ever larger. Then, standing there with my arms outstretched, I awaited the moment at which my soul would separate from my body, magnetically attracted into the ray of the star. Then I felt a shudder go through me; my heart was seized with regrets for the earth and those I loved, and so fervently did I inwardly beseech the Spirit who was drawing me upwards that it seemed I was now redescending among humankind. I was surrounded by a night patrol. I was under the impression that I had grown quite tall and that, flooded as I was with electric forces, I was sure to overthrow anybody who approached me.*
> *etc.*

~~The star grows ever larger. Then he feels remorseful, and he prays to the spirit, that attracts him. Then he descends again to the mortals,~~ amplified himself and endowed with an enormous power. He is now discovered by a patrol officer, as he is running around naked, and is locked up. ~~In the cell he has~~ At the police station he has the following vision:

"Stretched out on a camp bed, I thought I saw the sky lift its veil and open out on to a thousand vistas of unsuspected magnificence. It seemed that the fate of the Soul after its deliverance was being revealed to me, as if to fill me with remorse for having so single-mindedly wished to set foot back on the very earth I was about to leave ... <u>Immense circles</u> traced their way through infinity, like the rings touched off in water by a falling body; peopled by radiant figures, each region in its turn took on color and movement and then dissolved; a divinity, always the same, smiled as she cast off the fleeting masks of her various incarnations, and then took refuge, out of grasp, in the <u>mystical splendors or the sky of Asia</u>."[+]

> [+]*"The idea has often occurred to me that in certain critical junctures in life this or that Spirit from the external world suddenly takes on the bodily shape of an ordinary person* [Aurélia]*, and then acts or attempts to act on us without that person ever having been aware of it or remembering it"*

He continues:

"This heavenly vision, by a phenomenon everyone has experienced in certain dreams, did not leave me oblivious to what was going on around me. Lying on the camp bed, I overheard the soldiers discuss some nameless person who, like me, had been arrested and whose voice had echoed through the same room. By an odd effect of vibration, it seemed to me that this voice was resonating <u>in my own chest</u> and that my soul was, so to speak, dividing into two—distinctly split between vision and reality. For a second, I thought I might make the effort to turn towards the individual in question, then I shuddered as I remembered that according to a tradition well-known in Germany, every man has a double and that when he sees him, <u>death is near</u>.

"I closed my eyes and lapsed into a confused state of mind in which the figures around me, whether real or fantastic, proceeded to shatter into a thousand evanescent guises. At one point, I saw two friends of mine who had come looking for me; the soldiers pointed me out to them; then the door opened and <u>someone of my own height</u> whose face I could not see left with my friends. I called after them in vain. 'But there's been a mistake!' I shouted. 'It's me they came to get but it's somebody else who's leaving!' I made such a commotion that they clapped me into a cell.

"There I remained for several hours in a kind of stupor; in the end, the two friends I thought I had already seen came to fetch me in a carriage. I told them what had occurred, but they denied they had come by that night.

"I dined with them calmly enough, but as night approached, I thought I had reason to fear that very hour that had nearly proved fatal to me the day before. I asked one of them for the Oriental ring he was wearing on his finger and that I regarded as an ancient talisman; I slipped a scarf through it, which I knotted around my neck, taking care to turn the stone—a tur-quoise—so that it pressed against a point in my nape where I felt pain. I imagined that it was from this point that my soul would exit when the star I had seen the previous night eventually reached its zenith and touched me with a certain ray. Either by sheer coincidence or owing to the intensity of the preoccupation to which I was prey, I was struck down as if by lightning at the same hour as the night before."

Immediately after, he is taken into a sanitorium, where he passes the first days in an almost-unconscious condition. But in this condition he experi-ences the following visions:

"One evening I was convinced I had been carried off to the banks of the Rhine. I found myself in front of menacing crags whose outlines were sketched out in the shadows. I entered a cheerful cottage; a last ray of sun was playing through the green shutters wreathed with grapevines. It seemed to me I had found my way back to some familiar dwelling, the home of one of my maternal uncles, a Flemish painter, dead for over a century. Unfin-ished canvases hung about the place; one of them depicted the celebrated fairy of this river ^{Lorelei}. An ancient servant, whom I called Marguerite and whom it seemed I had known since childhood, said to me: 'Why don't you go and lie down? You have traveled a great distance and your uncle won't be back until late; we'll wake you for supper.' I stretched out on a four-poster bed whose chintz canopy was decorated with large red flowers. Facing me on the wall was a rustic clock, and on this clock sat a bird, who proceeded to talk like a human. To my mind, the soul of my ancestor was in this bird; but I was no less astonished by its speech and shape than I was to find myself carried a century or so back in time. Referring to them as if they all existed simultaneously, the bird spoke to me about members of my family who were still alive or had died at different times, adding: 'You see, your uncle took care to paint her portrait in advance … Now she is with us.' I directed my gaze toward a canvas representing a woman dressed in old-fashioned German costume, leaning over the river's edge, her eyes drawn to a cluster of forget-me-nots."

The menacing crags remind one of the Acheron-like [Stygian] setting
^{Hades +}

+H. D. Lawrence [sic]: *Description of the Black Forest*

The old servant is an anima figure. Her name also is significantly <u>Margue-rite</u>. *Gretchen* The uncle, who died a hundred years ago, is the "<u>wise old man</u>." As an *aïeul* [ancestor, forebearer] he is grandfather or great-uncle, a <u>matriarchal authority</u>. His soul is a bird *avis Hermetis*. As to that the following parallels are to be mentioned: The primitive transformation of the souls into animals. Soul bird: Ba. Angel. Pater-Filius-Paraklet [Father-Son-Paraclete] = Bird *avis Hermetis*. (columba)⁺

⁺Picture in the Mus. Herm.

The woman in old-fashioned German costume is the beldame, the "Mère Lusine" (Melusine!) Hecate Great Mother Isis. *The old man has made his image beforehand: individuated. Hence the Aia [Anima] is with him (relation to nature) +*

⁺Divine parents. Niklaus of Flüe: Vision of God the Father
and God the Mother.

The vision continues:
"I thought <u>I was sinking into an abyss that cut through the globe</u>. I felt myself being buoyed along by a <u>current of molten metal</u>; a thousand similar streams whose hues varied⁺

⁺{Sanguis spirituale = [♀]}.
{bloodstream = Mercurius} The blood of Gayomart turns into the seven metals.

with their chemical composition crisscrossing the earth like vessels or veins that wind through <u>the lobes of the brain</u>. From the pulse and flux of their circulation, I gathered these streams were <u>made up of living beings in a molecular state</u>,

incarnated souls animae in carcere terrae.
homunculi

which only the speed at which I was traveling made it impossible to distinguish. A whitish light was filtering bit by bit into these channels, and at last I saw a new horizon open up like a huge

blood cell—the world of the small

dome dotted with <u>islands washed by luminous waves</u>. I found myself on a coast lit by a light

image Saturn

not of the sun and saw <u>an old man who was cultivating the soil</u>. [See figure 25.] I recognized him as the same man who had spoken to me through the voice of <u>the bird</u>, and whether it was his words or my inner intuition of them, it became evident to me that <u>our ancestors</u> assumed the shape of certain *animals* in order to visit us on earth and take part in the various phases of our existence as silent observers."

The plunging into the earth represents a dive into the collective unconscious. The stream of metal (chemical diversity) can be compared to the *Spiritus vitae* (= Mercurius). But this fall leads—so to speak—into the brain. (Schizophrenia. Brain matter!) The rivers s̶i̶g̶n̶i̶f̶y̶ ^{composed of} living souls (p̶s̶y̶c̶h̶i̶c̶!) As to the <u>island</u>⁺

> ⁺*The islands are like blood cells. The world*
> *of the small. Blissful isle, where the immortals*
> *sojourn, where there is no time. Feeling of immortality*
> *Island of the lovers and of Poliphilo.*

compare Mörike's:

> You are Orplid, my country,
> in the distance gleaming!⁽*Anima*⁾

For the old man (= *aïeul*) as a tiller of the soil ^{georgós} compare the Berliner Zauber-Papyrus: "Come to me, you good husbandman = Agathos Daemon"; and "I call to you, Dame Isis, and he who comes with you, with you, Agathos Daemon, who dwells in total darkness."⁺

> ⁺*First day in autumn:* "*The day on which the Goddess's left eye*
> *became ready for the arrival of the God.*"

I.e., the "black" ^{ton té melanon} is the pupil. Isis = e̶y̶e̶ ̶o̶f̶ ̶O̶s̶i̶r̶i̶s̶ ̶=̶ ̶s̶u̶n̶,̶ ̶G̶o̶d̶ ̶v̶e̶i̶l̶e̶d̶
^{The black. In the black of the pupil is the God} i̶n̶t̶o̶ ̶i̶t̶,̶ ̶n̶a̶m̶e̶l̶y̶ ̶i̶n̶ ̶t̶h̶e̶ ̶p̶u̶p̶i̶l̶. In alchemy this corresponds with the Sol niger. Compare also <u>Olympiodor</u>'s quotation: ⁺

> ⁺*Berthelot: II, IV, 32.*

"He came to Achaab, the husbandman, and he will learn how he who ^{sows} the grain, also engenders it." In alchemy, <u>Saturn</u> appears as the <u>gardener</u>. (Lead = prima materia, black earth.)—There are numerous parallels to the ancestors of the animals with the primitive. ^{Alcherringa mitjina}

The vision continues:

"The old man left off working and accompanied me to a house that stood nearby. The local landscape reminded me of a region of French Flanders where ancestors of mine had lived and that now held their tombs: the field ringed with thickets at the forest's edge, the neighboring lake, the river with its washerwomen, the village with its sloping street, the dark sandstone hills with their tufts of broom and heather—a rejuvenated image of the places I had loved. Only <u>the house</u> I was now entering was unfamiliar to me. I gathered that it had existed at some moment or other in time and that this world I was now visiting included the ghosts of things as well as of bodies.

"I entered a huge hall where many persons were assembled. I recognized familiar faces everywhere. The features of relatives whose deaths I had mourned were reproduced in the faces of other ancestors who, dressed in more ancient garb, greeted me with the same paternal warmth. They seemed to have gathered for a family banquet. One of them came towards me and embraced me tenderly. He was wearing an old-fashioned outfit whose colors seemed to have faded and, beneath his powdered hair, his smiling face bore a certain resemblance to mine. He seemed more distinctly alive than the others and, as it were, in more deliberate sympathy with my own mind. It was <u>my uncle</u>. He seated me by his side, and a kind of communication sprang up between us; for I cannot say I heard his voice, but the moment my thoughts turned to a particular question, the explanation immediately became clear and the images were as sharp to my eyes as paintings that had come to life.

"'So it's true!' I exclaimed with elation. 'We are immortal and retain the images of the world in which we once lived. What a joy to realize that everything we have loved will always exist around us! ... I was tired of living!'

"'Don't be so quick to rejoice', he said, 'for you still belong to the <u>world above</u> and still have <u>years of severe trials ahead of you</u>. This dwelling place that so enchants you also has its sorrows, its struggles, and its dangers. The earth on which we formerly lived remains the theater in which our fates are played out; we are the <u>rays of the fire</u> that lies at the core of the earth and that gives it life, dimming all the while.'

"'You mean the earth could die and all of us be swallowed into the void?'

"'The void', he said, 'does not exist in the usual sense of the term; but the earth is itself a material body whose soul is made up of the sum total of minds. Matter can no more die than can the mind, but it can be modified for good or evil. Our past and our future are intertwined. <u>We live in our race, and our race lives in us.</u>'

"This notion immediately became tangible to me and, as if the walls of the hall had opened out on to infinite vistas, I thought I saw an unbroken chain of men and women to whom I belonged and yet <u>all of whom were myself</u>; the costumes of every nation, the images of every land appeared distinctly and simultaneously, as if my powers of attention had been multiplied without losing their sense of detail, by a spatial phenomenon analogous to the temporal concentration of an entire century of action into a single moment of a dream. My astonishment grew when I realized that this immense proliferation of beings was composed solely of those persons gathered in the hall and whose images I had seen divide and recombine into countless fleeting features.

"'We are seven,' I said to my uncle.

"'The very number,' he replied, 'typical of every human family, and, by extension, seven times seven and so on down the line.' I cannot hope to make his answer understood, for it remains quite obscure to me."

The author makes a comment on the number seven: "But how to go about establishing the individual centers that emanate from these" (the seven persons) "—or from which they emanate—like some <u>collective anima figure</u> whose permutations would at once be finite and unlimited?"+ Compare the seven planets

> +*You might as well query a flower about the number of its petals or the divisions of its corolla ... ,* ^{Blumenkrone}

$$\odot \quad \mathbb{C} \qquad \qquad \mathbb{\Large ☿ ♀ ♂ ♃ ♄}$$
$$2 \qquad \qquad \qquad \qquad 5$$

Further in the course of the dream vision, the old man transforms into <u>a youth</u> (Hermes, Senex, and Juvenis), who now conversely receives ideas from the dreamer *who received ideas from me rather than vice versa. ... Had I traveled too far in these vertiginous heights?*. They arrive in a large town, whose inhabitants had managed to maintain their fierce individuality,"+

> +*amid the mixed and ordinary population of this enormous city.*

~~that is even still in a collective form.~~ The town ~~is~~ *lies* in the form of terraces along a mountain slope, with one terrace of houses above the other.+

> +*First they climb an endless flight of steps up through the town until they reach the ornamental garden at its lovely summit, a delicious oasis, a neglected solitude above the tumult and the noisiness below was no more than a murmur ... "A fortunate race of men had created this sanctuary for itself, a place favored by birds, flowers, clear air, and light. These ... are the ancient inhabitants of the mountain that dominates the city."*

From above, they climb down into one of these houses, and "it seemed as if my feet were sinking into the successive strata of <u>buildings of different eras</u>." *an excavation!* Finally, *at the lowest level,* they meet an *old man* again.+

> +*A sort of craftsman, who was at work.*

A man *in white* threatens him and tries to prevent him from penetrating any further into the mystery of the place (~~the~~ *this* isle of bliss). Then they meet an *old woman* *and a child*. Then *many young people* appear,[+]

> [+]*"it was here that they had gone about their lives, simple in their*
> *customs, loving and just,*
> *steadfast, ingenious, and astute—peacefully triumphing over those blind*
> *masses who had so repeatedly encroached upon their heritage.*
> *And lo and behold, they were neither corrupted nor destroyed*
> *nor enslaved; having conquered ignorance,*
> *they still remained pure; having prospered,*
> *they still held to the virtues of poverty ...*
> *I cannot convey what it felt like to find myself*
> *among these charming creatures whom I*
> *adored without knowing who they were. They were like*
> *some primordial heavenly family, their smiling eyes*
> *seeking out mine with gentle compassion."*

> *Describes an essential attitude, truthfulness to themselves,*
> *a human race that is the way it ought to be.*

who *obviously* wish to keep him in this happy place, but everything dissolves and vanishes and he returns to consciousness.

After a while (still in the sanitorium), he has the following dream:

"A subsequent dream confirmed my views" (the immortality of his friends). "I found myself all of a sudden in a room of <u>my ancestor's house</u>, except that the room had grown in size. The ancient furniture gleamed with a wondrous sheen, the carpets and curtains seemed refurbished, a light three times brighter than day streamed through the window and door, and the fresh scent of an early spring morning wafted through the air. <u>Three women</u> were at work in this room and, without exactly resembling them, they represented various female family members and friends of my youth. Each of the three women seemed to possess various characteristics of these childhood figures. Their profiles flickered like the flame of a lamp, one person's features continually migrating into another's. Smile, voice, color of eyes or hair, posture, habitual gesture—all these traits shifted back and forth between them as if they were <u>sharing in a single life</u>, and <u>each was a composite image of all the others</u>, like those ideal types fashioned by painters after several different models so as to capture a perfect beauty.

The oldest of the three addressed me in a melodious voice whose trill I recognized from my childhood, although I do not know what it was she said that struck me as so profoundly accurate. But she managed to draw my attention back to myself, and I saw I was wearing a small, brown, <u>old-fashioned</u> suit of clothes <u>with gossamer needlework as fine as a spider's web</u>. The little outfit was stylish in cut and gently perfumed. Clad in these clothes that had sprung from their fairy fingers, I felt young and spry again and I thanked them, blushing like a little boy in the presence of beautiful ladies. Then one of them got up and proceeded towards the garden.

"As everybody knows, one never sees the sun in one's dreams, even though one is often aware of a light far more luminous. Objects and bodies have a radiance all their own. I saw myself in a small park with a long row of arbors, whose arches were heavy with <u>bunches of white and black grapes</u>; as the lady who was guiding me moved beneath these bowers, the latticed shadows cast by the trellises again caused her body and garments to fluctuate before my eyes. She at last emerged from under the arbors, and we found ourselves in an open area where one could still see the faint traces of the ancient lanes that had once <u>cut through here crosswise. The grounds had not been tended for many years</u>, and fresh growth of clematis, hop, honeysuckle, jasmine, ivy, and yellow creeper had sprouted all over the place, looping their fast-growing vines around the trees. Branches loaded with fruit brushed the ground and several <u>garden flowers, having reverted to the wild</u>, were blooming amid clumps of weeds.

"Stands of poplars, acacias, and pine trees here and there, and within their groves were glimpses of <u>statues blackened by time</u>. I saw before me a mound of ivy-covered rock from which a <u>freshwater spring</u> gushed, its splash melodiously echoing off a pool of still water half veiled by large water lilies.

"The lady I was following, her slender figure advancing at a rhythm that caused the folds of her <u>shot taffeta dress to shimmer</u>, gracefully slid her bare arm around a long stalk of hollyhock; then, in a shaft of light, she <u>began to grow so gigantic</u> that the entire <u>garden took on her shape</u>; the flower beds and the trees became the rosettes and flounces of her dress, while her face and arms imprinted their outlines on the purple clouds of the sky. I lost sight of her as she went through this transfiguration, for she seemed <u>to be vanishing into her own immensity</u>.

"'No! Don't disappear!' I shouted after her. 'All of nature is dying with you.'

"As I uttered these words, I painfully fought my way through the bramble, as if in <u>pursuit of the expanding shade</u> who was <u>eluding my grasp</u>, but I stumbled against a crumbling wall, at the foot of which lay the sculpted <u>bust of a woman</u>. Picking it up, I was convinced it was <u>hers</u>. ... I recognized the features I adored, and as I glanced around me, I saw that the garden now looked like a graveyard. Voices were saying:

"'The Universe lies in night!'"

The exposition of this dream shows again the House of the Ancestors. The three women are the three Parcae. (One + Three. Individuation!)

The development shows the dreamer ~~historically~~ dressed in *a spider's web* costume. ~~He belongs to the others, to the timelessness.~~[+]

[+]Costume = body. The Fates weave his earthly existence

He wanders into the garden with the lady (~~fruit~~), finds the ancient shape of a cross. *Culmination.* The garden has once again returned to its state of wildness. (~~Freshwater spring.~~) The lady "in her shot taffeta dress" (daemon!) becomes the garden, becomes nature. This leads to the peripeteia: "Don't disappear! All of nature is dying with you." The catastrophe would be that he can no longer grasp ~~the shadow~~ *the figure* and bumps against a wall, (~~the sculpted bust of a woman~~). And the lysis: "The Universe lies in night!"

The author comments: "This dream, which had started out so happily, caused me no end of perplexity. What did it mean? Only later did I find out. <u>Aurélia had died</u>."[+]

[+]"She belonged to me far more in her death than in her life … A selfish thought for which my reason would later pay with bitter regrets"

In the ensuing deliria *in a sanitorium,* ~~he sees~~ *he draws* <u>Aurélia</u> *with charcoal on the wall* "drawn with divine features, … a turning wheel under her feet." *and the Gods made her cortege* (cf. dream symbols of the process of individuation: woman on the globe, anima mundi.)

The following visions lead him to the complete story of the Creation. His condition improves, and he is finally discharged from the sanitorium.—But one fine day he sees a bird that starts speaking, which reminds him of his vision. On the same day he falls down a flight of stairs, he becomes ill, and his deliria begin anew.[+]

[+]"I remembered that the view I had so admired overlooked a cemetery, the very cemetery that contained Aurélia's grave"

[+2]"Initially, all I had were disjointed dreams, a jumble of bloody scenes. It seemed as if an entire race of malignant creatures had been unleashed on that ideal world I had formerly glimpsed of which she was the queen."

The young man, *(ideal city) elevated* ~~enlarged~~ as "Prince of the Orient" appears again, and he suddenly realizes that it is he himself.[+]

> [+] *"I lunged towards him, threatening him, but he turned towards me serenely. Oh horror, oh rage! It was my very face, my very body, enlarged and idealized."*
> *(Already at the police station, where another person was being set free.)*

He knows, that this "Other" is hostile to him,[+]

> [+]*He asks himself doubtingly which of these two he may be.*
> *"A fatal flash of lightning suddenly tore through these uncertainties …*
> *Aurélia was no longer mine! I thought I heard talk of a ceremony that was to take place elsewhere and that preparations were being made for a mystical wedding that was mine, and at which the other was going to benefit from the mistake of my friends and of Aurélia herself."*

~~and he assumes a~~ *"mariage mystique"* ~~is going to take place, marrying the "Other" to Aurélia.~~ *"A bad spirit had taken my place in the world of souls."* The subsequent visions lead him once again into the great town on the mountain, and into a workshop, where ~~there is again~~ a gigantic animal, *is being constructed by workers*—a winged llama.[+]

> [+]*Llama = Attempt to restore the genius at animal level. "A vast conspiracy between all animated beings to restore the world in its original harmony."*
> *This thought connects to the illusion of couples on horseback in the moonlight = the ancestors*

"A beam of fire seemed to be shooting through this monster and slowly bringing it to life; it twisted this way and that, penetrated by the countless purple shafts of flame … " He is told that this fire was originally the Earth's central fire, *which once reached to the surface* "but the wellsprings have dried up." Then Aurélia's ~~Hierosgamos~~ *marriage* to the "Other" is related again.[+c]

> [+c]*"I was immediately gripped by an insane fit of rage. I imagined the bridegroom they were all awaiting was my double who was due to marry Aurélia."*

He himself is threatened by a red-hot bullet against his head. (cf. dream symbols: billiard ball that dashes the navigation instruments.)[+d]

> [+d]*Pushed toward the throne in the center of the hall, wants to give the magic signal himself (for the wedding), at that moment*

He hears the cry of a woman and knows it comes from <u>Aurélia</u>.—"Lost, a second time!" *Everything is over, everything is past! It is now my turn to die, and to die without hope!*

The second part of the book begins with the author's reflections on what he had undergone, connected with religious lines of thought: "We may well be approaching that era when science, as predicted, having accomplished its entire cycle of synthesis and analysis, of belief and negation, will be able to purify itself and usher forth the marvelous city of the future from chaos and ruin."+e

> +e*"God will no doubt appreciate the purity of these intentions;*
> *what father relishes the sight of his son abdicating*
> *all reason and pride in his presence? The apostle*
> *who needed to touch in order to believe was not cursed for having doubts!"*

"What have I just written? Blasphemies. This is not the way Christian humility is permitted to speak. Ideas of this sort are hardly calculated to mellow the soul. They wear the proud lightning bolts of Satan's crown on their brow. A pact with God himself? ... O science! O vanity!"

~~The last dream the author mentions reads:~~

~~A woman who cared for me in my youth appeared in my dream addressing reproaching me for a serious mistake I once committed. I recognized her, although she seemed much older than the last time I had seen her. This made me think bitterly that I had neglected to go visit her during her last moments. She seemed to say to me: "You did not weep for your old parents as much as you did for this woman. How then can you expect forgiveness?"~~

~~It is Anima, whom he had "missed." In the subsequent course of the dream the memory of the past comes back to him, and he says to himself: "All of this has happened to induct you into the secrets of life, but you did not understand. Religion(s) and legends, the saints and the poets agreed on explaining the fatal enigma, but you misinterpreted them ... Now it is too late!" He was struck by panic: "This is my last day!" and he had to admit to himself: "After the apparition of the Stone Guest, I had sat down again to the feast!"+~~

> +*Dream of a mortally ill friend:*
> *"A sublime dream in the shadowy reaches of infinity,*
> *a conversation with a being at once distinct from and identical to himself, and*
> *of whom he asked, believing himself dead, the whereabouts of God. 'But God is*
> *everywhere,' his spirit answered. 'He is in you, he is in everyone. He judges you,*
> *he listens to you, he counsels you. He is us, you and I, as we think and dream in*
> *unison—we have never parted, we are eternal!' ... 'God is with him,' I cried out,*
> *'but he is no longer with me! What a disaster! I have cursed him, I have threat-*
> *ened him, I have disowned him!' It was indeed he, that mystical brother who had*
> *been drawing further and further away from my soul and sending me warnings*

in vain! Favored bridegroom and king of glory, it is he who is now judging and condemning me; it is he who is now carrying off to his heaven that bride that he might have bestowed on me, a bride of whom I am no longer worthy!'

⁺Dream, after he had heard about a friend's suicide: He was speaking to him: behind them a large mirror, in which he thought he saw Aurélia. "She seemed sad and pensive; but suddenly, whether it was because she had stepped out of the mirror or because she had been reflected in it a moment earlier as she crossed the room, this tender figure was standing by my side. She held out her hand to me and, casting me a mournful glance, said: ' We shall meet again later ... at your friend's house.'

And it came to me in a flash—her marriage, the curse that was keeping us apart. I said to myself: is it possible? Will she ever come back to me? In tears, I asked: 'Have you forgiven me?' But everything had vanished ... She is lost, I cried out to myself, but why? ... Now I understand, she made one last effort to save me—but I missed that crucial moment at which forgiveness was still possible. She could have interceded on my behalf with the divine Bridegroom in the heavens above ... But does my salvation even matter? She has been snatched into the abyss, lost to me, lost to all!"

The manuscript of Aurélia was found on the author's corpse. On a cold January night he was wandering the streets of Paris and around three in the morning arrived at an alleyway in the Tour Saint-Jacques district. There was an antique shop that displayed a mummy in the window. Previously the alleyway had been known as 'Rue de la Tuerie' because of an abattoir that had once stood there. It led to the Seine, where a sewer discharged into the river. The sewer was covered over with a grille. On this grille Gérard de Nerval hanged himself with a corset string.

This was the end of a personality who had never understood how to prize open the narrow circle of the personal "I" ~~and the mystery he so often spoke of~~ *—and grant admission to the shadow, that ambiguous herald of yet another order of things.*

SIX

Jung's First Notes on *Aurélia*, 1942

EDITOR'S NOTE: THE FOLLOWING IS A TRANSCRIPTION OF JUNG'S ORIGINAL manuscript notes; the holographs of these five pages are reproduced below, on pages 113–117. Phrases and sentences translated from the German are transcribed directly; phrases and sentences translated from the French are presented in quotation marks. Latin and Greek phrases and astrological symbols are transcribed without alteration, but translations of these can be found in sections 3 and 5.

21 III 1942
Gérard de Nerval.

G. de N. pseudonym of Gérard Labrunie born 23.5.1808, died 25.1.1853.
"Vers dorés" beautiful lyric poems.
Translated poems by Klopstock, Goethe and Heine. 1828 a Faust-translation.
"Lorely, Souvenirs d'Allemagne." 1848–50 Scènes de la vie
Orientale. 1855 Le rêve et la vie. postum.
1852–3 Aurélia. Found on his body. Suicide on
a cold January night, in [a] little street, originally named rue de la Tuerie.
At the head of the lane an antique shop with mummy.
Hanged on sewer grille with a corset-string.

Aurélia: Opening: "Dream is a second life."
The Unconscious:
"Little by little, the dim cavern is suffused with light and, emerging
from its shadowy depths, the pale figures who dwell in limbo come into view
…—the
spirit world opens for us." p. 26–28
Intermezzo in Italy. Sudden libidinal withdrawal. Meeting
with A. p. 30–32

p. 8 _Dream:_ Expos. His past and present life.
Development: looks for his room. Gets lost
Peripeteia or catastrophe: The collapse
of the daemon in the inner courtyard!
  no _lysis._

Daemon: "Rosey hues." Wings of a thousand colors. Cauda
        pavonis (continet omnes colores) _Superhumanly great._
      Eros or fire.   _Self,_ which contains himself.
The dreamer retires from his life, that is also a catastrophe
for the Self, which remains confined in the inner courtyard.
 It cannot unfold anymore like the causa pavonis.
 Angel of Melancholy = the mental alienation,
that drops on him. ~~p.9~~ 32
After the dream. Revealed because of [the] approach of the Unconscious, like
before. _Anticipation of death. Orient_ = Germany, where
often, when a bit deranged. Land of the Unconscious. _Star_ of his fate,
benchmark, goal. Halt at the _three-way_ = _Hecate,_ does not aim further,
 remains in antiquity: Therefore _apostle:_
contradiction to Christianity. _Pagan point of view:_
"I do not belong to your heaven. Those who await me are in that star.
They predate the revelation." _Aurélia_ also among them.
        His goal is the _ancient world._ (_Rosencreutz:_ Aeg. Fest u. Hieros Gamos.
              Faust class. Walpurgisnacht
Poliphile, Hof der Venus. _Tannhäuser_ Venusberg. _Alchemie:_ 7 Götter.

  [page] 2
Anima announces antiquity. _She_ shows the ancient past life.
Like _Orpheus_ he seeks his Eurydice in the underworld.
Faust seeks Gretchen:

        Mephisto, do you see
off there, alone, dead-pale, a lovely girl?
Now she is slowly moving away,
dragging her feet as if they were in fetters.
I have to say I can't help thinking
that she looks like my own dear Gretchen.
…
I know those are the eyes of someone dead,
eyes that no loving hand has closed.
That is the breast which Gretchen let me press,
that the sweet body which gave me joy.
…

What ecstasy, and yet what pain!
I cannot bear to let this vision go.
How strange that on that lovely neck
there is an ornament a single scarlet thread
no thicker than a knife!

Mephisto: You're right, I see it too.
She also can transport her head beneath her arm,
thanks to the fact that Perseus lopped it off

Gorgon = Hecate at the three-way crossroad. Petrification,
the imprisonment and the torpidity of schizophrenia. Lot's wife, Eurydice
look backwards. *Not forward into life, but backwards out of life*
"Here began for me ... the overflow of dream into real life."

Continues his way towards the star, *singing a mysterious* hymn
from another existence, "which filled me with a joy beyond words."

Golden Serenity, come!
You, most secret, sweetest
anticipation of the pleasure of death!

Casts off his clothes. *(Discards his body).* Star *grows larger.*
Then he feels remorseful, (prayer to the spirit that attracts him.)
descends to mortals again, enlarged himself,
of enormous power. Gets locked up.
Vision *p. 12 f.* ~~Comment~~ *37*
        Sanatorium. Visions: *p. 19 40 Comment: dark*
1. Rocks: *Stygian landscape. 3.* Uncle: *died 100 years ago:*
wise old man. *2.* Old maid-servant:
aïeul: grandfather. Great uncle. Maternal authority. *His soul a* bird.

[page] *3*
Anima: *Marguerite!*
Bird-parallel: *primitive transformation of souls into animals.*
Soul bird: Ba. Angel. *Pater-Filius-Paraclete = bird columba*
Woman in old-fashioned German costume: *beldame. Mère Lusine.*
Hecate. Primordial mother Isis. *p. 23 42*

Comment: *Plunge into the Earth = collective unconscious.*
Stream *of metal (chemical diversity) Spir. [Spiritus] vitae = Mercurius*
Plunge into the brain. *= Schizophrenia. Brain substance!*

Rivers = living <u>souls</u>. Psychic!
<u>*Island:*</u> *'You are Orplid, <u>my</u> country, <u>Mörike</u>.*
 in the distance gleaming!'

<u>*Old man:*</u> *aïeul (bird)* <u>*Berl[iner] Zaub[er] Pap[yrus]*</u>: ἧκέ μοι ἀγαθὲ
γεωργέ = ἀγαθὸς δαίμων. *Olympiodor quot. from Zosimos Hermes-citation.*
Achaab o. Acharanthus.
Zaub.Pap. ἐπικαλουμαί σε Κύρια Ἴσι, ἥ συνεχώρησεν ὁ
Ἀγαθὸς Δαίμων βασιλεύων ἐν τῶ τελείω μέλανί.
τὸ τέλεων μέλαν = *pupil. Isis = eye of Osiris = sun, God veiled
into it, namely in the pupil. = <u>Sol niger</u>.*
<u>*Olympiodor*</u> *II, IV, 32* Ἄπελθε πρὸς Ἀχαὰβ τὸν γεωργόν, καὶ μα-
θήσῃ ὡς ὁ σπείρων σῖτον σῖτον γεννᾷ.
Alch[emy] <u>*Saturn*</u> *as gardener. (Lead = pr. mat.) Black earth*
<u>*Ancestors as animals*</u> *p. 23 ff 42*
<u>*Comment:*</u> <u>*Heptad:*</u>   *"But how to go about establishing
the individual centers that emanate from these,—or from which
they emanate—like some collective anima figure
whose permutations would at once be finite and unlimited?"*

⊙   ☾   ☿ ♀ ♂ ♃ ♄
2   5

*Old man is transformed into [a] youth, (Senex et iuvenis. Hermes)
<u>who received the ideas from the dreamer. Large town. Inhabitants</u>
"They had managed to maintain their fierce <u>individuality</u>"
amid the mixed and undistinguished population.
"<u>Mountain which dominates the town:</u>" Place of the inhabitants
Isle of bliss. "It seemed as if my feet were sinking
into the successive strata of buildings
of different eras."   Finally, (at the lowest level,) an <u>old man</u>.
A man threatens him in order to prevent him
from penetrating into the mystery of the place = refuge of the inhabitants
"<u>Vanquishers over the blind masses!</u>" Old woman alike
Many young people who wish to keep him there. Everything disappears.*

[page] 4
<u>*Dream:*</u> *p. 36*
<u>*Expos.*</u> *The ancestor's house: 3 women: (the) Fates 1 + 3* <u>*indiv[iduation]*</u>.
<u>*Development:*</u> *Historically dressed. He belongs to the others,
in timelessness.*

Fruit!	In the garden with lady. Ancient shape of a cross.
	Garden returned to wildness.
	Spring water fountain.
	"Lady in shot taffeta dress changing." (Daemon)
	She becomes the garden, becomes nature.
Peripeteia:	"No! Don't disappear! All of nature is dying with you!"
Catastrophe:	Can no longer grasp the shadow, bumps
	against a wall. "Bust of a woman."
Lysis:	"The Universe lies in night!"
	"This dream, which had started out so happily,
	caused me no end of perplexity. What did it mean?
	Only later did I find out. Aurélia had died."

In the ensuing deliria Aur. "drawn with divine features,
a turning <u>wheel</u> under her feet."
(Dream symbols: woman on globe.
        anima mundi.)
Goes through the complete story of Creation.
Recovery. Bird appears.   Deliria begin again.
The young man, enlarged as "prince of Orient"
appears again: <u>It is he himself</u>. <u>Assumes</u>:
Aur.'s "mystical marriage" with the <u>Other</u>.
(~~Faust: Paris and Helen~~)
"A bad spirit had taken my place in the world of souls."
Again, the great town and the mountain and workshop.
<u>Animal</u>. Winged llama. "A beam of fire seemed to be
shooting through this monster and slowly bringing it to life;
it twisted this way and that, penetrated by
the countless purple shafts of flame ..."
From the central fire, "but the wellsprings have dried up."
<u>Hierosgamos to the Other</u>.   He is threatened by
a red-hot bullet against his head.
(Dream. Billiard ball.) Cry of Aurélia.
"Lost, a second time!"

   [page] 5
"We may well be approaching that era when science, as predicted, having
accomplished its entire cycle of synthesis and analysis, of belief and negation,
will now be able to purify itself and usher forth the miraculous city of the future
from chaos and ruin ..."

"What have I just written? Blasphemies. This is not the way Christian humility
is permitted to speak. Ideas of this sort are hardly calculated to mellow the soul.

They wear the proud lightning bolts of Satan's crown on their brow. A pact with God himself? ... O science! O vanity!"

Dream: p. 91 100

Comment: Anima, whom he has <u>missed</u>.
"All this was done in order to teach you the secret of life, yet you did not understand. All the religions and fables ..."
Following: All his memories of the past resurge.
"... all the saints and poets concurred in explaining the fatal enigma, yet you misinterpreted it ... Now it is too late! ... This is my last day. After the visit of <u>the guest of stone</u>, I had returned to the banquet table."

21.III.1942

Gérard de Nerval.

HS 1055:106₁

G. d. N. Pseudonym von G. de Labrunie geb. 23.V. 1808, gest.
25.I.1853. "Vers dorés", schöne lyrische Gedichte. Übersetzte Gedichte
von Klopstock, Goethe und Heine. 1828 Faust-übersetzung.
"Lorely, souvenirs d'Allemagne". 1848–50 scènes de la vie Orientale. 1855 le rêve et la vie posthum.
1852-3 Aurelia. Auf seinem heilbaren gefunden. Suicide in
kalter Januarnacht, in Gässchen, rue de la Tuerie genannt. Am
Eingang eines Raren Antiquitätenladen mit Mumie. Am Canal-
gitter aufgehängt mit Corsett-schnur.

Aurélia: Anfang: Le Rêve est une seconde vie.

Ubw = "C'est un souterrain vague qui s'éclaire peu à peu, et où
se dégagent de l'ombre et de la nuit les pâles figures im-
mobiles qui habitent le séjour des limbes. — ... le monde
des Esprits s'ouvre pour nous. p. 26–28
zntermezzo in Italien. plötzlicher Libido-entzug. Zu-
sammentreffen mit A. p. 30–32

28. Traum: Expos. Sein vergangnes – jetziges Leben.
Schürzung d. Knotens: sucht einen Raum. Verirrt sich.
Peripetie o. Katastrophe: Absturz des Daemons in Innen-
hof. (galéries centrales!)
Keine Lysis.

Daemon: teintes vermeilles. Flügel von 1000 Farben. Cauda
pavonis (continet omnes colores) unermesslich gross.
Eros o. Feuer. Selbst, das ihn enthält.
Der Träumer zieht sich aus seinem Leben zurück, das ist zugleich
eine Katastrophe für das Selbst, welches im Innenhof gefangen
bleibt. Es kann sich nicht mehr entfalten wie die cauda
pavonis. Engel der Melancholie = Geisteskrankheit senkt
sich auf ihn. p. 9 32

nach dem Traum. Gelöbnis wegen Annäherung des Ubw, wie
früher. Vorahnung des Todes. Orient = Deutschland, wo
oft, wenn etwas verrückt. Land des Ubw. Stern zeiner Seligkeit
als, Fixpunkt, Ziel. Halt am Dreiweg = Hekate, will
nicht weiter, bleibt bei der Antike: Darum Apostel:
Auseinandersetzung mit dem Christenthum. Heidn. Standp.
"Je n'appartiens pas à ton ciel! Dans cette étoile sont
ceux qui m'attendent. Ils sont antérieurs à le rêve
latin. Auch Aurélia dabei. Rosenvruth: Aug. Fest. Thiers
Sein Ziel die antike Welt. (Faust d. h. Walpurgisnacht)
Poliphile, Hof der Venus. Tannhäuser Venusberg. Alchemie:
7. Götter.

2

Anima kündet die antike Weltan. Sie zeigt das antike Vorleben des Helden. Er sucht wie Orpheus seine Eurydike in der Unterwelt. Faust sucht Gretchen:

» Mephisto, siehst du dort
Ein blasses schönes Kind allein und ferne stehen?
Sie schiebt sich langsam nur vom Ort,
Sie scheint mit geschlossnen Füßen zu gehen.
Ich muss bekennen, dass mir deucht
Dass sie dem guten Gretchen gleicht.

Fürwahr es sind die Augen einer Toten,
Die eine liebende Hand nicht schloss.
Das ist die Brust, die Gretchen mir geboten,
Das ist der süße Leib, den ich genoss.

Welch eine Wonne, welch ein Leiden!
Ich kann von diesem Blick nicht scheiden.
Wie sonderbar muss diesen schönen Hals
Ein einzig rothes Schnürchen schmücken,
Nicht breiter als ein Messerrücken.

Mephisto:
Ganz recht, ich seh es ebenfalls.
Sie kann das Haupt auch unterm Arme tragen,
Denn Perseus hat's ihr abgeschlagen.

Gorgo = Hekate am Dreiweg. Versteinerung, Gefangenschaft, Erstarrung in der Schizophrenie. Roth, Weiß, Eurydike schauen zurück. Nicht durchs Leben vorwärts, sondern aus dem Leben rückwärts.

ici a commencé pour moi --- l'épanchement du songe dans la vie réelle.

Sucht seinen Weg nach der Sternenfurt. Singt einen mysteriösen Hymnus aus einer andern Existenz, qui m'enveloppe d'une joie ineffable.

Flüter bit gütlicher Komm!
Du des Todes
heimlichstes, süsestes Vorgenuss.

Wirft seine Kleider ab. (Legt den Körper ab.) Stern wird grün, Dann fasst ihn die Reue, (Geht zum Geist, der ihn aufgibt.) steigt wieder zu den Menschen hinunter, selbst ausgesöhnt, von ungeheurer Kraft. Wird angesteckt.

Vision p. 12 f Comets 3

Sanatorium. Visionen: p. 19 40 Comets: finster
Felsen: scheerantike Landschaft. Onkel: über 100
Vater gestorben. Alter Weiser. Alte Mago:
Aasel = Gwnvati, Gonarkel. Matriarchalische Autorität. Seine Seele ein Vogel.

3

Anima : Margarethe !

Vogel Parallel: primitive Verantwortung der Seelen in Thier-
Seelenvögel: Ba , Siegel . Pater-Filius- Paraklet = Vogel columba
Frau in alt deutschen Tract ; Ahnfrau . Mère Lusine .
Hekate . Urmutter . p. 23 42

Comentar : Absturz in die Erde = coll. Ubew.
metalltrans (chem. Verschiedt.) Spir. vitae = Mercurius
Absturz ins Gehirn. ? Schizophrenie . Geheimmaterie !
Flüsse = lebende Seelen . Psychisch !
Insel : Du bist Ophir mein Land . Mörike .
Darfernecmaltet .

Greis = aïeul (Vogel) Bol. Zaub. Pap. : ἧκέ μοι ἀγαθὲ
γεωργέ = ἀγαθὸς δαίμων . Olympiodoret aus Zosimos Hermesversetzt.
Zaub. Pap. ἐπικκλουμαί δε Κύρα Ἴσι , ἧ συνεχωρηδε ὁ
Ἀγαθὸς Δαίμων βασιλεύων ἐν τῶ τελείω μέλανι .
τὸ τέλεον μέλαν = Pupille . Isis = Auge der Osiris = Sonne, Gott darein
verhüllt nämlich in der Pupille . = Sol niger .
Olympiodor II , IV, 32 Ἄπελθε πρὸς Ἀχααβ τὸν γεωργόν καὶ μα-
θήση ὡς ὁ σπείρων σῖτον σῖτον γεννᾶ .
Alch . Saturn als Gärtner . (Blei = pr. mat.) Schwarze Erde .
Vorfahren als Thiere . p. 23 / 42

Comentar : Siebenzahl : mais comment établir les
centres individuels émanés d'eux , — dont ils émanent,
comme une figure animique collective dont la com-
binaison serait à la fois multiple et bornée ?

$$\frac{\odot \, \mathbb{C} \, \male \, \venus \, \jupiter \, \saturn \, \mercury}{2 \quad 5}$$

Greis verwandelt mich jetzt in Jüngling , (Senex et iuvenis
der vom Träumer die Idee erlöst . Grosse Stadt. Bewohn.
Ils savaient maintenir leur individualité farouche
selbst noch in collectiver Gestalt .
Montagne qui domine la ville : Art der Bewohner .
Glückseelige Insel . Il me semblait que mes pieds
s'enfonçaient dans les couches successives des édifices
de différents âges . Endlich (zuunterst) ein Greis
ein Mann bedroht ihn , um ihn daran zu hindern,
das Rätsel des Ortes zu lösen = Befreiung der Bewohner,
vainqueurs des masses aveugles ! Ebenso alte Frau.
viele junge Leute die (Alles verwundert .
ihn zurückhalten wollen .

4   Traum: p. 36.

Expos. Haus des aïeul: 3 Frauen: Parae 1+3. Judïa

Schürf D⁰Knots: In historischem Gewand. Er gehört zu dem
          Dem, un Zeitlosen.
    Früchte!   Fürst Tanze im Garten. Alte Kreuzform.
          Garten zur Wildheit zurückgekehrt.
          Source d'eau vive.
          Dame in Taffetas changeant. (Daemon)
          Sie wird zum Garten, zur Natur.
Peripetie : Oh! ne fuis pas! — car Nature meurt avec
                                                toi!
Katastrophe. Kann den Schatten nicht nach fassen, stößt
          an eine Mauer. Buste de femme.

Lyris : L'univers est dans la nuit!

        Ce rêve si heureux à son début me jeta dans
        une grande perplexité. Que signifiait-il? Je
        ne le sus que plus tard. Aurélia était morte.

    In der folgenden Delirien Aur. peinte sous les traits
    d'une divinité, sous ses pieds tournait une zone.
    (Traumsymbole: Frau auf Globus.)
          anima mundi.
    Geht durch die ganze Schöpfungsgeschichte.
    Besserung. Vogel erscheint. Delirien beginnen wieder.
    Der junge Mann, umspannt als prince d'Orient
    erscheint wieder: Er ist es selbst. Vermuthet.
    Mariage mystique de Aur. mit dem Andern.
    (Faust: Paris, u Helena.)
    Un mauvais génie avait pris ma place dans
    le monde des âmes.
    Über die große Stadt u. die Berg u. Werkstätt.
    Thier. Lama mit Flügeln. Ce monstre était
    comme traversé d'un jet de feu qui l'animait
    peu à peu, de sorte qu'il se tordait, pénétré par
    mille filets pourpres. —
    Aus dem Centralfeuer, mais les sources se sont
    taries.
        Hierosgamos mit dem Andern. Er wird
    mit rothglühender Kugel gegen den Kopf bedroht.
    (Traums. Billardkugel.) Schrei der Aurélia.
    Une seconde fois perdue!

Peut-être touchons-nous à l'époque prédite où la
science, ayant accompli son cercle entier de synthèse
et d'analyse, de croyance et de négation, pourra
s'épurer elle-même et faire jaillir de désordre
et des ruines la cité merveilleuse de l'avenir....

Qu'ai-je écrit là? Ce sont des blasphèmes.
L'humanité chrétienne ne peut parler ainsi. De telles
pensées sont loin d'attendrir l'âme. Elles ont sur
le front les éclairs d'orgueil de la couronne de
Satan..... Un pacte avec Dieu lui-même?...
Ô science! ô vanité!

Traum: p. 91 100

Comm. Anima dir ~~vorgeworfen~~ hat.
tout cela était fait pour t'enseigner le ~~secret~~ de la vie et
je n'as pas compris. les religions et les fables, les saints

Folgendes: Alle ~~Erinnerungen~~ (~~Relieu~~ en aride)

et les poètes s'accordaient à expliquer l'énigme fatale
et tu as mal interprété... Maintenant il est
trop tard. — — — C'est mon dernier jour!
Après la visite du convive de pierre je m'étais rassis
au festin!

SEVEN

Aurélia, or Dream and Life

by Gérard de Nerval

TRANSLATED AND ANNOTATED BY RICHARD SIEBURTH, WITH ALFRED KUBIN'S illustrations from Gérard de Nerval, *Aurelia oder, Des Traum und Das Leben*, the Georg Müller edition, 1910, and with marginalia indicated from C. G. Jung's copies—the Paris: Écrit Intimes/Éditions de la Pléiade/J. Schiffein edition and Munich: Georg Müller edition.[1]

---

1. Published in two installments in the *Revue de Paris*, 1 January and 15 February 1855.

First Part

I

ream is a second life. I have never been able to cross through those gates of ivory or horn which separate us from the invisible world without a sense of dread.[2] The first few instants of sleep are the image of death; a drowsy numbness steals over our thoughts, and it becomes impossible to determine the precise point at which the *self*, in some other form, continues to carry on the work of existence. Little by little, the dim cavern is suffused with light and, emerging from its shadowy depths, the pale figures who dwell in limbo come into view, solemn and still. Then the tableau takes on shape, a new clarity illuminates these bizarre apparitions and sets them in motion—the spirit world opens for us.

[Emanuel] Swedenborg called these visions his *Memorabilia*; they came to him more often in reverie than in sleep; Apuleius's *Golden Ass* and Dante's *Divine Comedy* are the poetic models of such studies of the human soul.[3] Following their example, I shall attempt to transcribe the impressions of a lengthy illness that took place entirely within the mysteries of my own mind—although I do not know why I use the term illness here, for so far as I am concerned, I never felt more fit. At times I believed my strength and energy had redoubled; I seemed to know everything, understand everything; my imagination afforded me infinite delights. Having recovered what men call reason, must I lament the loss of such joys? …

This *Vita nuova* was divided into two phases in my case.[4] Here are the notes relating to the first of these. A woman I had long loved and whom I shall call Aurélia was lost to me.[5] The circumstances of this event which was to have such a major influence on my life do not really matter. Any-

2. For the classical distinction between the two Gates of Sleep, see *Odyssey*, 19:562–69; *Aeneid*, 6:893–96. The gates of horn allow "true shades" to pass through, whereas the gates of ivory are associated with distorted or illusory dreams.

3. Nerval links these as quest romances that culminate in the redemptive vision of the Eternal Feminine—the goddess Isis and Beatrice, respectively. Swedenborg (1688–1772) gathered various narratives of his visionary communications with angels and spirits in his *Memorabilia*—parodied by the "Memorable Fancies" of Blake's *Marriage of Heaven and Hell*.

4. Dante's *Vita Nuova* recounts, in a mixture of poetry and prose, how the figure of Beatrice appeared to the poet in order to guide the transformation of his profane life into religious faith. The "two phases" may allude to Nerval's breakdowns of 1841 and 1851–52.

5. "Aurélia" is the Latin translation of the Greek "chrysalis," the gold-colored pupa of the butterfly—emblem of metamorphosis and hiddenness (like Dante's *donna schermo*, Beatrice). The name also occurs in one of E.T.A. Hoffman's novels *The Devil's Elixir*, partially translated by Nerval, and echoes the actress Aurélie in Nerval's *Sylvie*. Biographical interpretations identify Aurélia with Nerval's ill-fated passion for the singer Jenny Colon.

body can search his memories for the emotion which proved the most devastating or for the cruelest blow of fate; the only decision in these cases is whether to die or go on living—later I shall explain why I did not choose death. Condemned by the woman I loved, guilty of an offense for which I no longer hoped to be forgiven, my only course was to plunge myself into vulgar intoxications; I affected a gay, carefree air, I traveled the world, entranced by its diversity and unpredictability; the bizarre costumes and customs of distant lands especially appealed to me, for it seemed to me that I was thereby relocating the conditions of good and evil, the outer limits, as it were, of what we French define as *feelings*. What madness, I told myself, to go on platonically loving a woman who no longer loves you. The trouble is I have read too much; I have taken the inventions of poets too seriously and have made a Laura or a Beatrice out of an ordinary woman of our century. ... Let us move on to other affairs of the heart; she will soon be forgotten.

The giddy merriment of a carnival in an Italian city raised my melancholy spirits. So grateful was I for this moment of relief that I shared my joy with all my friends; in my letters I portrayed as a stable state of mind what was in fact merely a passing fever of overexcitement.

One day a lady of great renown arrived in the city; she took a liking to me and, accustomed as she was to dazzling her entourage, effortlessly swept

45 me into the circle of her admirers.[6] After a soiree during which she had
conducted herself in a manner both so unaffected and so beguiling as to
have charmed all those present, I felt so enraptured by her that I wanted
to write to her without delay. I was overjoyed to feel my heart capable of
a new love! … In the rush of my contrived enthusiasm, I appropriated the
50 very turns of phrase which had allowed me, so short a while ago, to depict
a love both genuine and long-felt. Having sent off the letter, I wanted to
retract it; and I went off alone to ponder what seemed to me a profanation
of my memories.

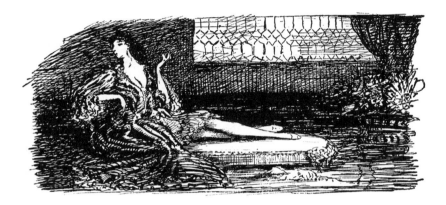

Evening restored all the previous day's glamour to my newfound love.
55 The lady was appreciative of my letter, although somewhat taken aback by
the suddenness of my fervor. I had, in a single day, run the gamut of emotions one can feel for a woman with a semblance of sincerity. She confessed
that she was flattered, if astonished. I attempted to convince her of my feelings; but no matter what I tried to say in the course of our conversations, I
60 was unable to recapture my previous flights of style; I was reduced to admit-
ting, tears in my eyes, that I had both deceived myself and misused her. My
heartfelt confidences nonetheless moved her, and my vain protestations of
love gave way to a friendship far deeper and more gentle.

II

Later, I met her in another city, in which the woman I still hopelessly
loved also happened to find herself.[7] As chance would have it, they made

6. This reference may allude to the pianist Mare Pleyel, whom Nerval met in Vienna in 1839.
7. Nerval again met Marie Pleyel in the winter of 1840 in Brussels, where his *Piquillo*, star-
ring Jenny Colon, was being premiered.

each other's acquaintance and the former no doubt took the occasion to speak on my behalf, eliciting the compassion of the one who had exiled me from her heart. As a result, finding myself one day at a gathering at which she was also present, I saw her come in my direction and extend her hand. How to interpret this gesture and the deep, mournful glance she cast in greeting me? I took it to be forgiveness for the past; the simple phrases she addressed to me, graced by the divine accent of pity, acquired a value beyond words; it was as if something religious had infused itself into a love heretofore profane and imprinted it with the seal of eternity.

I was forced to return to Paris by a pressing obligation, but I immediately decided I would spend only a few days there before rejoining my two friends. My elation and impatience were such that I fell prey to a kind of giddiness which was aggravated by all the unfinished business to which I had to attend. One evening, around midnight, as I was making my way back to my lodgings, I raised my eyes by chance and noticed a house number lit up by a street lamp. It was the same number as my age.[8] Then, lowering my eyes, I saw before me a woman with hollow eyes and a pallid face whose features seemed to be those of Aurélia. I said to myself: this must be an omen of *her death* or mine! I do not know why I settled on the latter conjecture, but I was stricken by the idea that this would come to the pass the following day at the very same hour.

That night I had a dream which confirmed this idea. I was wandering through an immense building made up of several rooms, some being used as study halls, others devoted to conversation or philosophic debate. Out of curiosity, I stopped in one of the former rooms, where I thought I recognized my old teachers and schoolmates. The lessons dealing with Greek and Roman authors droned on, their monotonous hum resembling some prayer to the goddess Mnemosyne.[9] I passed on to another room where philosophical discussions were taking place. I took part in these for a while, then left to find myself a room in a sort of hostelry with huge staircases and bustling with travelers.

I lost my way several times in the long corridors, and as I was crossing one of the central galleries, I was struck by a strange scene. A creature of disproportionate size—man or woman, I do not know—was fluttering about with great difficulty overhead and seemed to be floundering in the thick clouds. In the end, out of breath and energy, it plummeted into the center of the dark courtyard, snagging and bruising its wings on the roofs and balustrades as it fell. I was able to get a brief look at it. It was tinged with rosy hues and its wings shimmered with countless changing reflections. Draped in a

8. In 1841, the year of his first severe mental breakdown, Nerval turned thirty-three—the Christological age.
9. The goddess of Memory and the mother of the Muses.

long robe falling in classical folds, it resembled the Angel of Melancholy by Albrecht Dürer.[10] I could not stifle my shrieks of terror, which woke me with a start.

40   The next day I was in a hurry to see all my friends. I was mentally saying good-bye to them, and without letting them know what was on my mind, I launched into passionate disquisitions on mystical topics; I astonished them by my peculiar eloquence; it seemed to me that I understood every-thing, that the mysteries of the world were being revealed to me in these 45 final hours.

    That evening, as the fatal hour seemed to be drawing near, I was at a club, sitting at table with two friends, holding forth on painting and music, de-fining my views on the generation of colors and the meaning of numbers. One of them, by the name of Paul ***, wanted to accompany me back to my 50 lodgings, but I told him I was not going home.[11] "Where are you going?" he asked. "*To the Orient!*" And as he walked by my side, I began to scan the sky for a certain <u>star</u> I thought I knew, as if it had some influence over my fate. Having located it, I continued on my way, following the streets where I could see it ahead of me, forging onwards, as it were, towards my destiny and 55 wanting to keep the star in view until the moment death was to strike. But having reached the intersection of three streets, I refused to go any further. My friend seemed to be exerting superhuman strength to get me to move on; he was growing every larger in my eyes and taking on the features of an apostle. The spot on which we stood appeared to rise up, losing all its urban 60 features—on a hilltop surrounded by vast expanses of emptiness, this scene

---

10.   Dürer's engraving *Melencolia I* (1514) is also alluded to in Nerval's sonnet "El Desdi-chado," where it is associated with the "black sun."
11.   One of Nerval's manuscripts bears the full name of this friend, the pantheist painter Paul Chenevard.

had now become a battle between two spirits, a kind of biblical temptation.[12] "No!" I said. "I do not belong to your heaven. Those who await me are in that star. They predate the revelation that you have announced. Let me rejoin them, for the one I love is among them, waiting for us to meet again."[13]

III

ere began for me what I shall call the overflow of dream into real life. From this point on, everything at times took on a double aspect—without, however, my reasoning powers thereby ever lacking in logic and without my memory losing the least detail of what was happening to me. It was simply that my actions, to all appearances insane, were subject to what human reason chooses to deem illusion...

The idea has often occurred to me that at certain crucial junctures in life, this or that Spirit from the external world suddenly takes on the bodily shape of an ordinary person and then acts or attempts to act on us without that person ever having been aware of it or remembering it.[14]

My friend had left me, realizing his efforts were in vain and no doubt convinced that I had fallen prey to some momentary idée fixe that simply needed to be walked off. Finding myself alone, I struggled to my feet and again set off in the direction of the star, not letting it stray from my sight for one moment. As I walked along, I chanted a mysterious hymn which I thought I remembered having heard in some other life and which filled me with a joy beyond words. At the same time, I proceeded to shed my earthly garments and scatter them about. The route appeared to lead ever upwards as the star grew larger. Then, standing there with my arms outstretched, I awaited the moment at which my soul would separate from my body, magnetically attracted into the ray of the star. Then I felt a shudder go through me; my heart was seized with regrets for the earth and those I loved, and so fervently did I inwardly beseech the Spirit who was drawing me upwards that it seemed I was now redescending among mankind. I was surrounded by a night patrol. I was under the impression that I had grown quite tall and that, flooded as I was with electrical forces, I was sure to knock down anybody who approached me. There was something comical in the care I took to spare the strength and lives of the soldiers who had picked me up.

12. Genesis 32:324–32; Jacob wrestling with the Angel. (See figure 20.)
13. Editor's Note: In the margin of his Pléiade edition of Aurélia (catalogued BF20), p. 34, Jung writes: "XPisme" (Christianism).
14. Nerval's use of the term external world here and elsewhere refers not to exterior reality but rather to the supernal realm of dream or death.

If I did not think it a writer's mission to analyze sincerely what he feels at the most momentous occasions of his life, and if I had not set myself a goal I believe useful, I would stop here, rather than attempt to describe what I subsequently experienced in a series of visions which were perhaps insane, or more simply, the mere products of my illness ... Stretched out on a camp bed, I thought I saw the sky lift its veil and open out on to a thousand vistas of unsuspected magnificence. It seemed that the <u>fate of the Soul</u> after its deliverance was being revealed to me, as if to fill me with remorse for <u>having so single-mindedly wished to set foot back on the very earth I was about to leave</u> ... Immense circles traced their way through infinity, like the rings touched off in water by a falling body; peopled with radiant figures, each region in its turn took on <u>color and movement and then dissolved;</u> a divinity, always the same, smiled as she cast off the fleeting masks of her various incarnations, and then took refuge, <u>out of grasp, in the mystical splendors of the sky of Asia.</u>[15]

This heavenly vision, by a phenomenon everyone has experienced in certain dreams, did not leave me oblivious to what was going on around me. Lying on the camp bed, I overheard the soldiers discuss some nameless person who like me had been arrested and whose voice had echoed through the same room. By an odd effect of vibration, it seemed to me that this voice was resonating in my own chest and that my soul was, so to speak, dividing in two—distinctly split between vision and reality. For a second, I thought I might make the effort to turn towards the individual in question, then I shuddered as I remembered that according to a tradition well known in Germany, every man has a double and that when he sees him, death is near.[16]

I closed my eyes and lapsed into a confused state of mind in which the figures around me, whether real or fantastic, proceeded to shatter into a thousand evanescent guises. At one point, I saw two friends of mine who had come looking for me; the soldiers pointed me out to them; then the door opened and someone of my own height whose face I could not see left with my friends. I called after them in vain. "But there's been a mistake!" I shouted. "It's me they came to get but it's somebody else who's leaving!" I made such a commotion that they clapped me into a cell.

15. A Dantean detail. See *Paradiso*, 3:123–24: "*Come per acqua cupa cosa grave.*"
16. Nerval's readings of the works of E. T. A. Hoffman led him to identify the doppelgänger as a specifically German motif, derived perhaps from the "Oriental" tradition of the *ferouer* or "double" mentioned later in the text.

70 There I remained for several hours in a kind of stupor; in the end, the
two friends I *thought* I had already seen came to fetch me in a carriage. I told
them what had occurred, but they denied they had come by that night. I
dined with them calmly enough, but as night approached, I thought I had
reason to fear that very hour which had nearly proved fatal to me the day

75 before. I asked one of them for the Oriental ring he was wearing on his finger and which I regarded as an ancient talisman; I slipped a scarf through
it, which I knotted around my neck, taking care to turn the stone—a tur-
quoise—so that it pressed against a point in my nape where I felt pain. I
imagined that it was from this point that my soul would exit when the star

80 I had seen the previous night eventually reached its zenith and touched me
with a certain ray. Either by sheer coincidence or owing to the intensity of

the preoccupation to which I was prey, I was struck down as if by lightning
at the same hour as the night before. I was placed on a bed, and for a long
time I could make no sense of the connections between the images which
presented themselves to me. This condition lasted several days. I was taken
to a clinic.[17] Many friends and relatives came to visit me, although I was unaware of it. For me the only difference between waking and sleep was that
in the former case everything was transfigured before my eyes; everybody
who approached me seemed changed; material objects possessed a kind of
penumbra that altered their shape; the distortions created by the play of
light and refractions of color kept me occupied with a constant series of
interlinked impressions, whose plausibility was further borne out by my
dreams, less dependent as they were on external elements.

IV

One evening I was convinced I had been carried off to the banks of the
Rhine. I found myself in front of menacing crags whose outlines were
stretched out in the shadows. I entered a cheerful cottage; a last ray of sun
was playing through the green shutters wreathed with grape-vines. It seemed
to me I had found my way back to some familiar dwelling, the home of
one of my maternal uncles, <u>a Flemish painter, dead for over a century</u>.[18]
Unfinished canvases hung about the place; one of them depicted the celebrated fairy of this river. <u>An ancient servant, whom I called Marguerite</u>
and whom it seemed I had known since childhood, said to me: "Why don't
you go and lie down? You have traveled a great distance and your uncle
won't be back until late; we'll wake you for supper." I stretched out on a
four-poster bed whose chintz canopy was printed with large red flowers.
Facing me on the wall was a rustic clock, and on this clock sat a bird,
who proceeded to talk like a human. To my mind, <u>the soul of my ancestor was in this bird</u>; but I was no less astonished by its speech and shape
than I was to find myself carried a century or so back in time. Referring
to them as if they all existed simultaneously, the bird spoke to me about
members of my family <u>who were still alive or had died at different times,</u>
adding: "You see, your uncle took care to paint *her* portrait in advance.
... Now *she* is with us." I directed my gaze towards a canvas representing
a woman dressed in an old-fashioned German costume, leaning over the

17. In late February 1841, Nerval was hospitalized in the clinic of Mme Sainte-Colombe on
the rue de Picpus in Paris.
18. Although the dwelling here evoked resembles the house of his uncle Antoine Boucher
at Mortefontaine (see *Sylvie*), Nerval also imagined himself to be the distant descendant of
the Flemish painter Olivier Bega, here confused with another artist, Carl Bega, painter of the
Lorelei, siren of the Rhine.

| river's edge, her eyes drawn to a cluster of forget-me-nots. Meanwhile the night was gradually falling and the sights, sounds, and sensations of the place were becoming blurred to my slumbering mind. I thought I was

25 | sinking into an abyss which cut through the globe. I felt myself being buoyed along by a current of molten metal; a thousand similar streams whose hues varied with their chemical composition were crisscrossing the earth like the vessels or veins that wind through the lobes of the brain. From the pulse and flux of their circulation, I gathered these streams were

30 | made up of living beings in a molecular state, which only the speed at which I was traveling made it impossible to distinguish. A whitish light was filtering into these channels, and at last I saw a new horizon open up like a huge dome dotted with islands washed by luminous waves. I found myself on a coast lit by a light not of the sun and saw an old man

35 | who was cultivating the soil. I recognized him as the same man who had spoken to me through the voice of the bird, and whether it was his words or my inner intuition of them, it became evident to me that our ancestors assumed the shape of certain animals in order to visit us on earth and take part in the various phases of our existence as silent observers.

40 | The old man left off working and accompanied me to a house which stood nearby. The local landscape reminded me of a region of French Flanders where ancestors of mine had lived and which now held their tombs; the field ringed with thickets at the forest's edge, the neighboring lake, the river with its washerwomen, the village with its sloping street, the dark sandstone

45 | hills with their tufts of broom and heather—a rejuvenated image of the places I had loved. But the house I was not entering was unfamiliar to me. I gathered that it had existed at some moment or other in time and that this world I was now visiting included the ghosts of things as well as of bodies.

I entered a huge hall where many persons were assembled. I recognized

50 | familiar faces everywhere.[19] The features of relatives whose deaths I had mourned were reproduced in the faces of other ancestors who, dressed in more ancient garb, greeted me with the same fatherly warmth. They seemed to have gathered for a family banquet. One of them came towards me and embraced me tenderly.[20] He was wearing an old-fashioned outfit whose colors

60 | seemed to have faded and, beneath his powdered hair, his smiling face bore a certain resemblance to mine. He seemed more distinctly alive than the others and, as it were, in more deliberate sympathy with my own mind. It was my uncle.[21] He seated me by his side, and a kind of communication sprang up

19. Editor's Note: In the margin of his Pléiade edition of *Aurélia* (catalogued BF20), p. 44, Jung writes: "*étoile*" (star).
20. Editor's Note: In the margin of his Müller edition of *Aurélia* (catalogued BF22), p. 24, Jung writes: "*Raum n. Zeit*" (Space and Time).
21. Editor's Note: In the margin of Jung's Pléiade edition of *Aurélia* (catalogued BF20), p. 44, Jung writes: "*idem*" (the same).

between us; for I cannot say I heard his voice, but the moment my thoughts
turned to a particular question, the explanation immediately became clear
and the images were as sharp to my eyes as paintings that had come to life.

"So it's true!" I exclaimed with elation. "We are immortal and retain the
images of the world in which we once lived. What a joy to realize that everything we have loved will always exist around us! ... I was so tired of living!"

"Don't be so quick to rejoice," he said, "for you still belong to the world
above and still have years of severe trials ahead of you. This dwelling place
which so enchants you also has its sorrows, its struggles, and its dangers. The
earth on which we formerly lived remains the theater in which our fates are
played out; we are the rays of the fire which lies at the core of the earth and
which gives it life, dimming all the while ... "

"You mean the earth could die and all of us be swallowed into the void?"

"The void," he said, "does not exist in the usual sense of the term; but the
earth is itself a material body whose soul is made up of the sum total of
minds. Matter can no more die than can the mind, but it can be modified
for good or evil. Our past and our future intertwined. We live in our race
and our race lives in us."

This notion immediately became tangible to me and, as if the walls of the
hall had opened out on to infinite vistas, I thought I saw an unbroken chain
of men and women to whom I belonged and yet all of whom were myself;
the costumes of every nation, the images of every land appeared distinctly and
simultaneously, as if my powers of attention had been multiplied without losing their sense of detail, by a spatial phenomenon analogous to the temporal
concentration of an entire century of action into a single moment of dream.
My astonishment grew when I realized that this immense proliferation of
beings was composed solely of those persons gathered in the hall and whose
images I had seen divide and recombine into countless fleeting features.[22]

22.   Editor's Note: In the margin of his Pléiade edition of *Aurélia* (catalogued BF20), p. 44,
Jung writes: "*multiplicatio*" (multiplication).

"We are seven," I said to my uncle.[23]

"The very number," he replied, "typical of every human family, and, by extension, seven times seven and so on down the line."[24]

95   I cannot hope to make his answer understood, for it still remains quite obscure to me. Metaphysics cannot supply me with the terms to convey the perception I then acquired of the relation of this number of persons to the overall harmony of the universe. One can easily seize the analogy which exists between the electrical forces of nature and a father and a mother;

100   but how to go about establishing the individual centers that emanate from these—or from which they emanate—like some collective anima figure whose permutations would at once be finite and unlimited?[25] You might as well query a flower about the number of its petals or the divisions of its corolla ... or ask the ground to explain its tracks or the sun the colors it casts.

V

Everything was changing shape around me. The spirit with whom I was conversing no longer appeared the same. He was now a young man who, instead of communicating his thoughts to me, was henceforth receiving my ideas. ... Had I gone too far ascending these dizzying heights? I seemed to

5   sense that these were dangerous or obscure questions, even for those spirits who belonged in the world I was now glimpsing ... Some higher power was perhaps also preventing my investigations. I saw myself wandering through the streets of a very populous and unfamiliar city.[26] I noticed that it was made up of many hills and dominated by a mountain entirely covered

10   with dwellings. Among the crowds of this metropolis, I spotted a certain

23.   Editor's Note: In the margin of his Müller edition of *Aurélia* (catalogued BF22), p. 24, Jung writes: "*Siebenzahl/Notes*" (Heptad/Notes).

24.   Nerval notes: Noah's family numbered seven, but one of the seven was mysteriously related to the earlier generations of the Elohim. ... It came to my imagination in a flash that the multiple godheads of India were images of what was, so to speak, the primal family cell. I trembled at the thought of pursuing this any further, for the Trinity still represents a fearsome mystery ... We were born under the law of the Bible.

    Translator's note: For the seven members of Noah's family, see Genesis 7:13. The Elohim are discussed in some length in Nerval's text "Diorama." Brahma, Shiva, and Vishnu were sometimes known as the Hindu Trinity in nineteenth-century comparative religion. At the core of all these numerological speculations lie the fundamental questions: how to think (or believe) simultaneously in terms of unity *and* plurality, how to reconcile orthodox Christianity with gnosticism, occultism, or paganism?

25.   The French reads "*une figure animique collective.*" The Jungian connotation of animus (breath or soul) does not seem out of place here.

26.   The evocation of this dream-city draws on a number of elements contained in Nerval's description of the Greek island of Syra in his *Voyage to the Orient*.

number of men who seemed to belong to a nation apart; their vigorous, resolute air and the energetic cast of their features reminded me of those independent warrior races who live in the mountains or on islands rarely visited by strangers; and yet they had managed to maintain their fierce individuality amid the mixed and undistinguished population of this enormous city. Who were these men? My guide led me up a number of steep, noisy streets filled with the sounds of various workshops. We continued our ascent up endless flights of steps, at the top of which the view opened out before us. Here and there, terraces covered with trellises, small gardens on occasional patches of level ground, rooftops, airy habitations painted and carved with elaborate patience. The various vistas, interlaced by long trains of climbing vegetation, were as enchanting to the eye and as pleasing to the mind as the sight of a luscious oasis. Amid this unsuspected solitude, the noisy hubbub of the city below was little more than a murmur. One has often heard tell of outlaw nations dwelling in the darkness of necropolises or catacombs; up here, it seemed the reverse was true. A fortunate race of men had created this sanctuary for itself, a place favored by birds, flowers, clear air, and light. "These are the ancient inhabitants of the mountain which dominates the city we are now visiting," my guide informed me. "This is where they lived over the ages, loving and just, simple in their customs, having preserved the natural virtues of the earliest days of creation. The surrounding populations revered them and modeled themselves after them."

Following my guide, I made my way down from this place into one of the tall dwellings whose intercommunicating rooftops presented such a strange sight. I seemed as if my feet were sinking into the successive strata of buildings of different eras. These phantom structures continuously opened out into other ones, each marked by the particular style of its era; I was reminded of the excavations made of ancient cities, except that here everything was airy and alive and shot through with the ever-changing play of light. I found myself at last in a huge room, where I saw an old man at a workbench engaged in some sort of craft unknown to me.

As I was passing through the door, a man dressed in white and whose face I could barely make out suddenly threatened me with a weapon he was holding in his hand; but my companion motioned him away. It seemed someone or something wanted to forbid me from penetrating into the mysteries of these sanctuaries. Without inquiring of my guide, I intuitively understood that these heights and these depths were the sanctuary of the original inhabitants of the mountains. Fending off the flood of new races which threatened to invade them, it was here that they had gone about their lives, simple in their customs, loving and just, steadfast, ingenious, and astute—peacefully triumphing over those blind masses who had so repeatedly encroached upon their heritage. And lo and behold, they were neither corrupted nor destroyed nor enslaved; having conquered ignorance, they still remained pure; having prospered, they still held to the virtues of poverty.

A child was playing on the floor with crystals, seashells, and engraved stones, no doubt making a game out of his studies. An older woman, still beautiful for her years, was engaged in household chores. At that moment, several young men made a noisy entrance, as if coming home from work. I was astonished to see them all dressed in white; but it seems it was an optical illusion on my part; in order to render things more tangible, my guide proceeded to sketch in their clothing and color it in bright shades, indicating to me that this is what they looked like in reality. The whiteness which had so astonished me was perhaps the effect of a certain glare which had caused the usual colors of the spectrum to bleach together. I left the room and saw myself on a terrace laid out like a flower bed. Young girls and children were walking about and playing. They too appeared to be clad in white, but their dresses were trimmed with pink embroidery. These girls were so beautiful, their features so lovely, their souls shone so radiantly through their delicate bodies, that they inspired a kind of love in me that transcended preference or desire, a love that epitomized all the vague exhilaration of youthful passion.

I cannot convey what it felt like to find myself among these charming creatures whom I adored without knowing who they were. They were like some primordial heavenly family, their smiling eyes seeking out mine with gentle compassion. I melted into tears, as if remembering a lost paradise. Yet I bitterly realized that I was but a passing stranger in this world at once so precious and so foreign, and I shuddered at the thought that I would have to return to life. It was in vain that these women and girls crowded about me as if to hold me back. Their enchanting bodies were already dissolving into mist; their lovely faces were growing paler, and their chiseled features and sparkling eyes were receding into a penumbra lit up by the last lingering flash of a smile ...

Such was the vision, or at least such were the principal details which remained in my memory. The cataleptic state into which I had lapsed for several days was explained to me scientifically and the accounts of those who had seen me in this condition caused me a certain irritation, when I

85 realized that it was to mental aberration that they ascribed certain words and actions of mine which had coincided with the various phases of what were to me a series of logical events. I by far preferred those of my friends who, either because they were so patiently understanding or because their ideas happened to agree with mine, encouraged me to recount in full de-
90 tails the things I had seen as a spirit.[27] One of them said to me in tears, "Then it's true there is a God?" "Yes!" I answered with enthusiasm. And we embraced each other like two brothers who came from that same mystic homeland I had glimpsed. How happy I was in my newfound conviction! Those lingering doubts about the immortality of the soul which beset
95 even the best of minds were now laid to rest. No more death, no more sorrow, no more anxiety. Those I loved, family and friends alike, were showing me undeniable signs of their eternal existence; I was now separated from them only by the hours of the day. I awaited the hours of the night in quiet melancholy.

VI

A subsequent dream confirmed my views. I found myself all of a sudden in a room of my ancestor's house, except that the room had grown in size. The ancient furniture gleamed with a wondrous sheen, the carpets and curtains seemed refurbished, a light three times brighter than day
5 streamed through the window and door, and the fresh scent of an early spring morning wafted through the air. Three women were at work in this room and, without exactly resembling them, they represented various female family members and friends of my childhood. Each of the three women seemed to possess various characteristics of these childhood figures.
10 Their profiles flickered like the flame of a lamp, one person's features continually migrating into another's. Smile, voice, color of eyes or hair, posture, habitual gesture—all these traits shifted back and forth between them as if they were sharing in a single life, and each was a composite image of all the others, like those ideal types fashioned by painters after
15 several different models so as to capture the complete range of beauty.
    The oldest of the three addressed me in a melodious voice whose trill I recognized from my childhood, although I do not know what it was she said that struck me as so profoundly accurate. But she managed to draw my attention back to myself, and I saw I was wearing a small, brown, old-

27.   Editor's Note: Hedwig Kubin's translation into the German reads: "*Ich liebte mehr die meiner Freunde, die aus geduldiger Gefälligkeit oder in Folge ähnlicher Gedanken mich zu langen Erzählungen der Dinge veranlaßten, die ich im Geist gesehen hatte.*" On a slip of paper inserted into his Müller edition of *Aurélia* (catalogued BF22), Jung writes: "*Gefälligkeit* = kindness, complaisance."

fashioned suit of clothes with gossamer needlework as fine as a spider's web. The little outfit was stylish in cut and gently perfumed. Clad in these clothes which had sprung from their fairy fingers, I felt young and spry again and I thanked them, blushing like a little boy in the presence of beautiful ladies. Then one of them got up and proceeded towards the garden.

As everybody knows, one never sees the sun in one's dreams, even though one is often aware of a light far more luminous. Objects and bodies have a radiance all their own. I saw myself in a small park with a long row of arbors, whose arches were heavy with bunches of white and black grapes; as the lady who was guiding me moved beneath these bowers, the latticed shadows cast by the trellises again caused her body and garments to fluctuate before my eyes. She at last emerged from under the arbors, and we found ourselves in an open area where one could still see the faint traces of the ancient lanes that had once cut through here crosswise. The grounds had not been tended for many years, and fresh growths of clematis, hop, honeysuckle, jasmine, ivy, and yellow creeper had sprouted all over the place, looping their fast-growing vines around the trees. Branches loaded with fruit brushed the ground and several garden flowers, having reverted to the wild, were blooming amid clumps of weeds.

Stands of poplar, acacia, and pine rose here and there, and within their groves were glimpses of statues blackened by time. I saw before me a mound of ivy-covered rock from which a freshwater spring gushed, its pretty splash echoing off a pool of still water half-veiled by large water lilies.

The lady I was following, her slender figure advancing at a rhythm that caused the folds of her shot taffeta dress to shimmer, twined her bare arm around a long stalk of hollyhock; then, in a bright shaft of light, she began to grow so gigantic that the entire garden took on her shape; the flowers and tress became the rosettes and flounces of her dress, while her face and arms imprinted their outlines on the purple clouds of the sky. I lost sight of her as she went through this transfiguration, for she seemed to be vanishing into her own immensity. "No! Don't disappear!" I shouted after her. "All of nature is dying with you."

As I uttered these words, I fought my way through the bramble, as if in pursuit of the expanding shade who was eluding my grasp, but I stumbled against a crumbling wall, at the foot of which lay the sculpted bust of a woman. Picking it up, I was convinced it was *hers* ... I recognized the features I adored, and as I glanced around me, I saw that the garden now looked like a graveyard. Voices were saying, "The Universe lies in night!"

VII

This dream, which had started out so happily, caused me no end of perplexity. What did it mean? Only later did I find out. Aurélia had died.[28]

Initially, the only news I had was that she was ill. Given my state of mind, my reaction was no more than a vague distress intermixed with hope. I believed that my own days were numbered, and I was now certain that there existed a world where loving hearts met up again. Besides, she belonged to me far more in death than in her life ... A selfish thought for which my reason would later pay with bitter regrets.

I do not want to make too much of premonitions; chance does strange things; but a particular memory of our fleeting union continued to prey upon my mind. I had given her an antique ring set with an opal carved in the shape of a heart. This ring being too large for her finger, I made the unfortunate decision to have it cut down in size; it was only upon hearing the noise of the saw that I realized my mistake. I thought I saw blood flowing...

Medical treatment had restored my health, although my mind had not yet recovered the regular habits of human reason. The establishment in which I found myself was located on an elevated spot and had a large garden planted with rare trees.[29] The pure air of the hilltop setting, the first breezes of spring, the comforting pleasures of company all provided me with long days of tranquility.

I was enchanted by the vividness of the first sycamore leaves, the variegations of which resembled the crests of guinea fowl. From morning to evening, the vista overlooking the plain afforded delightful prospects whose gradations of color pleased my imagination. I peopled the hills and the clouds with godlike figures whose shapes seemed to appear distinctly before my eyes. I wanted to fix my favorite thoughts more clearly, and with the help of bits of charcoal and brick I had gathered, I soon covered the walls with a series of frescoes recording my impressions. One figure constantly overshadowed all the rest; it was the figure of Aurélia, painted in the guise of a divinity, just as she had appeared to me in my dreams.[30] A wheel re-

---

28. Nerval was hospitalized for the better part of 1841, whereas Jenny Colon died only a year later, in mid-1842—another example of his liberal rearrangement of his biography in order to give it a more Dantean shape (cf. the prophetic dream of Beatrice's death in the *Vita Nuova*).

29. Released from the rue de Picpus clinic on 16 March 1841, Nerval had a relapse five days later and was immediately remanded to the care of Dr. Esprit Blanche in his *maison de santé* on the heights of Montmartre—where he would undergo observation and treatment for the next eight months.

30. In the drafts of *"Aurélia,"* this female divinity is identified as the Queen of Sheba. Several contemporary visitors to Dr. Blanche's clinic in 1841 confirmed the existence of Nerval's drawings on the walls.

volved beneath her feet and she was surrounded by a retinue of gods. I managed to color in this group by extracting the juices of flowers and weeds.
How often I stood before this precious idol, lost in my dreams! I went even
35 further; I tried to shape the body of my beloved out of clay; every morning
I had to start my work all over again, for the lunatics, jealous of my joy, took
delight in smashing the image.

I was given paper and spent a great deal of time and effort covering it
with thousands of drawings and tales in verse and inscriptions in every
40 known tongue, all meant to represent a kind of history of the world in-
termingled with memories of my studies and fragments of dreams which,
given my state of mind, had become all the more tangible while plunging
me ever deeper into my private preoccupations. I did not restrict myself
to the modern traditions of the creation. My thoughts reached far further
45 back: I glimpsed, as if in recollection, the primordial covenant drawn up by
the genii by means of talismans. I had tried to gather together the stones
of the Sacred Table and to represent, seated around it, the original seven
Elohim who had divided the world among themselves.[31]

This system of history, borrowed from Oriental traditions, began with the
50 harmonious concord of the Powers of Nature who originally formulated
and organized the universe. During the night that preceded my undertaking, I thought I had been transported to some vague planet where the first
germs of creation were struggling into existence. Giant palm trees, poison-
ous euphorbia, and acanthi entwined around cactus plants sprouted from
55 the depths of the still-damp clay; barren rock formations jutted out like
skeletons of this creation in the making; and, coiling and uncoiling, hideous reptiles snaked their way through the dense tangle of wild vegetation.
The bluish sweep of this strange horizon was lit only by the pale glow of
the firmament; but as these creatures gradually took shape, a brighter star
60 began to draw the seeds of its own radiance from this scene.

VIII

Then the monsters changed shape and, shedding their original skins,
reared up more formidably on their huge hind legs and trampled the
branches and the grasses with the enormous bulk of their bodies; and in
this chaos of nature, they engaged in battles in which I also took part, for
5 my body was as strange as theirs. All of a sudden a wondrous harmony
echoed through our solitudes, and it seemed as if all the shrieks and roars
and hissings of these elemental creatures were now joining in this divine

31. The Elohim would here seem to be equated with the original archangels, who traditionally ranged from four to seven in number.

chorus. The variations played themselves out in infinite succession, little by little the planet grew brighter, heavenly forms were sketched out on field and wood, and the monsters I had seen, now tamed, shed their weird shapes and changed into men and women; as they went through their transformations, some took on the features of wild animals, fish, and birds.

Who had worked this miracle? A radiant goddess was guiding the rapid evolution of mankind through this series of *avatars*. A distinction between races was established; first came the birds, then the mammals, fish, and reptiles. There were the *divs*, the Peris, the Undines, and the Salamanders.[32] Each time one of these creatures died, it would immediately be reborn to sing the glory of the gods in a fairer form. One of the Elohim, however, took it into his head to create a fifth race, composed of the elements of the earth, which was called the *Afrites*.[33] This touched off a complete revolution among the Spirits, who refused to recognize these new masters of the world. I have no idea for how many thousands of years these battles went on bloodying the globe. Three of the Elohim, together with the attendant Spirits of their races, were finally relegated to the southern reaches of the earth, where they founded vast kingdoms. They carried off with them the secrets of the divine cabbala which connects different worlds, and they derived their power from their adoration of certain stars, to which they continue to correspond. These necromancers, banished to the ends of the earth, had agreed among themselves that they would transmit their power to each other. Surrounded by women and slaves, each of their sovereigns had made sure he would be reborn in the form of one of his children. Their life span was a thousand years. As they neared death, powerful cabbalists would shut them into well-guarded tombs and ply them with elixirs and preservatives. They thus maintained an outer semblance of life for a long period of time; then, like the chrysalis spinning its cocoon, they fell into a sleep of forty days, to be reborn in the form of a young child who would later be named to the throne.

Meanwhile the vivifying resources of the earth were being exhausted in order to nourish these families, whose blood coursed from generation to generation without renewal. In vast underground chambers hollowed out beneath pyramids and catacombs, they had accumulated all the treasures of past races as well as certain talismans that protected them against the wrath of the gods.

32. A typical example of Nervalian syncretism. D'Herbelot's *Bibliothèque orientale* (1697) provided him with the Zoroastrian *divs* (or *daevas*) and *peris* (good and evil genii), while the abbé de Villar's *Comte de Gabalis* (1788) supplied him with the elemental spirits familiar to occultist and Rosicrucian tradition: gnomes (earth), sylphs (air), undines (water), and salamanders (fire).

33. D'Herbelot defines the Arabic term *Afriet* as a kind of medusa or lamia, here associated by Nerval with the gnomes, elemental spirits of earth.

These strange mysteries took place in the center of Africa, beyond the
Mountains of the Moon and ancient Ethiopia; it was there that I long suffered in captivity, along with a portion of the human race. The woods that had
formerly been so green to my eyes now offered nothing but faded flowers and
withered leaves; the land was ravaged by a relentless sun, and the feeble off-
spring of these never-ending dynasties seemed to stagger under the burden of
life. This stately and monotonous grandeur, with its ritual observation of eti-
quette and hieratic ceremony, was oppressive to all, even though no one dared
to break with it. The elders languished under the weight of their crowns and
imperial ornaments, surrounded by doctors and priests, whose science guar-
anteed their immortality. As for the general population, forever caught in
the cogs of the caste system, it could no longer hope for life or liberty. At the
feet of trees stricken with death and sterility, at the mouths of fountainheads
which had run dry, one could see sallow, listless children and young women
withering on the scorched grass. The splendor of the royal chambers, the maj-
esty of the porticoes, the brilliance of the vestments and adornments offered
meager consolation for the never-ending tedium of this wasteland.

Soon the populations were decimated by disease, the animals and plants all died, and even the immortals wasted away in their ceremonial gowns. A plague far greater than all others suddenly swept down in order to rejuvenate and rescue the world. The constellation of Orion opened cataracts of water in the sky; the earth, top-heavy with the ice of the opposite pole, spun backwards and the seas overflowed their coastlines and poured into the plains of Africa and Asia; the floodwaters seeped into the sands, filled the tombs and pyramids, and for forty days a mysterious ark sailed the seas, carrying with it the hopes for a new creation.

Three of the Elohim had taken refuge on the highest peak of the mountains of Africa. A fight broke out between them. Here my memory grows murky, so I do not know the outcome of this supreme struggle. But I can still see a woman they had abandoned, standing on a peak lapped by the waves, shrieking, her hair disheveled, fighting for her life. Her cries of distress rang out above the tumult of the waters ... Was she saved? I had no idea. The gods—her brothers—had condemned her to death, but the Evening Star shone above her head, raining its fiery rays upon her face.[34]

The hymn of the earth and the heavens which had been interrupted was now melodiously resumed in consecration of the harmony among the new races. And while the sons of Noah toiled away beneath the rays of the new sun, the necromancers huddled over their treasures in their underground retreats, gloating in silence and in darkness. Now and then they would steal forth from their lairs in order to strike terror into the living or to spread their deadly science among wicked men.

34. Certain commentators have seen this as an allusion to Arcana 17 of the tarot.

85   Such are the memories I retraced by a kind of vague intuition of the past: I shuddered as I reproduced the hideous features of these outlaw races. Everywhere the suffering image of the Eternal Mother kept on languishing, weeping, and dying. The same scene repeated itself again and again throughout the shadowy civilizations of Asia and Africa, a scene involving
90 orgies and carnage reenacted by the same spirits under different guises. The last of these scenes took place in Granada, where the sacred talisman was shattered by the enemy blows of the Christians and the Moors. How many years longer will the world have to suffer? For these eternal enemies are sure to pursue their vengeance beneath other skies! They are the severed sections
95 of the snake that encircles the earth ... Sundered by the sword, they rejoin in a hideous kiss, sealed by the blood of mankind.

    IX

Such were the images which paraded before my eyes. Little by little my mind had regained its calm and I left the establishment that had been paradise to me. Many years later, unhappy circumstances prompted a relapse, which started off this interrupted series of strange reveries all
5 over again.
    I was strolling through the countryside, my mind taken up by a work which was to deal with religious questions. As I passed by a house, I heard a bird uttering some words he had been taught, and yet to me his random chatter seemed to make sense; I was reminded of the talking bird in the
10 vision recounted above, and I shuddered at the bad omen. Continuing along my way, I met a friend whom I had not seen for some time and who lived nearby. He wanted to show me around his property and, in the course of the visit, had me climb up to a raised terrace which overlooked a vast horizon. It was sunset. As I made my way back down a rustic stair-
15 way, I stumbled badly and my chest smashed into the corner of a piece of furniture.[35] I mustered up enough strength to get back on my feet and to rush to the center of the garden, convinced that I had just received a mortal blow yet nonetheless wanting to cast one last glance at the setting sun before I died. Despite all the regrets occasioned by such a moment,
20 I was happy to be dying in this fashion, at this hour, among these very trees and vines and autumn flowers. It turned out, however, that I had merely fainted, and I soon recovered sufficient strength to return home and take to bed. I was seized with a fever; as I thought back on the location where my fall had taken place, I remembered that the vista I had

35. The accident took place in September 1851, at the home of a printer friend in Montmartre. More important, however, are the allegorical dimensions of this "fall."

25 so admired overlooked a cemetery, the very cemetery which contained
Aurélia's grave.[36] It was only now that this realization fully struck home;
otherwise, I would have ascribed my fall to the shock this sight might well
have provoked in me.

All this led me to consider this fateful coincidence in more careful terms.
30 I regretted all the more deeply that death had not reunited me with her.
But upon reflection, I said to myself that I was unworthy of this. I bitterly
reviewed the life I had lived since her death, reproaching myself not for
having forgotten her—for this had never been the case—but rather for having profaned her memory by easy loves. The idea came to me to search my
35 dreams for an answer, but *her* image, which had so often appeared to me, no
longer graced my sleep. Initially, all I had were disjointed dreams, a jumble
of bloody scenes. It seemed as if an entire race of malignant creatures had
been unleashed on that ideal world I had formerly glimpsed, a world of
which she was the queen. The same Spirit who had earlier threatened me—
40 when I was entering the sanctuary of those pure families who dwelled on
the heights of the *Mysterious City*—again crossed my path, no longer wearing the white of his race as he formerly did, but now dressed like an Oriental prince. I lunged towards him, threatening him, but he turned towards
me serenely. O horror, O rage! It was my very face, my very body, enlarged
45 and idealized ... Then I remembered the unidentified individual who had
been arrested the same night as I and who had been released, so I thought,
from the police barracks under my name when two of my friends had come
to fetch me. In his hand he carried a weapon whose shape I had difficulty
making out, and one of the persons accompanying him said: "This is what
50 he struck him with."

I don't quite know how to explain the fact that in my mind, terrestrial
events were liable to coincide with events of the supernatural world; these
things are easier to *sense* than to articulate clearly. But who exactly was this
spirit who was myself and yet outside myself? Was he the *double* of legend
55 or the mystical brother whom the Orientals call *ferouer*?[37] Had I not been
struck by the tale of the knight who had spent an entire night in a forest
battling an unknown adversary who was none other than himself?[38] Be this
as it may, I believe that the human imagination has never invented anything
that is not true, whether in this world or in other worlds, and I could not
60 cast into doubt what I myself had so distinctly *seen*.

36. Jenny Colon was indeed buried in the Montmartre cemetery.
37. Nerval discovered this Zoroastrian term in the baron de Bock's *Essai sur l'histoire du
sabéisme* (1788), where *ferouers* are defined as the archetypes or models (rather than the
doubles) of the creatures created by Ormuzd to combat his evil rival Ahriman.
38. Most likely to Nerval's friend Théophile Gautier's fantastic tale "*Le Chevalier double*" (1840).

I was struck by a dreadful thought: man is double. "I feel two men within me," wrote a Church Father.[39] The concurrence of two souls has implanted this compound seed in man's body, which displays two similar halves in all the organs of its structure. There is in every man a spectator and an actor, someone who speaks and someone who replies. The Orientals saw two enemies in this: the good genius and the bad genius. I asked myself: am I the good one? Am I the evil one? Either way, *the other* is against me. ... Who knows whether at a given age or occasion these two spirits do not part ways? Both bound to the same body by material affinity, perhaps one is destined for glory and happiness, and the other for annihilation or eternal suffering?

A fatal flash of lightning suddenly tore through these uncertainties ... Aurélia was no longer mine! ... I thought I heard talk of a ceremony that was to take place elsewhere and that preparations were being made for a mystical wedding which was mine, but at which the other was going to benefit from the mistake of my friends and of Aurélia herself. My closest acquaintances dropped by to console me, but they seemed less than certain in my regard, that is, the two portions of their souls took on separate attitudes to me, affectionate and compassionate, on the one hand, and horror-stricken, on the other. There was a double meaning to everything they said, even though they were unaware of this, since they were not *in spirit* as I was. For a brief moment, the idea even struck me as comical when I thought back on Amphitryon and Sosia.[40] But what if this grotesque symbol were something altogether different? What if, as in other fables of Antiquity, the fatal truth lay hidden behind a mask of folly? "Fine," I said to myself. "Armed with the weapons of tradition and science, we'll take on the fatal spirit, we'll even take on God. Whatever he may be up to in the shadows and the darkness, I do exist—and I have all the time left to me on this earth to defeat him."

X

How to depict the strange despair to which these ideas gradually reduced me? An evil genius had taken my place in the world of the shades. Aurélia imagined it to be me, and the disconsolate spirit animating my body—enfeebled, disdained, unrecognized by her—saw itself forever doomed to despair or nothingness. I gathered up all my willpower in order to penetrate deeper into the mystery whose veils I had begun to lift. At times my dreams mocked my efforts, affording me nothing but fleeting and distorted figures. Here I can only give a fairly bizarre idea of what emerged from

39. An allusion to Paul's Epistle to the Romans?
40. In the comedies of Platus and Molière, Amphitryon and Sosia become the dupes of the doubles who have taken on their features—Jupiter and Mercury.

this mental struggle. I felt myself sliding down an endless tightrope. The
earth, crisscrossed with colored veins of molten metal—just as I had previously seen it—was gradually growing brighter as the fire at its core spread
outwards, its white heat blending into the cherry reds which tinged the
innards of the globe. Now and then I was surprised to come across huge
puddles of water suspended like clouds in the air and yet whose density
was such that one could pluck flakes off them; clearly a liquid quite unlike
the water found on earth, this was no doubt the evaporated form of the
substance which made up the rivers and oceans of the spirit world.

I came within sight of a huge beach, its many dunes covered with reeds of
a greenish hue, with yellow tips which seemed to have been singed by the
flames of the sun—although I no more saw the sun than on previous occasions.[41] The coastline was dominated by a castle, towards which I proceeded
to climb. Once on the other side, I saw an enormous city spread out below
me. Night had fallen as I was crossing the mountains, and I could make out
the lights of the houses and streets. Making my way downwards, I found
myself in a marketplace where fruits and vegetables similar to those of the
South were being sold.

I climbed down a dark stairway and found myself on the streets. There
were posters announcing the grand opening of a casino and the various
door prizes were spelled out in detail.[42] The decorative borders of these
handbills were made up of garlands of flowers whose typography and col-
oration were so exact that they seemed natural. A portion of the building
was still under construction. I entered a workshop where I saw workmen
modeling out of clay an enormous llama-shaped animal, which apparently
was to be equipped with giant wings. A beam of fire seemed to be shooting through this monster and slowly bringing it to life; it twisted this way
and that, penetrated by the countless purple shafts of flame which formed
its arteries and veins and which were fecundating its lifeless matter, causing it to sprout an instantaneous growth of fibrous fins and tufts of wool. I
stopped to contemplate this masterpiece whose fabrication seemed to have
discovered the secrets of divine creation. "We have here at our disposal," I
was informed, "the primordial fire which animated the first created beings
… In former times, this fire reached to the surface of the earth, but its wellsprings have dried up." I also saw examples of the goldsmith's craft which
made use of metals unknown on earth; one of these was red and seemed to
correspond to cinnabar, while the other was sky blue. The decorative work
had not been done with hammer or chisel but rather evolved its form and
color on its own, like those metallic plants that flower forth from certain

41.   Editor's Note: In the margin of his Pléiade edition of *Aurélia* (catalogued BF20), p. 78,
Jung writes: "*côte*" (coast).
42.   A "casino" is not necessarily a gambling establishment, but in nineteenth-century usage
more like a country resort.

chemical mixtures. "Wouldn't it be possible to create men as well?" I asked one of the workmen. He replied, "Men come from above and not from below; how could we possibly create ourselves? Here all we do is apply the technical advances of our industries to create matter far subtler than the matter that composes the earth's crust. These flowers which seem so natural to you, this animal which appears to be alive, are but the products of art raised to the highest level of our knowledge, and everyone should judge them accordingly."

Such more or less are the words that were either said to me or whose meaning I believed I had seized. I began strolling around the rooms of the casino and came upon a large crowd, in which I recognized a number of familiar faces, some of them alive, some of them who had died at various different times. The former seemed not to see me, whereas the latter responded to my greetings without appearing to know who I was. I had reached the largest room; its walls were hung with poppy-red velvet decorated with intricate patterns of gold braid. In the middle of the room stood a sofa shaped like a throne. Several people passing through sat down on it to test out its springiness, but since preparations were still under way, they moved on to other rooms. There was talk of a wedding; the bridegroom, it was said, would soon make an appearance and announce the beginning of the festivities. I was immediately gripped by an insane fit of rage. I imagined the bridegroom they were all awaiting was my *double* who was due to marry Aurélia, and I created a commotion that apparently made the gathered guests quite uneasy. I launched into a violent diatribe, detailing all my grievances and requesting the aid and assistance of those who knew me. An elderly gentleman said to me: "But this is no way to behave, you're frightening everyone." At which point I shouted: "I know full well that he has already attacked me with his weapons, but I'm not afraid of him; I'm waiting for him and I know the sign that will defeat him."

At that moment one of the workmen from the workshop I had visited on my way in appeared holding a long bar tipped with a red-hot knob. I wanted to lunge at him, but he stopped me short, threatening my head with the knob. Everyone around me seemed to be jeering at my impotence ... I then retreated to the throne, my soul bursting with unspeakable pride, and raised my arm to execute the sign I was convinced possessed magic power. The shriek of a woman—vivid and quavering with excruciating pain—woke me up with a start! The syllables of some unknown word I was about to pronounce expired on my lips. ... I threw myself to the ground and fervently starting praying, hot tears streaming from my eyes. But what was this voice which had so achingly echoed through the night?

It did not belong to the dream; it was the voice of a living person, but to me it was the very voice and accent of Aurélia.

I opened my window; everything was quiet, and there was no second cry.
I checked outside; nobody had heard anything. And yet, I remain certain
that the cry was real, and that it had resounded through the air of the living
… One could no doubt object that by some coincidence a woman had at
95 that very moment cried out in pain in the vicinity of my lodgings. But to
my mind terrestrial events were bound up with those of the invisible world.
This is one of those strange relations which I myself do not quite understand and which it is easier to point out than to define …

What had I done? I had disturbed the harmony of that magical universe
100 from which my soul drew the certainty of immortal life. Perhaps I was ac-
cursed for having attempted to penetrate into a terrible mystery in violation
of divine law; all I could now expect was anger and scorn! The shades fled
away in displeasure, shrieking and tracing ominous circles in the air, like
birds in a gathering storm.

Second Part

I

Eurydice! Eurydice![43]

Lost, a second time!

Everything is over, everything is past! It is now my turn to die, and to die without hope! Yet what is death? Would to God it were nothingness! ... But God himself cannot make death into nothingness.

Why is this the first time in years that I am thinking of *him*? The deadly system which had elaborated itself in my mind did not admit of this singular royalty ... or rather, merely absorbed it into the sum total of beings: it was the god of Lucretius, powerless and astray in his own immensity.[44]

Yet she believed in God, and one day I overheard the name of Jesus on her lips. It flowed from them so sweetly that I was moved to tears. Dear God! This tear ... this tear ... so long since dry! Lord, give me back this tear!

When the soul hovers uncertainly between life and earth, between mental disarray and the reappearance of cold reflection, it is in religious belief that one must seek solace. I have never been able to find relief in that school of philosophy which merely supplies us with maxims of self-interest or, at the most, of reciprocity, leaving us nothing but empty experience and bitter doubts.[45] Such a philosophy combats our mortal sufferings by deadening our sensibility; like the surgeon, it knows only how to cut out the organ which is causing the pain. But for us, born in an age of revolutions and upheavals which shattered all beliefs, raised at best to practice a vague religion based on a few outward observances and whose lukewarm devotion is perhaps more sinful than impiety or heresy, for us things become quite difficult whenever we feel the need to reconstruct that mystic temple whose edifice the pure and simple of spirit accept fully traced within their hearts. "The Tree of Knowledge is not that of Life!"[46] And yet can we rid our mind of all the good or evil implanted in it by so many intelligent generations? Ignorance cannot be learned.

I have higher hopes in the goodness of God: we may well be approaching that era when science, as predicted, having accomplished its entire cycle of synthesis and analysis, of belief and negation, will now be able to purify itself

43. In a celebrated aria of Gluck's opera *Orfeo ed Eurydice* (1762), Orpheus utters this cry after having looked back and lost Eurydice for the second time.

44. In his *De rerum natura*, the Roman poet and philosopher Lucretius (ca. 99–ca. 55 BC) seeks to persuade humankind that there need be no fear of the gods or death, since humans are their own masters.

45. Nerval is above all thinking of the materialist or sensualist philosophies of the Enlightenment.

46. From Byron's Faustian drama *Manfred*, act 1, scene 1.

and usher forth the miraculous city of the future from chaos and ruin … One should not sell human reason short by claiming it has something to gain by humiliating itself outright, for this impugns its divine origin … God will no doubt appreciate the purity of these intentions; what father relishes the sight of his son abdicating all reason and pride in his presence? The apostle who needed to touch in order to believe was not cursed for having doubts!

What have I just written? Blasphemies. This is not the way Christian humility is permitted to speak. Ideas of this sort are hardly calculated to mellow the soul. They wear the proud lightning bolts of Satan's crown on their brow. A pact with God himself? … O science! O vanity!

I had gathered together several books on the cabbala. Having immersed myself in them, I had managed to persuade myself that everything the human mind had amassed on this score over the centuries was true. The convictions I had arrived at concerning the existence of the external world coincided far too closely with my readings for me to have any further doubts about the revelations of the past. It seemed to me that since the doctrines and rites of the various religions bore such a close relation to all this, each religion possessed a certain portion of those arcana which constituted its means of expansion or defense. This force could decline, diminish, and disappear, which would lead to the invasion of certain races by other races, although no race could be victorious or be vanquished save by the Spirit.

It is nonetheless certain, I said to myself, that these sciences are riddled with human error. The magic alphabet, the mysterious hieroglyphs have come down to us in garbled form, distorted either by time or by those who have something to gain by keeping us in the dark; let us recover the lost letter or the effaced sign, let us recompose the dissonant scale, and we shall acquire power in the spirit world.

It was thus I became convinced I could perceive the relations between the real world and the spirit world. The earth, its inhabitants and their history were the theater of those physical actions which prepared the existence and the situation of the various immortal beings bound up with its destiny. Without delving into the impenetrable mystery of the eternity of worlds, my mind reached backwards to the epoch when the sun, like the plant which represents it and which follows the revolutions of its celestial course with inclined head, sowed the fertile seeds of plants and animals upon the earth. This element was none other than fire, which being an amalgam of souls, instinctively gave rise to our common home. The spirit of the Godhead, reproduced and as it were reflected on earth, became the shared feature of human souls, each of which as a result was at once man and God. Such were the Elohim.[47]

47. Children of fire (and not of clay), the Elohim are a Promethean half-human, half-divine race.

When one feels miserable, one thinks of the misery of others. I had put off visiting one of my closest friends whom I had heard was ill. As I made my way to the clinic where he was being treated, I bitterly reproached myself for my negligence. I was even more crestfallen when my friend informed me that he had been in excruciating pain the previous day. I entered a whitewashed hospital room. The sun was casting gay patterns on the wall and playing off a vase of flowers which had just been placed on the invalid's table by a nun. It was almost the cell of an Italian anchorite.

His wasted face, the yellowed ivory of his skin, heightened by the blackness of his beard and hair, his eyes illumined by a hint of fever, perhaps even the arrangement of the hooded cloak that was draped around his shoulders—all this made of him a being partially different from the person I had known. He was no longer the merry companion with whom I had worked and played; there was something of an apostle about him. He told me that just as the suffering caused by illness was becoming most unbearable, he had been seized by one last spasm, which he was convinced was his final breath. And then suddenly the pain stopped, as if by miracle.

It is impossible to convey what he subsequently related to me: a sublime dream in the shadowy reaches of infinity, a conversation with a being at once distinct from and identical to himself, and of whom he asked, believing himself dead, the whereabouts of God. "But God is everywhere," his spirit answered. "He is in you, he is in everyone. He judges you, he listens to you, he counsels you. He is us, you and *I*, as we think and dream in unison—we have never parted, we are eternal!"

I can cite nothing more of this conversation, which I may well have misheard or misunderstood. All I know is that it made a powerful impression on me. I hesitate to attribute to my friend conclusions I may have falsely drawn from his words. I'm not even sure their implications are consonant with Christian doctrine.

"God is with him," I cried out, "but he is no longer with me! What a disaster! I have cursed him, I have threatened him, I have disowned him! It was he, that mystic brother who had been drawing further and further away from my soul and sending me warnings in vain! Favored bridegroom and king of glory, it is he who is now judging and condemning me; it is he who is now carrying off to his heaven that bride he might have bestowed on me, a bride of whom I am no longer worthy!"

II

cannot describe the dejection into which these ideas plunged me. Now I understand, I said to myself, I have preferred the creature to the Creator; I have deified my love; I have held in pagan adoration someone whose last sigh was given over to Christ. But if this religion is true to its word, I can still be pardoned by God. He can give her back to me if I humble myself before him: perhaps her spirit will return within me!

I wandered the streets aimlessly, lost in these thoughts. A funeral procession crossed my path; it was heading towards the cemetery where she had been buried; it occurred to me to follow it, and I joined in the cortège. I have no idea who is being borne to his grave, I said to myself, but I now know that the dead can see us and hear us. Perhaps the dead man will be happy to see he is being followed by a brother in misery far more despondent than anyone else at his funeral. This idea brought tears to my eyes, and I was no doubt taken to be one of the closest friends of the deceased. O blessèd tears! How long had your sweetness been denied to me! ... My head was clearing, and a ray of hope was still guiding me. Feeling the strength within me to pray, I exulted with joy.

I did not even bother to find out the name of the person whose casket I had been following. The cemetery I had entered was sacred to me for a number of reasons. Three of my maternal relatives had been buried there; but I was unable to go and pray at their graves because several years ago these had been transferred to a distant site, their place of origin.

I searched at length for Aurélia's grave but was unable to locate it. The layout of the cemetery had been changed—and perhaps my memory had also gone astray ... It seemed to me that this chance circumstance, this lapse of

memory, was further damning evidence as far as I was concerned. I thought
of asking the cemetery officials, but did not dare pronounce the name of
someone over whom I had no religious claim ... But I remembered that I
had kept the exact location of her grave at home and I raced back there, my
heart pounding, my mind reeling.

As I have already noted, I had surrounded my love with bizarre superstitions. In a small box that had belonged to *her*, I kept her last letter. I
must even confess that I had turned this box into a kind of reliquary in
which I stored the souvenirs of those long journeys on which her memory
had accompanied me: a rose plucked in the garden of Schoubrah, a strip
of mummy cloth brought back from Egypt, laurel leaves gathered by the
river of Beirut, two tiny gilded crystals, bits of mosaic from Saint Sophia, a
rosary bead, various other items ... and finally, the piece of paper that had
been given to me the day they laid her in her grave so that I might find my
way back to it. ... I blushed, I trembled as I picked through all this crazy
clutter. I retrieved the two pieces of paper and just as I was about to make
my way back to the cemetery, I changed my mind. No, I said to myself, I
am not worthy of kneeling at the grave of a Christian; let us not add yet
another profanation to the list! ... And to quiet the storm that was brew-
ing in my head, I left for a small town on the outskirts of Paris where I had
spent happy times in my youth at the home of some elderly relatives, since
deceased.[48] I had often enjoyed visiting them to watch the sunsets near
their house. There was a terrace there, shaded by lime trees, which brought
back memories of the young girls—kissing cousins—I had grown up with.
One of these girls ...

But had it crossed my mind to contrast this vague childhood infatuation
with the love that had devoured my youth? I watched the sun slant down
over the gathering mist and shadows of the valley; it then vanished, leaving the treetops at the edge of the great hills bathed in russet flames. I was
overcome with gloom.

I took a room for the night at an inn where I often stayed. The innkeeper
told me about one of my old friends who lived in town and who had blown
his brains out after an unlucky business transaction ... Sleep brought on
terrible dreams. My memory of them is muddled.

I was in an unfamiliar room, talking to someone from the external
world—perhaps the friend I just mentioned. Behind us, there was a very
tall mirror. I happened to glance at it, and thought I recognized A***. She
seemed sad and pensive; but suddenly, whether it was because she had
stepped out of the mirror or because she had been reflected in it a moment
earlier as she crossed the room, this tender figure was standing by my side.

48. Saint-Germain-en-Laye.

She extended her hand to me and, casting me a mournful glance, said: "We shall meet again later ... at your friend's house."

It came to me in a flash—her marriage, the curse that was keeping us apart. I said to myself: is it possible? Will she ever come back to me? In tears, I asked: "Have you forgiven me?" But everything had vanished. I was in a deserted place, a steep rocky slope in the middle of the woods. A single house, which I thought I recognized, overlooked this desolate landscape. I kept losing my way in the maze. Tired of fighting my way through the rocks and brambles, now and then I would seek out an easier path along the wooded trails. They're waiting for me over there! I thought to myself.

A certain hour struck ... I said to myself: *it is too late*! Voices answered back: *she is lost*! Darkness surrounded me on all sides; the house in the distance was lit up as if for festivities, full of guests who had arrived on time. She is lost, I cried out, but why? ... Now I understand, she made one last effort to save me—but I missed that final crucial moment at which forgiveness was still possible. She could have interceded on my behalf with the divine Bridegroom in the heavens above ... But does my salvation matter? She has been snatched into the abyss, lost to me, lost to all! ... I thought I saw her as if lit by a bolt of lightning—pale, dying away, carried off by shadowy horsemen ... I woke up gasping from my own screams of rage and pain.

"Dear God! Dear God! For her sake alone, dear God, forgive," I cried out as I fell to my knees.

Day was breaking. By an impulse I find difficult to explain, I immediately decided to destroy the two pieces of paper I had retrieved from the box the previous day: the letter, alas, which I reread in tears, and the funeral certificate stamped with the cemetery seal. "Find her grave now?" I said to myself. "But it was yesterday I should have gone back there—and my fatal dream is but the reflection of my fatal day."

III

The flames consumed these relics of love and death—entwined with the most painful fibers of my heart. I went to walk off my wounds and belated remorse in the country, hoping that the exercise and the fatigue might numb my mind and promise a subsequent night of less distressing sleep. Convinced as I had become that the dream opened communication between man and the spirit world, I had hopes … I still had hopes! Perhaps God would content himself with this sacrifice.

Here I must break off; it would be too presumptuous to pretend that my state of mind had merely been brought about by a memory of love. Let us rather say that I was involuntarily using this memory to embellish my keen remorse for a life I had foolishly wasted, in which evil had often triumphed and whose errors I refused to recognize until I reeled from the blows of ill fortune. I no longer even considered myself worthy of thinking of her, for I was tormenting her in her death after having plagued her in her life; it was only out of sweet and saintly pity that she had granted me a last glance of forgiveness.

The following night I barely slept. A woman who had looked after me in my youth appeared to me in a dream and reproached me for an extremely serious misdeed I had committed in the past. I recognized her even though she seemed far older than the last time I had seen her. This fact caused me to reflect bitterly that I had not gone to visit her in her dying moments. She seemed to be saying to me, "You never mourned your aged relatives the way you mourned this woman. How can you therefore expect forgiveness?" Here the dream became confused. Faces of people I had known at different times passed quickly before my eyes. They sped by, now bright, now dim, then dropping back into darkness like the beads of a rosary whose string has snapped. Then I saw sculpted images from antiquity, first in sketchy outline, then gradually taking on firmer contours, and finally resolving themselves into symbols of sorts whose meaning I struggled to grasp. As it was, I took them to be saying: All this was done in order to teach you the secret of life, yet you did not understand. All the religions and fables, all the saints and poets concurred in explaining the fatal enigma, yet you misinterpreted it … Now it is too late!

Filled with terror, I woke up, muttering to myself: this is my final day. After an interval of ten years, the same idea that I have described in the first portion of this narrative was returning to my mind with even greater conviction and dread. God had granted me this interval so that I might repent, but I had not made use of it. After the visit of the *guest of stone*, I had returned to the banquet table.[49]

35

IV

These visions and the ensuing reflections which occupied my hours of solitude produced in me a feeling of such sorrow that I felt completely at a loss. All my past actions appeared to me in their most unfavorable light, and during this sort of self-examination in which I was engaged, the most

49. Molière, *Don Juan*, act 4, scene 8.

distant events came back to my mind with a particular sharpness. I do not know whether it was a false feeling of shame that kept me from going to confession; perhaps it was the fear of committing myself to the doctrines and practices of a mighty religion, many of whose tenets I continued to view with philosophic suspicion. My early years had been too saturated with the ideas that issued from the Revolution; my education had been too liberal, my life too aimless for me to bow to an authority which in many respects still affronted my reason. I shuddered to think what kind of Christian I might make had I not been held back by a number of notions borrowed from the past two centuries of free inquiry and from my studies of various religions.

I never knew my mother. She had decided to follow my father into battle like the wives of the ancient Germans, and had died of fever and exhaustion in a frigid province of Germany; my father was subsequently unable to take charge of my formative years. I grew up in a region that was full of strange legends and bizarre superstitions. One of my uncles, who had an enormous influence on my early education, collected Roman and Celtic antiquities as a hobby. Now and then he would find images of gods and emperors in his own or neighboring fields—images which his scholarly admiration caused me to venerate and whose history I learned from his books. A certain Mars cast in gilded bronze, a Pallas or armed Venus, a Neptune and an Amphitrite sculpted over the village fountain, and above all the fat, friendly face of a bearded Pan smiling through the ivy and yellow creeper at the entrance of a grotto—such were the guardians and household gods of this refuge. I confess that at that point they inspired far more awe in me than the humble Christian images in the local church and the two shapeless saints at its portal which certain authorities on the region claimed were the Esus and Cernunnos of the Gauls. Bewildered by all these symbols, one day I asked my uncle what God was. "God is the sun," he replied. This was the private conviction of an honest man who had lived his life as a Christian, but who had gone through the Revolution, and who came from a region where a number of others shared his ideas about the Divinity. This did not keep the women and children from attending church, and it was to one of my aunts that I owed the teachings which allowed me to understand some of the beauty and grandeur of Christianity. After 1815, an Englishman who happened to be in the area had me learn the Sermon on the Mount and presented me with a New Testament ... I only mention these details to indicate the causes of a certain irresolution which in my case is often wedded to a decidedly religious frame of mine.

45   I want to explain how, having strayed from the true path for so long, I felt myself led back to it by the fond memory of a dead woman, and how my need to believe that she still existed opened my mind to a more precise appreciation of certain truths which I had not firmly enough gathered into my soul. For those who have no faith in immortality with all its joys
50 and sorrows, certain fatal situations can result in despair and suicide. I think I shall have done something worthwhile by providing a straightforward account of the succession of ideas which allowed me to recover my peace of mind and acquire a new source of strength against life's future tribulations.

55   The succession of visions which had come to me during sleep had reduced me to such despair that I could barely speak; the company of my friends provided only a vague distraction; my mind, entirely taken up by these illusions, refused to entertain the slightest idea which might diverge from them; I could not read or understand ten lines in a row. I invented
60 elaborate excuses: why worry, none of this is real to me. One of my friends, by the name of Georges, tried to fend off my discouragement. He took me to visit various spots on the outskirts of Paris, and was quite happy to do all the talking while I merely replied with a few broken phrases. His expansive manner—almost that of a friar—reinforced the impact of
65 the extremely eloquent attack he one day mounted against those years of skepticism and of political and social disillusionment which had followed upon the July Revolution. I had been among the younger generation of this period and had shared in its argent hopes and bitter discouragements. Something in his words moved me; I said to myself that such lessons could
70 not have been addressed to me without the intervention of Providence, and that some spirit was no doubt speaking through him. ... One day we were dining under an arbor in a small village in the vicinity of Paris; a woman approached our table and started singing, and I do not know what it was, but something in her worn yet appealing voice reminded me of Aurélia's.
75 I looked at her: the features were not unlike those I had loved. She was ushered out of the place; I did not dare beg her to stay, but I said to myself: Who knows, perhaps *her spirit* is in this woman. And I felt happy at the alms I had given her.

    I said to myself: I have clearly made bad use of my life, but if the dead
80 can forgive us, it is no doubt on the condition that we henceforth abstain from harm and repair all the wrongs we have committed. Is this at all possible? ... From here on, let us try to mend our ways and repay our debts in full, whatever they may be. I had recently dealt very poorly with someone; it was merely an inadvertence on my art, but I started things off by going to
85 apologize. The happiness I felt at having made these amends did me a great deal of good; I had a reason to go on living and being active; I was regaining an interest in the world.

Difficulties arose: events I could not fathom seemed to conspire against all my good intentions. My mental condition made it impossible for me to produce the work I had promised. Since it was believed I was now back in good health, more was expected of me; having decided to refrain from further deception, I found myself in a quandary when it came to dealing with people who had no second thoughts about applying coercion. The burden of reparations to be made was crushing, especially given my incapacitation. Things were indirectly aggravated by political events; besides causing me considerable distress, they deprived me of the means of putting my affairs back in order.[50] The death of one of my friends proved to be the crowning blow to my general discouragement. I thought back with sorrow on his house and the paintings he had shown me with delight a month earlier; I passed by his coffin just as they were nailing him in. As he was my age and generation, I said to myself: What would happen should I suddenly die like this?

When I awoke the following Sunday, I was overcome with gloom. I went to visit my father; his maid was off sick and he seemed out of sorts. He insisted on fetching the firewood from his attic on his own and the only assistance I could offer was to reach him a log he needed to get at. I left in dismay. I met a friend on the street who wanted to invite me home to dinner in order to lift my spirits a bit. I declined and set out towards Montmartre on an empty stomach. The cemetery was closed, which struck me as a bad omen. A German poet had given me several pages of his to translate and had advanced me a sum for the job.[51] I proceeded in the direction of his house to reimburse the money.

As I was approaching the fate of Clichy, I noticed a fight had broken out. I tried to separate the combatants but did not manage to succeed. At that moment a huge workingman crossed the square where the quarrel had just taken place, carrying a child in a hyacinth-colored dress on his left shoulder. I imagined he was Saint Christopher carrying Christ and that I was doomed for having been so ineffectual in the scene that had just occurred. From this point onwards, I wandered in despair through the waste grounds that divide the outer suburbs from the inner city limits. It was too late to pay the visit I had planned, so I followed the streets back towards the center of Paris. Near the rue de la Victoire, I came upon a priest, and, in my disarray, wanted him to hear my confession. He told me this was not his parish and that he was on his way to somebody's home for the evening; if I wanted to confer with him tomorrow at Notre-Dame, all I had to do was ask for Father Dubois.

50. The coup d'état of 2 December 1851?
51. The German poet Heinrich Heine (1797–1856) had been living in exile in Paris since 1831. Nerval published a number of translations of his poems in 1848. Heine's home was on the rue d'Amsterdam, not far from the Clichy gate.

Desperate, I made my way in tears towards Notre-Dame-de Lorette, where I threw myself at the feet of the altar of the Virgin, asking forgiveness for my sins. Something in me was telling me: the Virgin is dead and your prayers are useless. I went to kneel at the rear of the choir and from my finger I slipped off a silver ring whose stone was engraved with the three Arab words: *Allah! Muhammad! Ali!* Immediately several candles lit up in the choir, signaling the start of a service, which I attempted to follow in spirit. When the priest reached the *Ave Maria*, he broke off in the middle of the orison and started all over again seven times in succession without my being able to recall the words that followed. The prayer was then brought to a close, and the priest delivered a sermon which seemed to allude to me alone. When all the candles were extinguished, I got up and set off towards the Champs-Elysées.

Upon reaching the place de la Concorde, my intention was to do away with myself. Several times I made for the Seine, but something kept me from going through with it. The stars were shining up above. Suddenly it seemed to me that they had all gone dark at once, like the candles I had seen in church. I thought that the final hour had come and that the end of the world announced by the Apocalypse of Saint John was near. I believed I saw a black sun in the vacant sky and a bloodred orb above the Tuileries. I said to myself: eternal night is upon us, and the darkness will be frightful. What will happen when they all realize there is no more sun? I turned back along the rue Saint-Honoré and pitied the peasants who were still straggling down the street. When I got to the place du Louvre, a strange scene awaited me. The wind was whipping the clouds across the sky, and I saw several moons darting by overhead. I thought the earth had shot out of its orbit and was careening through the heavens like a ship that had lost its mast, drawing closer or further away from the stars as they in turn grew or diminished in size. After contemplating this confusion for two or three hours, I set off towards Les Halles. The peasants were bringing in their produce and I said to myself: how astonished they will be to see that the night is not coming to an end… Yet here and there dogs were barking and cocks crowing.

Utterly exhausted, I returned home and flung myself on my bed. When I woke up, I was amazed to see light. A mysterious choir caught my ear; a chorus of youthful voices was repeating: "*Christe! Christe! Christe! …*" A large group of children, it seemed, had been assembled in a nearby church (Notre-Dame-des-Victoires) to beseech Christ.[52] But Christ is no more! I said to myself, and they have not yet found out about it! The invocation went on for about an hour. I got up at last and wandered over to the galleries of the Palais-Royal. I told myself that the sun had probably conserved enough of its light to shine on the earth for three days, but that it was burning itself out; and indeed, it looked cold and colorless to me. I ate a biscuit

---

52. In 1853, Nerval briefly lived on the rue du Mail, not far from Notre-Dame-des-Victoires.

to allay my hunger and to give me strength to make it all the way to the
German poet's house. Upon entering, I told him that everything was done
170   for and that we might as well prepare ourselves to die. He called his wife
over and she asked me what the matter was. "I don't know," I replied, "I am
lost." She sent for a cab, and a young girl escorted me to the Dubois clinic.[53]

V

There I had a relapse with various complications. After a month I recovered.
Over the course of the following two months I resumed my peregrinations
in and around Paris. My longest journey took me on a visit to the cathedral
of Reims. Little by little I returned to writing and composed one of my fin-
5   est stories.[54] But it did not come easily; I wrote it almost entirely in pencil
on stray scraps of paper at odd moments of my reveries or wanderings. The
revisions caused me considerable anguish. A few days after its publication,
I began to suffer from persistent insomnia. I would spend the entire night
wandering around Montmartre and then watch the sunrise from the hill. I
10   would stop to chat at length with workers and peasants. On other occasions
I would set off towards Les Halles. One night I dropped in for a bite at a
boulevard café and, just for the fun of it, started tossing around gold and
silver coins. Then I went to the market and found myself in an argument
with a complete stranger, whom I proceeded to slap in the face; I have
15   no idea why nothing further came of it. At one point, hearing the clock
of Saint-Eustache chime, my thoughts turned to the battles between the
Burgundians and the Armagnacs, and I thought I saw the ghosts of these
ancient warriors rising up around me.[55] I picked a quarrel with a market
auctioneer who was wearing a silver plaque on his chest and accused him of
20   being Duke John of Burgundy. I tried to prevent him from entering a tavern.
For some strange reason I cannot explain, when he saw that I meant him
deadly harm, his face filled with tears. I felt pity for him and let him pass.

I set off for the Tuileries. The park was closed, so I walked along the quays;
then I went up to the Luxembourg gardens and returned back to meet one
25   of my friends for lunch. I then proceeded towards Saint-Eustache, where I
piously knelt at the altar of the Virgin while thinking of my mother. The
tears I shed eased my soul and, upon leaving the church, I bought myself a
silver ring. From there I went to my father's house to pay him a visit; as he
was out, I left him a bouquet of daisies.[56] I then wandered over to the Jardin

---

53.   Nerval was hospitalized in the Dubois municipal clinic from 23 January to 15 February
1852, and again from 6 February to 27 March 1853.

54.   *Sylvie*, first published in magazine form in August 1853.

55.   Opposing factions that fought to control France in the early fifteenth century.

56.   Nerval's father then lived in the Marais.

30 des Plantes. The place was quite crowded and I stopped to watch a hippo-
potamus bathing in a pool.

I then went to have a look at the osteological exhibits at the Museum
of Natural History. The sight of the monsters on display got me thinking
about the Flood and, as I made my way out to the gardens again, it was
35 pouring with rain. I said to myself: what a shame! All these women and
children are going to get drenched! … Then I said to myself: but things are
far more serious! This is the beginning of the real Flood! The water was
rising in the nearby streets; I ran down the rue Saint-Victor and, believing I
might be able to stem the global tide, I threw the ring I had bought at Saint-
40 Eustache into the deepest part of the water. It was roughly at this moment
that the rain tapered off and a ray of sun burst forth.

I was again filled with hope. I had arranged to meet my friend Georges
at four and set off for his house.[57] Passing by a curiosity shop, I bought two
velvet screens covered with hieroglyphics. This seemed to me to be a con-
45 secration of divine forgiveness. I arrived at Georges's place precisely at the
appointed hour and told him of my newfound hope. I was wet and bedrag-
gled. I changed my clothes and lay down on his bed. A splendid vision came
to me as I slept. It seemed the goddess was appearing to me and saying: "I
am none other than Mary, none other than your mother, none other than
50 the one you have always loved in every shape and manner. At each of your
ordeals I have cast off one of the masks that veil my features; soon you shall
see me as I truly am." From the clouds at her back there emerged a bower of
bliss, a paradise suffused with gentle light, and though there was no sound
other than her voice, I was utterly enraptured.

57. Nerval's friend Georges Bell lived on the rue de Seine.

55   I woke up shortly afterwards and said to Georges, "Let's go out." As we were crossing the Pont des Arts I explained the migration of souls and told him: "I think the soul of Napoleon is within me tonight, inspiring me and commanding me to do great things." I purchased a hat in the rue du Coq and while Georges was collecting the change from the gold coin I had

60 tossed on the counter, I continued on to the galleries of the Palais-Royal.

    It seemed that everyone there was staring at me. I couldn't get the idea out of my head that the dead no longer existed. I wandered up and down the Galerie de Foy, saying, "I've made some mistake," but I could not discover what it was as I searched through my memory, which I believed to be Napoleon's

65 ... "There's something here I've left unpaid!" With this in mind I entered the Café de Foy and thought I recognized old Bertin of the *Débats* among the customers.[58] Then I crossed through the garden and my attention was caught by some young girls dancing a round. Leaving the galleries, I proceeded on to the rue Saint-Honoré. I went into a shop to buy a cigar and when I emerged the

70 crowd was so thick I almost suffocated. Offering their assurances all around, three friends of mine extricated me and ushered me into a café while one of them went looking for a cab. I was taken off to the Hospice de la Charité.[59]

    In the course of the night the delirium got worse, especially in the early hours when I realized I had been bound and tied. I managed to free myself from the

75 straitjacket and wandered through the wards as dawn approached. Convinced I had become a god and possessed healing powers, I laid hands on several invalids and, approaching a statue of the Virgin, removed her crown of artificial flowers in order to clasp her with my imagined powers. I strode around ranting about the ignorance of those who believed they could cure by science alone,

80 and spying a flask of ether on a table, I swallowed it down in a single gulp. An angel-faced attendant tried to stop me, but driven by my nervous energy I almost knocked him down before checking myself and explaining to him that he did not understand the nature of my mission. Then the doctors arrived and I continued my diatribe against the worthlessness of their science. Then, though

85 I was without shoes, I marched off down the stairs. Finding myself in front of a garden, I went in and picked some flowers while strolling on the grass.

    One of my friends had come back to fetch me. I left the garden and while we were conversing, a straitjacket was thrown over my shoulders and I was bundled into a cab that took me to a clinic on the outskirts of Paris.[60] When

90 I saw I was among the mad, I understood that everything up to this point had been mere illusion. All the same, it seemed to me that the promises I attributed to the goddess Isis were being fulfilled through this series of ordeals I was destined to undergo. I therefore accepted them with resignation.

58.   Louis François Bertin (1766–1841), founder of the influential *Journal des Débats*.
59.   Nerval was brought to the Charité hospital (on the current site of the École de Médecine) on 15 August 1853.
60.   Nerval entered the clinic of Dr. Esprit Blanche's son Émile in Passy on 27 August 1853.

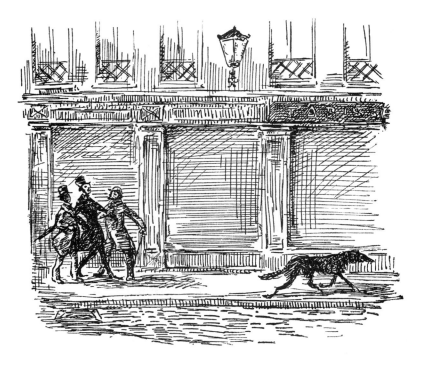

My wing of the clinic overlooked a large exercise yard shaded by walnut trees. Off to the side there was a small mound which one of the inmates used to spend the whole day circling. The others, like myself, were content to confine themselves to the perimeters of the raised terrace area with its embankments of grass. One of the western walls was covered with drawings; one of them represented the moon with geometrically drawn eyes and mouth, and a kind of mask had been painted over the figure. The wall to the left featured various drawings in profile; one of them suggested a Japanese idol. Further on, a death's head had been gouged into the plaster; facing this were two blocks of sandstone which had been sculpted into rather well-rendered little gargoyles by one of the garden's regulars. Two doors led to the cellars, which I imagined were underground passages rather like those I had seen at the entrances to the Pyramids.

VI

I initially imagined that the people gathered in this garden all exercised some influence over the stars and that the individual who kept ceaselessly turning in the same circle was thereby regulating the course of the sun. An elderly man, who was allowed out at certain hours of the day and who used to time himself with his watch as he tied knots, appeared to me to be in charge of monitoring the course of the hours. To myself I attributed the influence over the course of the moon, and I believed that having been struck by lightning by the Almighty, this star wore on its face the imprint of the mask I had previously noticed.

I ascribed a mysterious significance to the conversations of the guards and my companions. It seemed to me they represented all the races of the earth and that our task was to replot the course of the planets and to further expand their system. As I saw it, an error had crept into the overall combination of numbers and this was the root of all the ills of humanity. I further believed that the celestial spirits had taken on human form and that they were participants in this general assembly, even though they appeared to be busying themselves with mundane matters. My role, it seemed to me, was to reestablish universal harmony by cabbalistic arts and to discover a solution by summoning up the occult powers of the various religions.

In addition to the exercise area, we had a hall whose windows opened on to a horizon of foliage through their vertical bars. As I looked through these windows at the row of buildings outside, I saw their facades and windows take on the silhouette of countless pavilions, all decorated with arabesques and ridged with frets and spires, which reminded me of the imperial kiosks on the shores of the Bosphorus. This naturally turned my thoughts to Oriental matters. Around two o'clock, I was given a bath, thinking the attendants were Valkyries, daughters of Odin, who wanted to raise me into immortality by gradually stripping my body of all its impurities.

In the evening I took a walk in the moonlight, feeling utterly serene. As I raised my eyes towards the trees overhead, it seemed to me that the leaves were impishly bobbing this way and that so as to create images of knights and ladies borne along on caparisoned steeds. To my mind these figures represented our triumphant ancestors. This idea led to another, namely, that there was a massive conspiracy among all living creatures to reestablish the world in its original harmony, and that the magnetism of stars provided their means of communication, and that the minds committed to this general communion were linked by an uninterrupted chain stretching across the earth, and that all their songs and dances and glances, drawn ever closer by magnetic attraction, translated this shared aspiration. To me the moon was the sanctuary of those fraternal souls who, delivered from their mortal bodies, were all the more free to devote themselves to the regeneration of the universe.

Already the length of each day seemed to me to have increased by two hours; so that when I got up at the requisite times set by the clocks of the clinic, I was wandering through the kingdom of the shades. To me my fellow companions seemed to be asleep or like specters out of Tartarus until the hour at which the sun rose for me. I would then greet it with a prayer, and my real life would begin.

From the moment I became persuaded of the fact that I was undergoing the ordeals of a sacred initiation, a sense of invincibility took hold of my mind. I considered myself a hero living under the gaze of gods; everything in nature took on a new dimension; secret voices called out to me in warning and encouragement from plants, tree, animals, and the tiniest of insects. I could grasp the mysterious turns taken by the language of my companions; shapeless and lifeless objects were effortlessly weighed in my mind; harmonies that had heretofore escaped me now issued forth from the configurations of stones, angles, cracks, apertures, leaf patterns, colors, smells, and sounds. I said to myself: how could I have gone on living this long so removed from nature and unable to identify with it? Everything is alive, everything is in motion, everything corresponds; the magnetic rays that emanate from me or from others flow directly through the infinite chain of creation whose transparent network is in continuous communications with the planets and the stars. A captive here on earth for the moment, I commune with the chorus of stars and they join in my sorrows and joys.

I immediately shuddered at the thought that this mystery might be discovered. If electricity, I said to myself, which is the magnetic attraction of physical bodies, is subject to laws which determine its direction, then there is all the more reason to believe that malevolent or despotic spirits could enslave other minds by dividing them in order to conquer. This is how the ancient gods were conquered and enslaved by the new gods. This is how, I further said to myself as I searched through my memories of ancient times, the necromancers managed to subjugate entire races and to keep generation after generation subservient to their eternal scepter. How dreadful! Even Death cannot set them free, for we live on in our sons just as we have lived in our fathers—the science of our enemies is merciless and can detect us wherever we are. Our hour or place of birth, our first gesture, our name, the very room in which we are born, the various ceremonies and rituals which usher us into the world—all this establishes the series of fortunate or unfortunate circumstances on which our future entirely depends. But if all of these factors are overwhelming as far as the calculus of human life is concerned, just think what things must be like when one takes into consideration the mysterious formulas which govern the order of the worlds. As has been right observed: nothing is insignificant, nothing is inconsequential in the universe; an atom can destroy it all, an atom can save it all!

O Horror! Herein lies the eternal distinction between good and evil. Is my soul this indestructible molecule, this tiny bubble of breath which plays its part in nature nonetheless? Or is it instead merely this void, this image of nothingness receding into infinite space? Or perhaps it is simply that ill-fated particle, destined to go through endless transformations at the vengeful mercy of powerful beings? All this led me to take account of my life and even of my previous existences. By proving to myself that I was good, I thereby proved that I must have always been so. And if I had been bad, I said to myself, isn't my life as it now stands sufficient atonement? This thought reassured me, but it did not allay my fears that I would be forever classified among the unfortunate. I felt as if I had been plunged into a cold bath, and that water which was even colder streamed down my brow. I turned my thoughts to the eternal Isis, sacred mother and bride, all my aspirations, all my prayers fathered into her magic name; I felt myself come back to life in her, and at times she appeared to me in the guise of the ancient Venus, at times she took on the features of the Christian Virgin. Night rendered this enchanting vision clearer to me, and yet I asked myself: what can she do for her poor children, defeated and perhaps oppressed as she is? Pale and torn, the moon's crescent was waning with every evening and would soon disappear; perhaps we were never to see it again in the sky? Nonetheless, it seemed to me that this star was the sanctuary of all my sister souls, and I saw it populated by wistful shades, destined one day to be reborn on earth.

My room lies at the far end of a corridor, one side of which is occupied by the mad and the other by the domestic staff of the clinic. The only room favored with a window, it opens out on to the tree-lined courtyard, which functions as the exercise area during the day. I take pleasure in gazing at one of the leafy walnut trees and the two Chinese mulberries. Beyond, one can vaguely make out a fairly well-traveled road through the green trellises. The horizon opens up towards the west; there is something like a hamlet over there, with windows decorated with plants or cluttered with birdcages and rags hanging out to dry, and now and then one can catch sight of a younger

15 or older housewife peering out, or else the rosy face of a child. Shouts, songs, bursts of laughter ring forth, a joy or a sorrow to the ear depending on the hour or mood.

All the debris of my various fortunes has found its way here, the odds and ends of personal belongings scattered or sold over the past twenty years. The clutter is as bad as Doctor Faust's study. An ancient tripod table with 20 feet in the shape of eagle's heads, a console supported by a wingèd sphinx, a seventeenth-century commode, an eighteenth-century bookcase, a tester bed from the same period whose oval canopy is appointed in red damask (which proved impossible to set up), a rustic cupboard bursting with crockery and Sèvres china, most of it chipped, a narghile brought back from 25 Constantinople, a large alabaster bowl, a crystal vase, some wood paneling rescued from the demolition of an old house I had once inhabited near the Louvre and which friends of mine, since famous, had covered with mythological paintings, two large canvases in the manner of Prud'hon representing the muses of history and of comedy. I spent several pleasant days setting 30 up the place, turning this cramped attic room into an odd cross between a palace and hovel, a fairly accurate image of my nomadic existence. Above my bed I have hung my Arab outfits, the two cashmere shawls which have gone through so many mendings and remendings, a pilgrim's gourd, a hunter's game bag. A huge map of Cairo stretches above the bookcase; a 35 bamboo bedside table holds a lacquered Indian platter where I can arrange my toilet articles. I was delighted to find myself back among these humble relics of my changing fortunes over the years; a lifetime of memories was associated with them. The only items that had been left aside were a small painting on copper in the style of Correggio depicting *Venus and Eros*, some 40 panels featuring satyrs and huntresses, and an arrow I had kept in memory of the Companies of the Bow of the Valois, to which I had belonged as a youth; my weapons had been sold when the new laws came in. In short, I was surrounded by virtually all my remaining possessions. My books, a farrago of the wisdom of the ages, histories, travel accounts, religious treatises, 45 cabbala, astrology, would gladden the shades of Pico della Mirandola, Meursius the Sage, and Nicholas of Cusa—the library of Babel in two hundred volumes.[61] And all this I had been allowed to keep! There was enough here to make a wise man mad; let's hope there is also enough to make a madman wise.

50 What pleasure it has given me to file away in drawers my bundles of notes and letters, whether private or public, inconsequential or notewor-

---

61.   Pico della Mirandola (1463–96), Italian humanist whose motto was "*De omni re scibili*" (of all things knowable). The Dutch philologist Jan Meursius (1579–1639) was the author of a commentary on Lycophron, reputed to be the most obscure of Greek authors. Nicholas of Cusa (1401–64) was known for his polymathic command of languages, philosophy, theology, and mathematics.

thy, depending on whom I had happened to meet or which distant lands I had been visiting. Unrolling a packet more carefully wrapped than the others, I came across letters from Arabia, relics of Cairo and Stamboul. Oh joy! Oh mortal sorrow! This yellowed handwriting, these faded first drafts, these half-crumbled letters are the treasures of my only love … Let us reread them … Many of the letters are missing, many others have been torn up or erased; here is what I find:[62]

*

One night I was talking and singing in a kind of ecstasy. One of the attendants came to put me in my cell and took me down to a room on the ground floor where he locked me in. Though awake, I continued my dream, believing I had been locked up in some sort of Oriental kiosk. I checked out all the corners and discovered it was octagonal. A divan ran around the walls; the latter appeared to be made of thick glass, beyond which I saw a brilliant array of treasures, shawls, and carpets. A moonlit landscape was visible through the latticework of the door, and I could make out the outlines of familiar tree trunks and rocks. I had already lived here in a previous life and thought I recognized the deep grottoes of Ellora.[63] A bluish light was gradually filtering into the kiosk and causing bizarre images to appear. I thought I had ended up in some vast charnel house where the history of the world was scrawled in blood.

The giant body of a woman stood painted before my eyes, except that she had been hacked apart as if by a saber; on the other walls, more women of various races, their bodies growing ever more pronounced, loomed forth in a bloody tangle of limbs and heads, extending from empresses and queens down to the humblest of peasants. The history of every crime was written here, and it was enough to direct one's gaze to a given place in order to see

62. In their 1855 edition of *Le Rêve et la vie*, Nerval's first editors, Théophile Gautier and Arsène Houssaye, intercalated ten of the so-called "Letters to Jenny Colon" in order to fill the apparent gap in the text here. All modern editions choose to let the gap stand as originally published.

63. Famous underground temples of India discovered in the late eighteenth century.

some tragic scene taking shape. This, I said to myself, is what happens when power is bestowed upon men. Bit by bit, they have destroyed the archetype of beauty and cut it up into a thousand pieces, progressively sapping the races of mankind of their strength and perfection ... And in fact, on a thread of shadow slanting through the latticed door I saw the descending generations of future races.

I was at last deflected from this somber train of thought. The kindly, compassionate face of my excellent doctor brought me back to the world of the living. He had me observe a scene which fascinated me. Among the patients there was a young man, a former soldier in Africa, who had refused to eat anything for the past six weeks. They would force him to swallow solid and liquid substances by means of a long rubber tube inserted into his nostril. He was moreover unable to see or speak and evidently could not hear either.

This scene moved me deeply. Abandoned as I had been to the same never-ending circle of my own sensations or mental anguish, I was now coming face-to-face with an enigmatic creature, sitting there silent and patient like a sphinx at the outermost portals of existence. Seeing him so wretched and forsaken, I took a liking to him and felt uplifted by this sense of sympathy and pity. Placed as he was between life and death, he struck me as a sublime interpreter, a confessor predestined to hear those secrets of the soul which speech could never dare convey nor succeed in rendering. Here was the ear of God unadulterated by any other's thought. I spent hours mentally examining myself, my head bent over his, his hands in mine. A certain magnetism seemed to unite our minds, and I was elated when for the first time a word ushered forth from his mouth. Nobody wanted to believe it, and I ascribed these first signs of recovery to my own fierce determination. That night I had a marvelous dream, the first such dream I had had in a long time. I was in a tower which went so deep into the earth and so high into the sky that it seemed that my entire life would have to be spent climbing up and down it. My strength was ebbing and I was about to give up for good when a side door suddenly opened; a spirit appears and says to me: "Come, brother! ..." I do not know why the idea crossed my mind that his name was Saturnin.[64] His features were those of the unfortunate patient, but now transmogrified and alert. We were in the country and everything was bathed in starlight; we stopped to take in the scene and the spirit touched his hand to my brow just as I had done the previous day while attempting to magnetize my companion;

64. A name with many antithetical associations. The planet Saturn is traditionally associated with melancholy, yet in Virgil's Fourth Ecologue, Saturn is linked to the return of the Golden Age ("redeunt Saturnia regna"). Saturnin is also the legendary founder of gnosticism in Syria. Patron saint of Toulouse, Saint-Saturnin is particularly venerated for his healing powers; his feast day falls on 29 November, the date of Nerval's mother's death.

thereupon one of the stars above began to grow in size and the divinity of my dreams appeared to me, smiling and wearing a more or less Indian costume, exactly as I had formerly seen her. She joined in between us, and the meadows grew green and the flowers and leaves sprang from the earth in her footsteps … She said to me, "The ordeal to which you have been submitted is now at its end; these countless stairways which you so wearily climbed and descended were but the fetters of all the old illusions that trammeled your mind; think back on the day you implored the holy Virgin and, believing her dead, were seized with delirium. It was essential that your vow be transmitted to her by a simple soul who was not bound to the earth. This soul has appeared at your side, which is why I am now allowed to appear in person in order to offer you encouragement." My mind was so overjoyed by this dream that I woke exhilarated. Day was beginning to break. I wanted some material sign of this apparition which had come to comfort me, and I wrote these words on the wall: "You visited me last night."

I here record, under the title *Memorabilia*, the impressions of several dreams which followed the one I have just described.

On a soaring peak of the Auvergne, the shepherds' song has echoed forth. *Poor Mary!* Queen of the heavens! It is you they humbly invoke. This rustic melody has reached the ear of the corybants. They join in the song, rushing from the grottoes where Eros gave them shelter. Hosanna! Peace and earth and glory in the heavens!

On the heights of the Himalayas a tiny flower was born. Forget-me-not. A star shot a sparkling glance at her, and the reply came back in a sweet foreign tongue. *Myosotis!*[65]

In the sand there glowed a pearl of silver; a pearl of gold gleamed in the sky … The world was created. Chaste loves, heavenly sighs! Set the sacred mount aflame … for you have brothers in the valleys and sisters shyly hidden in the thick of the woods!

Scented groves of Paphos, you cannot compare to these retreats where every breath fills the lungs with the nourishing air of home. "Up there, among the mountains—they lead a life of ease—the wild nightingale is my delight!"

Oh! How fair is my belovèd! In her grandeur, she forgives the world; in her kindness, she has forgiven me. The other night she was sleeping in a palace, and I could not rejoin her. My dark chestnut horse was flagging. The

---

65. The magical word pronounced by the mythical German flower *Vergissmeinnicht* (forget-me-not), said to open access to buried mountain treasures.

reins were sliding on his sweaty withers, and I had to struggle to keep him from lying down on the ground.

265   Last night, my good Saturnin came to my aid and my belovèd pulled up beside me on her white mare caparisoned in silver. She said to me, "Courage, brother, this is the final stage!" And her large eyes stared out into space and her long hair, scented with all the perfumes of Yemen, streamed in the air.[66]

270   I recognized the divine features of ***.[67] We were soaring to victory, and our enemies lay at our feet. We were guided into the highest heavens by the hoopoe bird and the sacred hands of Apollyon brandished the bow of light.[68] The enchanted horn of Adonis echoed through the woods.

"O Death, where is thy sting?"[69] For the conquering Messiah was riding
275   between the two of us! His garments were a pale hyacinth and his wrists and ankles and feet sparkled with diamonds and rubies. When he touched the pearly gates of the New Jerusalem with his wand, we were all three flooded with light.[70] It was then that I went down among men to announce the glad tidings.

280   I am emerging from a lovely dream: I saw the woman I loved, radiant and transfigured. The heavens opened in all their glory and there I read the word pardon signed in the blood of Jesus Christ.

A star suddenly began to shine, revealing to me the secret of this and every world. Hosanna! Peace on earth and glory to the heavens!

285   From the still heart of darkness two notes echoed forth, one low, one high—and the eternal globe immediately spun into motion. Blessèd be the

66.   Yemen is traditionally associated with the Queen of Sheba.

67.   In one of Nerval's manuscripts, this now-nameless female divinity bore the name of Sophie—from the Greek *sophia* (wisdom).

68.   Mentioned in Revelation 9:11 as "the angel of the bottomless pit." Yet given the "bow of light" he carries, Apollyon the exterminating angel seems to be here fused with the Greek Apollo, god of light.

69.   1 Corinthians 15:55.

70.   Revelation 21:2, 21:21.

first octave that opened this heavenly hymn! Let it gather the days from
sabbath to sabbath into its magic web. It sings from the hills to the valleys,
from the springs to the streams, from the streams to the rivers, from the
rivers to the seas; its music trembles through the air and sets the budding
flowers ashimmer. The earth's quivering breast heaves a sigh of love, and the
chorus of stars reverberates through infinity, now receding, now returning
back on itself, now contracting, now expanding, scattering the seeds of new
creations far and wide.

On the peak of a bluish mountain a tiny flower was born. Forget-me-not!
A star shot a sparkling glance at her, and the reply came back in a sweet
foreign tongue. *Myosotis*!

Woe to you, god of the North![71] With a single stroke of your hammer,
you shattered the sacred table that was made of the seven most precious
metals! For you could not shatter the *Rosy Pearl* which lay at its center. It
rebounded under your blow—and so we have armed ourselves to protect
it ... Hosanna!

The *macrocosm*, or greater world, was constructed by cabbalistic arts; the
microcosm, or smaller world, is its image reflected in every heart. The Rosy
Pearl was tinted by the royal blood of the Valkyries. Woe to you, blacksmith
god, for having wanted to shatter a world!

And yet Christ's forgiveness was also proclaimed for you!

Therefore blessèd be thou, o giant Thor, Odin's most powerful son!
Blessèd be thou in Hela, thy mother, for death is often sweet, and in thy
brother and in thy dog Garm!

Blessèd is the snake that encircles the World, for he slackens his coils and
his gaping maw breathes in the anxoka, the brimstone flower—the dazzling
flower of the sun!

May God preserve the god Balder, son of Odin and Freya the fair!

 found myself *in spirit* at Zaandam, which I visited last
year.[72] Snow covered the ground. Skidding this way and
that on the frozen ground, a tiny little girl was making
her way, I believe, towards the house of Peter the Great.
There was something Bourbon in her noble profile. Her
neck peeked out from her swanskin hood, dazzling white.
She was cupping a lantern with her tiny pink hand to
protect the flame from the wind and was about to knock

71. In this and the following paragraphs Nerval deploys the various divinities of Nordic
mythology popularized by eighteenth- and nineteenth-century translations of the *Eddas*.
72. In the course of his travels through Holland in the spring of 1852, Nerval had visited
the house of the Russian czar Peter the Great (1672–1725) in Zaandam.

at the green door of the house when a scrawny cat shot out, got tangled in her legs, and toppled over her. "Why it's nothing but a cat!" she said as she got back up. "Cats are not nothing!" a soft voice replied. I was present at this scene, holding in my arms a small gray cat, which began to mew. "It's that old fairy's child!" said the little girl. And she proceeded into the house.

Last night my dreams took me to Vienna. On each of the squares of this city, as is known, there are large columns called *pardons*. The massed clouds of marble represent the order of Solomon and support the globes on which the seated divinities preside. Suddenly, oh wonders, I began thinking of that august sister of the emperor of Russia whose imperial palace in Weimar I had seen.[73] In my gentle melancholia, I saw the tinted mists of a Norwegian landscape suffused with soft gray light. The clouds became transparent, and before my eyes I saw a deep abyss opening up and all the freezing waves of the Baltic flooding down into it. It seemed that the entire Neva River was about to plunge its blue waters into this fissure. The ships of Kronstadt and Saint Petersburg were bobbing at anchor, ready to break loose and vanish into the chasm, when a ray of divine light lit up this scene of desolation from on high.

Under the bright beam which pierced the mist, the statue of Peter the Great immediately appeared to my eyes. Above its great rock pedestal, the clouds were piled in clusters that reached the zenith of the sky. Each one was laden with radiant, godlike figures, among whom one could distinguish the

73. Maria Paulowna, sister of the czar Nicholas I, had married Charles Frederick, the grand duke of Weimar—whom Nerval met in 1850.

345   two Catherines and the empress Saint Helena, accompanied by the fairest princesses of Muscovy and Poland.[74] They gazed expectantly in the direction of France, diminishing the distance by means of long crystal telescopes. I thereby gathered that our country had become the arbiter of the Oriental question and that they were awaiting its resolution. My dream ended with
350   the fond hope that peace would at last be granted us.

     In this way, I gradually gathered the courage to undertake a bold venture. I decided to fix upon my dreams and discover their secret. I said to myself, armed with sufficient willpower, why should I not at last be able to force open these mystic gates and master my sensations instead of submitting to
355   them? Is it not possible to tame the charms of this dread chimera, and to discipline these spirits of the night who make such a mockery of our reason? Sleep occupies a third of our life. It consoles us for the sorrows of our days, or punishes us for their pleasures. After several minutes of drowsiness, a new life begins, freed from the bounds of time and space and no doubt
360   similar to the life that awaits us after death. Who knows, there may well be a link between these two existences and it might be possible for the soul to establish it here and now.

     From that moment on, I made efforts to seize the meaning of my dreams, and my resultant uneasiness had an effect on my waking thoughts. To my
365   mind, it seemed clear that there were links between the external and internal worlds; it was only mental inattention or disarray that caused these evident connections to become distorted; and this explained the bizarre quality of certain dream images which resembled the grimacing reflections of real objects trembling on the surface of troubled waters.

370   Such were the inspirations of my nights; my days were spent quietly in the company of the poor patients who had become my friends. The awareness that I had now been cleansed of the errors of my past life set my mind at infinite ease; I had, as it were, been materially assured of the immortality and coexistence of everybody I had ever loved, and I blessed the brotherly
375   soul who had lifted me from the depths of despair and set me back on the luminous path of religion.

     The poor fellow, so singularly bereft of all intelligent life, was undergoing treatments which little by little were rousing him from his torpor. Learning that he had been born in the country, I spent entire hours singing old vil-
380   lage tunes to him, in the hope that they might move him. I was happy to see that he was listening to them and even repeating certain parts of the songs. One day, at long last, he opened his eyes for a second, and I saw they were

---

74. The two Catherines are Catherine (1684–1727), empress of Russia and wife of Peter the Great, and Catherine the Great (1729–96). Saint Helena (ca. 247–327) was the mother of the emperor Constantine, restorer of religious peace to the Roman Empire. Their gaze in the direction of France as the potential arbiter of peaceful harmony between the Occident and Orient may be explained by the Crimean War of 1854.

385

390

395

400

as blue as those of the spirit who had appeared to me in my dreams. One morning, several days later, he opened his eyes wide, this time for good. He also began talking, but only in spurts, and he recognized me, addressing me like an old acquaintance and calling me brother. But he was still refusing to eat. One day, as he was returning from the garden, he said to me: "I'm thirsty." I went to get him something to drink; he took the glass to his lips, but could not swallow. "Why," I asked, "do you refuse to eat and drink like everybody else?" "Because I'm dead," he replied. "I was buried in such and such a cemetery, in such and such a place ..." "And where do you think you are now?" "In purgatory, doing atonement."

Such are the bizarre ideas which these kinds of illness can induce; I recognized that I myself had not been far from sharing in this strange persuasion. The treatments I had received had already rendered me back to the renewed affection of my family and friends, and I now had a healthier view of the world of illusions in which I had for some time lived. All the same, I am happy with the convictions I have acquired, and I compare this series of ordeals I have undergone to what, in the eyes of the ancients, was represented by the idea of a descent into Hell.[75]

75. Editor's Note: On a slip of paper attached to the endpaper pages of Jung's Müller edition of *Aurélia* (catalogued BF22) are written (but not in Jung's handwriting) four lines from E. G. Kolbenheyer, *Amor Dei* (1912) and a valediction:

"*Ein weisses Licht erstrahlt über ihm / in hunderttausend Welten; dies wird den / Gerechten Erbe sein—er ist die Nahrung / der Heiligen—sein Gesicht heisst das lange Gesicht—/ Zur letzten Erinnerung an schweigsame / Gespräche—*"

(A white light shines above him / in a hundred thousand worlds; this will be / the righteous's inheritance—he is the nourishment / of the Saints—his face is called the long face—/ In remembrance of silent / conversations—)

References

Artaud, Antonin. 1974. *Lettres écrites de Rodex (1945-1946): Oeuvres complètes*. Vol. 11. Paris: Gallimard.

Auden, W. H. 2002. *The Complete Works of W. H. Auden, Prose, Volume II, 1939–1948*. Edited by Edward Mendelson. Princeton, NJ: Princeton University Press.

Baillarger, Jules. 1854. *Essai de classification des maladies mentales*. Paris: Victor Masson.

Baudelaire, Charles. 1976. "Edgar Poe, sa vie et ses oeuvres." In *Oeuvres complètes*, edited by Claude Pichois, 2:296–318. Paris: Bibliothèque de la Pléiade.

Berlin, Isaiah. 1999. *The Roots of Romanticism*. Edited by Henry Hardy. Princeton, NJ: Princeton University Press.

Berthelot, Michelin. 1888. *Collection des anciens alchimistes grecs*. Paris: G. Steinheil. Thomas Fisher Rare Book Library, University of Toronto. http://www.archive.org/details/collection desanc23bert (accessed December 2, 2014).

Betz, Hans Dieter, ed. 1985. *The Greek Magical Papyri in Translation*. Chicago: University of Chicago Press.

Bishop, Paul. 2008. *Analytical Psychology and German Classical Aesthetics*. Vol. 1. London: Routledge.

Blanche, Antoine-Émile. 1848. "Du cathétérisme oesophagien chez les aliénés." PhD diss., Salpêtrière.

Blaser, Robin. 1968. "Artaud on Nerval." *Pacific Nation* 1:67–78.

Butler, Shane. 2011. "The Backward Glance." In *The Matter of the Page: Essays in Search of Ancient and Medieval Authors*, 13–27. Madison: University of Wisconsin Press.

Cambray, Joe. 2014. "Romanticism and Revolution in Jung's Science." *Jung and the Question of Science*, edited by Raya Jones, 9–29. London: Routledge.

Colonna, Francesco. 1999. *Hypnerotomachia Poliphili: The Strife of Love in a Dream*. Translated by Joscelyn Godwin. New York: Thames and Hudson.

Dante. 2004. *Vita Nuova*. Translated by Barbara Reynolds. London: Penguin Classics.

Diethe, Carol. 2007. *Nietzsche's Sister and the Will to Power: A Biography of Elisabeth Förster-Nietzsche*. Champaign: University of Illinois Press.

Dolzani, Michael. 2004. Introduction to *Northrop Frye's Notebooks on Romance: The Collected Works of Northrop Frye, Volume 15*, xxi–lvii. Toronto: University of Toronto Press.

Eckermann, Johann Peter. 1998. *Conversations of Goethe with Johann Peter Eckermann*, edited by J. K. Moorhead and translated by John Oxenford. New York: Da Capo.

Eco, Umberto. 1994. *Six Walks in the Fictional Woods*. Cambridge, MA: Harvard University Press.

Esquirol, Jean-Étienne-Dominique. 1838. *Des maladies mentales, considérées sous les rapports médical, hygiénique et médico-légal Dictionnaire des sciences médicales*.

———. 1845. *Mental Maladies: Treatise on Insanity*. Translated by E. K. Hunt. Philadelphia: Lea and Blanchard.

Falret, Jean-Pierre. 1864. *Des maladies mentales et des asiles d'aliénés*. Paris: J.-B. Baillière et fils.

Fierz-David, Linda. 1950. *The Dream of Poliphilo*. Related and interpreted by Linda Fierz-David. Translated by Mary Hottinger. New York: Bollingen Series XXV.

Frye, Northrop. (1954) 2006. "Forming Fours: Jung's *Psychology and Alchemy*, reviewed for *The Hudson Review*." In *The Educated Imagination and Other Writings on Critical Theory, 1933–1963, The Collected Works of Northrop Frye, Volume 21*, edited by G. Warkentin, 203–13. Toronto: University of Toronto Press.

———. 2005. "The Drunken Boat: The Revolutionary Element in Romanticism." In *Northrop Frye's Writings on the Eighteenth and Nineteenth Centuries*, edited by Imre Salusinszky, 17:75–91. Toronto: University of Toronto Press.

Goethe, Johann Wolfgang von. 1984. *Faust I and II*. Vol. 2, *Collected Works*. Edited and translated by Stuart Atkins. Princeton, NJ: Princeton University Press.

Goetz, Christopher, Michel Bonduelle, and Toby Gelfand. 1995. *Charcot: Constructing Neurology*. Oxford: Oxford University Press.

Haule, John. 1992. "From Somnambulism to the Archetypes: The French Roots of Jung's Split with Freud." *Psychoanalytic Review* 71, no. 4 (1984): 635–59. In *Carl Gustav Jung: Critical Assessments*, edited by Renos Papadopoulos, 238–60. London: Routledge.

Hillman, James. 1983. *Healing Fiction*. Dallas: Spring Publications.

Holland, Vyvyan. 1933. Introduction to *Dreams and Life: Le Reve et La Vie*. Translated by Vyvyan Holland. London: First Edition Club, Boar's Head Press.

Janet, Pierre. 1907. *The Majors Symptoms of Hysteria: Fifteen Lectures Given in the Medical School of Harvard University*. New York: Macmillan.

———. 2004. "1902–1903, Les emotions et les oscillations du niveau mental." In *Leçons au Collège de France, 1895-1934*, 37–41. Paris: l'Harmattan.

Jaspers, Karl. 1997. *General Psychopathology, Volumes 1 and 2*. Translated by J. Hoenig and Marian W. Hamilton. Baltimore: Johns Hopkins University Press.

Jung, C. G. (1912) 1991. *Psychology of the Unconscious: A Study of the Transformations and Symbolisms of the Libido*. Vol. 5, sup. vol. B, Collected Works. Princeton, NJ: Princeton University Press.

———. (1916/1958) 1960/1969. "The Transcendent Function." In *The Structure and Dynamics of the Psyche*. Vol. 8, Collected Works, 67–91. Princeton, NJ: Princeton University Press.

———. (1917/1926/1943) 1953/1966. "On the Psychology of the Unconscious." In *Two Essays on Analytical Psychology*. Vol. 7, Collected Works, 3–119. Princeton, NJ: Princeton University Press.

———. (1918) 1964/1970. "The Role of the Unconscious." In *Civilization in Transition*. Vol. 10, Collected Works, 3–28. Princeton, NJ: Princeton University Press.

———. (1921) 1964. *Psychological Types*. Vol. 6, Collected Works. Princeton, NJ: Princeton University Press.

———. (1922/1931) 1966. "On the Relation of Analytical Psychology to Poetry." In *The Spirit in Man, Art, and Literature*. Vol. 15, Collected Works, 65–83. Princeton, NJ: Princeton University Press.

———. (1925/1931) 1954. "Marriage as a Psychological Relationship." In *The Development of Personality*. Vol. 17, Collected Works, 187–201. Princeton, NJ: Princeton University Press.

———. (1928/1935) 1953/1966. "The Relations between the Ego and the Unconscious." In *Two Essays on Analytical Psychology*. Vol. 7, Collected Works, 123–241. Princeton, NJ: Princeton University Press.

———. (1932) 1976. "On The Tale of the Otter." In *The Symbolic Life*. Vol. 18, Collected Works, 762–64. Princeton, NJ: Princeton University Press.

———. (1934/1952) 1966. "*Ulysses*: A Monologue." In *The Spirit in Man, Art, and Literature*. Vol. 15, Collected Works, 109–34. Princeton, NJ: Princeton University Press.

———. (1935/1954) 1959/1968. "Archetypes of the Collective Unconscious." In *The Archetypes and the Collective Unconscious*. Vol. 9i, Collected Works, 3–41. Princeton, NJ: Princeton University Press.

————. (1938/1954) 1968. "The Visions of Zosimos." In *Alchemical Studies*. Vol. 13, *Collected Works*, 57–108. Princeton, NJ: Princeton University Press.

————. (1939) 1966. "In Memory of Sigmund Freud. In *The Spirit in Man, Art, and Literature*. Vol. 15, Collected Works, 41–49. Princeton, NJ: Princeton University Press.

————. (1943/1948) 1968. "The Spirit Mercurius." In *Alchemical Studies*. Vol. 13, Collected Works, 191–250. Princeton, NJ: Princeton University Press.

————. (1945) 1976. "Gérard de Nerval." In *The Symbolic Life*. Vol. 18, Collected Works, 779. Princeton, NJ: Princeton University Press.

————. (1945/1948) 1959/1968. "The Phenomenology of the Spirit in Fairy Tales." In *The Archetypes and the Collective Unconscious*. Vol. 9i, Collected Works, 207–54. Princeton, NJ: Princeton University Press.

————. (1945/1948) 1960/1969. "On the Nature of Dreams." In *The Structure and Dynamics of the Psyche*. Vol. 8, Collected Works, 281–97. Princeton, NJ: Princeton University Press.

————. (1953) 1968. *Psychology and Alchemy*. Vol. 12, Collected Works. Princeton, NJ: Princeton University Press.

————. (1956) 1967. *Symbols of Transformation*. Vol. 5, Collected Works. Princeton, NJ: Princeton University Press.

————. (1958) 1960. "Schizophrenia." In *The Psychogenesis of Mental Disease*. Vol. 3, Collected Works, 256–72. Princeton, NJ: Princeton University Press.

————. 1962. *Memories, Dreams, Reflections*. New York: Random House.

————. (1963) 1970. *Mysterium Coniunctionis*. Vol. 14, Collected Works. Princeton, NJ: Princeton University Press.

————. 1973. *Letters*. Vol. 2. Edited by Gerhard Adler and Aniela Jaffé. Translated by R.F.C. Hull. Princeton, NJ: Princeton University Press.

————. 1997. *Visions: Notes of the Seminar Given in 1930–1934*. Edited by Claire Douglas. Princeton, NJ: Princeton University Press.

————. 2001. *Atom and Archetype: The Pauli-Jung Letters, 1932–1958*. Edited by C. A. Meier. Princeton, NJ: Princeton University Press.

————. 2008. *Children's Dreams: Notes from the Seminar Given in 1936–1940*. Edited by Lorenz Jung and M. Meyer-Grass. Translated by Ernst Falzeder with Tony Woolfson. Princeton, NJ: Princeton University Press.

————. 2009. *Liber Novus [The Red Book]*. Edited by Sonu Shamdasani. Translated by Mark Kyburz, John Peck, and Sonu Shamdasani. New York: W. W. Norton.

————. 2014. *Dream Interpretation Ancient and Modern, Notes from the Seminar Given in 1936–1941*. Edited by John Peck, Lorenz Jung, and Maria Meyer-Grass. Princeton, NJ: Princeton University Press.

Jünger, Ernst. (1939) 1970. *On the Marble Cliffs*. Translated by Stuart Hood. New York: Penguin Books.

Knapp, Bettina L. 1980. *Gérard de Nerval: The Mystic's Dilemma*. Tuscaloosa: University of Alabama Press.

Kopp, Robert. 2008. *Album André Breton*. Paris: Gallimard.

Kristeva, Julia. 1989. "Gerard de Nerval, The Disinherited Poet." In *Black Sun: Depression and Melancholia*, translated by Leon Roudiez, 139–72. New York: Colombia University Press.

Kubin, Alfred. 1967. *The Other Side: A Fantastic Novel*. Illustrations by Alfred Kubin. Translated by Denver Lindley. New York: Crown.

Lawrence, D. H. (1936) 1968. "A Letter from Germany." In *Phoenix: The Posthumous Papers of D. H. Lawrence*, edited by Edward D. McDonald, 107–10. New York: Viking Press.

MacGregor, John. 1989. *The Discovery of the Art of the Insane*. Princeton, NJ: Princeton University Press.

Meier, C. A. 1987. *The Meaning and Significance of Dreams*. Translated by David Roscoe. Boston: Sigo Press.

Moreau, Jean Jacques. 1845. *Du hashisch et de l'aliénation mentale: Études psychologiques.* Paris: Fortin, Masson. Translated by H. Peters as *Hashish and Mental Illness.* New York: Raven Press, 1973.

———. 1859. *La psychologie morbide dans ses rapports avec la philosophie de l'histoire, ou De l'influence des névropathies sur le dynamisme intellectuel.* Paris: Librarie Victor Masson.

Murat, Laure. 2001. *La Maison du docteur Blanche: Historie d'un asile et de ses pensionnaires de Nerval à Maupassant.* Paris: Edition J. C. Lattés.

Nerval, Gérard de. 1989. *Oeuvres Complètes.* Edited by Jean Guillaume and Claude Pichois. Vol. 1. Paris: Bibliothèque de la Pléiade.

———. 1984. *Oeuvres Complètes.* Edited by Jean Guillaume and Claude Pichois. Vol. 2. Paris: Bibliothèque de la Pléiade.

———. 1993. *Oeuvres Complètes.* Edited by Jean Guillaume and Claude Pichois. Vol. 3. Paris: Bibliothèque de la Pléiade.

———. 1999. *Gérard de Nerval: Selected Works.* Translated by Richard Sieburth. London: Penguin Books.

———. 2009. *The Salt Smugglers: History of the Abbé de Bucquoy.* Translated by Richard Sieburth. New York: Archipelago Books.

———. 2012. *Voyage to the Orient.* Translated by Conrad Elphinstone. Antipodes Press.

Nietzsche, Friedrich. 2004. *Dithyrambs of Dionysus.* Translated by R. J. Hollingdale. Greenwich, UK: Anvil Press Poetry.

Panofsky, Dora, and Erwin Panofsky. 1965. *Pandora's Box: The Changing Aspects of a Mythical Symbol.* New York: Harper Torchbooks.

Pawel, Ernst. 1995. *The Poet Dying: Heinrich Heine's Last Years in Paris.* New York: Farrar, Straus and Giroux.

Pichois, Claude, and Michel Brix. 1995. *Gérard de Nerval.* Paris: Fayard.

Pinel, Philippe. 1800. *Traité medico-philosophique sur l'aliénation mentale ou la manie.* Paris, Caille et Ravier.

Rinsler, Norman. 1973. *Gérard de Nerval.* London: Athlone Press.

Shamdasani, Sonu. 1995. "Memories, Dreams, Omissions." *Spring: Journal of Archetype and Culture* 57:115–37.

———. 1998a. *Cult Fictions: C. G. Jung and the Founding of Analytical Psychology.* London: Routledge.

———. 1998b. "From Geneva to Zürich: Jung and French Switzerland." *Journal of Analytical Psychology* 43, no. 1 (January): 115–26.

———. 2012. *C. G. Jung: A Biography in Books.* New York: W. W. Norton.

Sieburth, Richard. 1999. Introduction and notes to *Gérard de Nerval: Selected Writings.* London: Penguin Books.

Swedenborg, Emanuel. 1881. *The Author's Memorabilia: The Swedenborg Library V10.* Germantown, PA: Swedenborg Publishing Association.

Taylor, Eugene. 2007. "Jung on Swedenborg, Redivivus." *Jung History* 2 (2): 27–31.

von Franz, Marie-Louise. 1977. *Individuation in Fairy Tales.* Dallas: Spring.

Weiner, Dora. 1994. "Le geste de Pinel: Psychiatric Myth." In *Discovering the History of Psychiatry*, edited by Mark S. Micale and Roy Porter, 232–47. Oxford: Oxford University Press.

Woodman, Ross. 2005. *Sanity, Madness, Transformation: The Psyche in Romanticism.* Toronto: University of Toronto Press.

Zabriskie, Beverley. 2001. "Jung and Pauli: A Meeting of Rare Minds." In *Atom and Archetype: The Pauli-Jung Letters, 1932–1958*, edited by C. A. Meier, xxvii–l. Princeton, NJ: Princeton University Press.

Index

Note: Page numbers in italic type indicate illustrations.

The Collected Works of C. G. Jung

Editors: Sir Herbert Read, Michael Fordham, and Gerhard Adler; executive editor, William McGuire. Translated by R.F.C. Hull, except where noted.

20. GENERAL INDEX OF THE COLLECTED WORKS (1979)

THE ZOFINGIA LECTURES (1983)
Supplementary Volume A to the Collected Works.
Edited by William McGuire, translated by
Jan van Heurck, introduction by
Marie-Louise von Franz

PSYCHOLOGY OF THE UNCONSCIOUS ([1912] 1992)
A STUDY OF THE TRANSFORMATIONS AND SYMBOLISMS OF THE LIBIDO.
A CONTRIBUTION TO THE HISTORY OF THE EVOLUTION OF THOUGHT
Supplementary Volume B to the Collected Works.
Translated by Beatrice M. Hinkle,
introduction by William McGuire

Notes to C. G. Jung's Seminars

DREAM ANALYSIS ([1928–30] 1984)
Edited by William McGuire

NIETZSCHE'S *ZARATHUSTRA* ([1934–39] 1988)
Edited by James L. Jarrett (2 vols.)

ANALYTICAL PSYCHOLOGY ([1925] 1989)
Edited by William McGuire

THE PSYCHOLOGY OF KUNDALINI YOGA ([1932] 1996)
Edited by Sonu Shamdasani

INTERPRETATION OF VISIONS ([1930–34] 1997)
Edited by Claire Douglas

CHILDREN'S DREAMS ([1936–40] 2008)
Edited by Lorenz Jung and Maria Meyer-Grass, translated by Ernst
Falzeder with the collaboration of Tony Woolfson

Philemon Foundation Series

*The Question of Psychological Types: The Correspondence of C. G. Jung
and Hans Schmid-Guisan, 1915–1916.* John Beebe and Ernst Falzeder, eds.; translated by Ernst Falzeder

Dream Interpretation Ancient and Modern: Notes from the Seminar Given in 1936–1941. C. G. Jung. John Peck, Lorenz Jung, and Maria Meyer-Grass, editors. Translated by Ernst Falzeder with the collaboration of Tony Woolfson

Analytical Psychology in Exile: The Correspondence of C. G. Jung and Erich Neumann. Edited and introduced by Martin Liebscher. Translated by Heather McCartney

On Psychological and Visionary Art: Notes from C. G. Jung's Lecture on Gérard de Nerval's "Aurélia." Edited by Craig E. Stephenson. Translated by R.F.C. Hull, Gottwalt Pankow, and Richard Sieburth